HIGHWAY OF TEARS

HIGHWAY OF TEARS

A TRUE STORY *of* RACISM,

INDIFFERENCE, *and the* PURSUIT *of* JUSTICE

for MISSING *and* MURDERED

INDIGENOUS WOMEN *and* GIRLS

JESSICA McDIARMID

ATRIA BOOKS

New York   London   Toronto   Sydney   New Delhi

ATRIA
BOOKS

An Imprint of Simon & Schuster, Inc.
1230 Avenue of the Americas
New York, NY 10020

First Atria Books hardcover edition November 2019

ATRIA B O O K S and colophon are trademarks of
Simon & Schuster, Inc.

For information about special discounts for bulk purchases, please contact
Simon & Schuster Special Sales at 1-866-506-1949 or
business@simonandschuster.com.

The Simon & Schuster Speakers Bureau can bring authors to your live
event. For more information or to book an event, contact the Simon &
Schuster Speakers Bureau at 1-866-248-3049 or visit our website at
www.simonspeakers.com.

Manufactured in the United States of America

1   3   5   7   9   10   8   6   4   2

Library of Congress Cataloging-in-Publication Data has been applied for.

ISBN 978-1-5011-6028-8
ISBN 978-1-5011-6030-1 (ebook)

*For the women and girls who
never came home, and for their families*

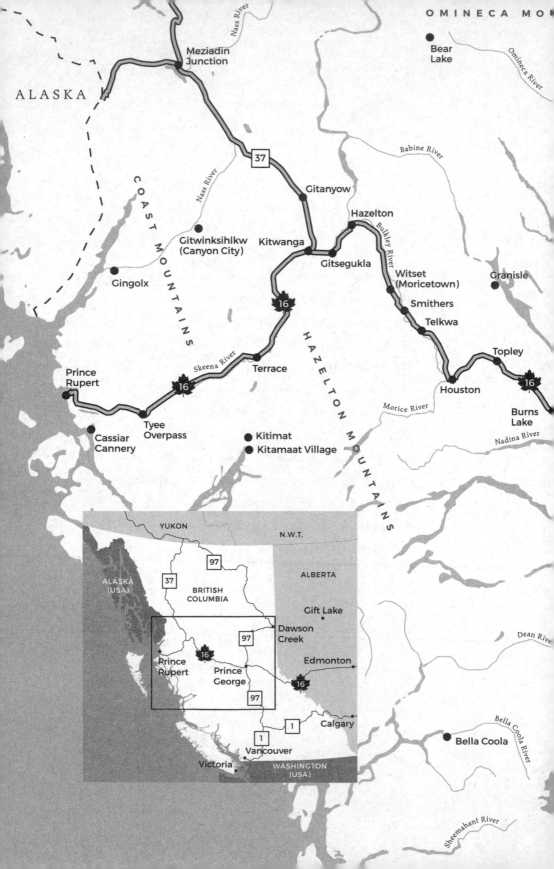

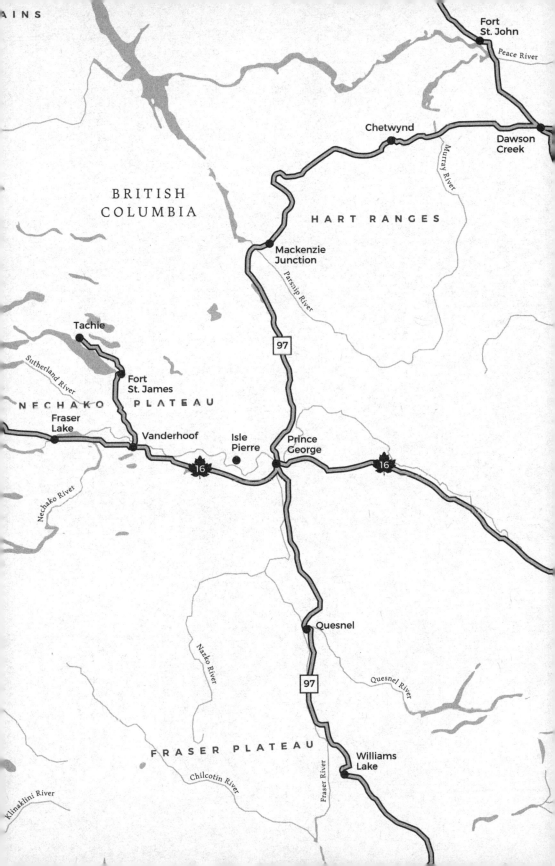

BECAUSE I AM AN INDIGENOUS WOMAN, I am six times more likely to be murdered than my non-Indigenous sisters. I am considered high risk just by virtue of being Indigenous and female. This is my reality. I am a statistic. Jessica McDiarmid's book brings life and a face to the statistics. The girls and women whose stories are presented in this book were someone's daughter, sister, mother, aunt, grandmother, friend, etcetera, and they were loved and important. They are still loved and important, but now they are also missed.

Over many years, I have worked locally, regionally, nationally and internationally to raise awareness of the issue of missing and murdered Indigenous women in Canada. I have done so because this issue is personal: my first cousin, a most treasured young woman, was lost along Highway 16 in British Columbia. Ramona Wilson went missing in 1994, and her remains were found a year later. Ramona was not only beautiful, she was smart, tenacious and had an effervescent personality—she was going places. She was loved. The pride my aunty Matilda and her siblings felt for her radiates from them every time they speak about her. The abrupt end of her life at the tender age of sixteen left an indelible mark on the heart of our family.

This book is a timely reminder that those who fail to learn from history are doomed to repeat it. Jessica paints a clear picture of the political and social climate in which many young women went missing along Highway 16. It was a time of political unrest due to the perceived threat of losses of jobs, properties and resources that would result from treaties with First Nations governments. There was an influx of workers into the resource sector, increasing the number of male-dominated camps. There was a lack of transportation options and a lack of essential health, social and education services.

In the north today we are facing the same factors that leave Indigenous women and girls vulnerable. There is friction between Indigenous and non-Indigenous northerners due to conflicting opinions on resource extraction. The planned liquefied natural gas plant in Kitimat and other resource extraction projects will see an increase in work camps, and the lack of services and access to those services is ongoing. Although a transportation plan developed for northern British Columbia has provided limited bus services along the Highway 16 corridor, Greyhound no longer offers bus service in the province.

In 2006, Carrier Sekani Family Services and Lheidli T'enneh hosted the Highway of Tears Symposium for approximately 700 participants. It was the start of a collaborative effort between every level of government, Indigenous communities, families of the victims and service providers to meet, engage and discuss. The symposium yielded a report with thirty-three recommendations toward solutions to the systemic, historic and ongoing problems confronted by people living along the highway. From those recommendations, the Highway of Tears governing body, composed of family members of the victims, government and service organizations representatives, was established, and the Highway of Tears (HOT) Initiative was born. The HOT Initiative would coordinate and oversee the implementation of the HOT recommendations. It was my honour to chair the HOT governing body and guide the work of the initiative through the Carrier Sekani Family Services.

When Jessica approached me about her desire to write a book on the Highway of Tears, I brought forward her request to the governing body, which supported and endorsed her work. After her years working in Africa for human rights and writing for the *Toronto Star*, Jessica returned home to the north to provide her in-depth perspective on the Highway of Tears. Jessica has put her blood, sweat and tears into this book, evident by her countless hours of research and interviews. Truly, she has given justice to a very sensitive and complex issue.

I am thankful that Jessica has so succinctly and thoroughly documented the history of the Highway of Tears and that the stories of our girls and women will never be forgotten. I am thankful that the work, energy and spirit that has gone into raising aware-ness of our missing and murdered girls and women is captured in the telling of our story. In Jessica's words, "Ramona has been here all these years: in the courage in her mother's eyes, the strength in her sister's voice, in all the work they've done." We have much work still to do.

This book is a tribute to all our warriors who demand justice for those who no longer have a voice. Through her words, Jessica McDiarmid has lent her voice in the fight for justice for those we can no longer hear. In the telling of the story of the Highway of Tears, Jessica has become one of us warriors. For this, my family will be forever grateful.

—Mary Teegee
Maaxsw Gibuu (White Wolf)
Executive Director,
Child and Family Services,
Carrier Sekani Family Servcies
Chair, B.C. Delegated Indigenous Agencies
President, B.C. Aboriginal Childcare Society

HIGHWAY
OF TEARS

THE HIGHWAY OF TEARS

THE HIGHWAY OF TEARS is a lonesome road that runs across a lonesome land. This dark slab of asphalt cuts a narrow path through the vast wilderness of the place, where struggling hayfields melt into dark pine forests, and the rolling fields of the Interior careen into jagged coastal mountains. It's sparsely populated, with many kilometres separating the small towns strung along it, communities forever grappling with the booms and busts of the industries that sustain them. At night, many minutes may pass between vehicles, mostly tractor-trailers on long-haul voyages between the coast and some place farther south. And there is the train that passes in the night, late, its whistle echoing through the valleys long after it is gone.

Prince George lies in a bowl etched by glaciers over thousands of years on the Nechako Plateau, near the middle of what is now called British Columbia, at the place where the Nechako and Fraser Rivers meet. It is a small city, as cities go, but with a population of about eighty thousand, it is by far the largest along the highway, a once prosperous lumber town that fell on hard times. Hunkered under towering sand bluffs carved by the rivers, the once bustling downtown is quieter these days, though a push for economic diversification has, in the past few years, brought in a new wave of boutique shops, pubs and upscale eateries.

From the city, the highway runs northwest, passing ranches with sagging barbed-wire fences and billboards advertising farm supply stores and tow truck companies. It winds down from the plateau toward the coast, through ever-narrower valleys where cedar and Sitka spruce and hemlock rise from beds of moss and ferns to form a near canopy. As the skies sink lower, the mountains loom higher. The air grows heavier as the highway draws closer to the Pacific, clinging to a ledge above the Skeena River blasted from the mountainsides to make way for trains and trucks, where the margin of error is only a few feet in either direction. Those who err are often gone forever, lost to a river that swallows logging trucks and fishing boats alike. Those who disappear in this place are not easily found.

The towns owe their existence to the railway that carved a path from the Rocky Mountains to Prince Rupert just over a hundred years ago, propelled by fears in Ottawa of an American invasion and hopes of selling prairie grain to Asia from a port on the northern Pacific. The last spike of the Grand Trunk Pacific Railway went into the ground April 7, 1914, just a few months before Europe erupted into the First World War. Settlements grew along the railway as livelihoods were wrested from farms forever beset by late springs and early frosts, from towering forests that carpeted the hills and from mines from which men chipped out silver, copper and gold to load onto boxcars going somewhere else.

But before these towns named for railway men, fur traders and settlers, there were other communities here. People inhabited this land long before history was recorded in any European sense. Before the Egyptians erected the pyramids, before the Maya began to write and study the sky, before the Mesopotamians built the first cities, Indigenous people lived in this place. Only about two hundred years ago did Europeans arrive in the Pacific Northwest, seeking sea otter, gold and, later, lumber. Soon, the nascent government of Canada would claim the territory as its own and seek to assimilate or destroy those who had been here for so long. Settlers arrived on foot and in canoes, then on railcars and steamboats, and then on the highway. By the early 1950s, a road connected Prince Rupert to Prince George, though it was little more than a gravel strip in places and often rendered impassable by snowfall, avalanches and landslides. Soon, Highway 16 was extended across the Rockies to connect the northwest of British Columbia to Edmonton and beyond, opening this vast region to the rest of the country. The road was dubbed the Yellowhead after the Iroquois-Metis fur trader Pierre Bostonais, known as Tête Jaune for his shock of bright yellow hair. And so it remained, until what it brought earned it a new name: the Highway of Tears.

No one knows who the first Indigenous girl or woman to vanish along the highway between Prince Rupert and Prince George was, or when it happened. Nor does anyone know how many have gone missing or been murdered since. In more recent years, grassroots activists, many of whom are family members of missing and murdered Indigenous girls and women, have travelled from community to community to collect the names of those lost. Their lists suggest numbers far higher than those that make their way into most media reports, but they are still incomplete—people who have been gathering names for many years continue to hear about cases they were unaware of.

The RCMP has put the number of missing and murdered Indigenous women in Canada at about 1,200, with about a thousand of those being victims of homicide. The actual number is likely higher; the Native Women's Association of Canada, or NWAC, and other advocacy groups have estimated it could be as high as four thousand. And although the RCMP reported that the proportion of homicide cases that were solved was about the same for Indigenous and non-Indigenous women and girls—88 and 89 per cent respectively—NWAC research into 582 cases suggested that 40 per cent of murders remained unsolved.

According to the RCMP, a third of the 225 unsolved cases nationwide were in British Columbia, with thirty-six homicides and forty unresolved missing person cases, more than twice the next-highest province, Alberta. The entirety of northern British Columbia is home to only about 250,000 people, or about 6 per cent of the province's population. Around the Highway of Tears alone, a region that is just a fraction of northern B.C., at least five Indigenous women and girls went missing during the time period covered by RCMP statistics—more than 12 per cent of the provincial total. And, in addition to the missing, there are at least five unsolved murders, or about 14 per cent.

The Highway of Tears is a 725-kilometre stretch of highway in British Columbia. And it is a microcosm of a national tragedy—and travesty. Indigenous people in this country are far more likely to face violence than any other segment of the population. A 2014 Statistics Canada report found Indigenous people face double the rate of violence of non-Indigenous people. Indigenous women and girls, in particular, are targets. They are six times more likely to be killed than non-Indigenous women. They face a rate of serious violence twice as high as that of Indigenous men and nearly triple that of non-Indigenous women. This is partly because they are more likely to confront risk factors such as mental illness, homelessness and poverty, which afflict Indigenous people at vastly disproportionate rates—the ugly, deadly effects of colonialism past and present. But even when controlling for those factors, Indigenous women and girls face more violence than anyone else. Put simply, they are in greater danger solely because they were born Indigenous and female. As one long-time activist put it, "Every time we walk out our doors, it's high risk."

Across Canada, as across the Highway of Tears, no one has counted the dead. But whatever the number, too often forgotten is that behind every single death or disappearance is a human being and those who love them, a web of family and community and friendship, those bonds we form that make us strong; those bonds that, when broken, tear us apart.

I was ten years old the first time I saw Ramona Wilson. A photo of her, smiling, black hair cloaking her left shoulder, was printed on sheets of eight-by-eleven paper and hung up around Smithers, the B.C. town where we both grew up. Over the picture was a banner that read: "MISSING." Under it was a description: "16 years old, native, 5 foot 1, 120 pounds, last seen June 11, 1994." The posters plastered telephone poles and gas station doors and grocery store bulletin boards throughout town and the surrounding areas for months. But in April the following year, the posters were taken down. She was gone.

I would learn later that Ramona wasn't the only First Nations girl or young woman to vanish from the area. In 1989, it was Alberta Williams and Cecilia Anne Nikal. The following year, Cecilia's fifteen-year-old cousin Delphine Nikal disappeared. In 1994, the same year Ramona didn't come home, Roxanne Thiara and Alishia Germaine were murdered, their bodies later found near the highway. In 1995, Lana Derrick went missing. The posters went up, and they came down, but not because the girls got home alive.

There wasn't a great fuss about these missing and murdered girls. "Just another native" is how mothers and sisters and aunties describe the pervasive attitude. Police officers gave terrified, grieving families the distinct impression that they didn't care and didn't try very hard. Nor did the public rally to the cause in large numbers with donations for reward money or attendance at vigils, searches or walks. Families were often left to search, raise funds, investigate and mourn alone. It was not unusual in the 1990s to hear comments about the "error" a girl must have committed to encounter such a fate, whether it was hitchhiking, prostitution, drinking or walking alone at night. It is still not uncommon. Too often, these deaths and disappearances are seen as the result of the victim's wrongdoing rather than as what they truly are: an ongoing societal failure. Many of the girls who vanished here were not hitchhiking, nor were they sex workers, nor were they doing anything much different than many other young people. But to many of the people living in predominantly white communities, it seemed as though disappearing off the face of the earth was something that happened to other people. And it was, because this is a country where Ramona Wilson was six times more likely to be murdered than me.

I left northwestern British Columbia in my late teens and never planned to return, aside from the odd week or two to visit family. I reported from across the country and overseas, focusing when I could on human rights abuses and social injustice—that was what I cared about, what I wanted to shed light upon, in hopes of playing some small role in fixing it. Over those years, I watched as women and girls in northwestern B.C. continued to disappear—Nicole Hoar, Tamara Chipman, Aielah Saric-Auger, Bonnie Joseph, Mackie Basil—and long felt that I needed to come home to this story. The first time I spoke with local family members who have become some of the strongest advocates—quite literally, national game changers—for missing and murdered Indigenous women and girls was in 2009. But it wasn't for another seven years that circumstances aligned and I returned home to research and write this book.

In June of 2016, not long after I arrived back in Smithers, I had the honour of walking the Highway of Tears with Brenda Wilson, Ramona's sister; Angeline Chalifoux, the auntie of fourteen-year-old Aielah Saric-Auger; and Val Bolton, Brenda's dear friend, along with dozens of family members and supporters who joined them for part of the way. Called the Cleansing the Highway Walk, it marked the ten-year anniversary of the first Highway of Tears walk. At the end of it, when we arrived in Prince George after three weeks of leapfrogging down the highway's length from Prince Rupert, Angeline stood on a stage alongside Brenda and Val. It was June 21, National Aboriginal Day, and hundreds of people had turned out to celebrate at Lheidli T'enneh Memorial Park on the banks of the Fraser River. Angeline told Aielah's story, and then she read to the crowd her favourite quote, from Martin Luther King Jr. "He who passively accepts evil is as much involved in it as he who helps to perpetrate it," she read out. "He who accepts evil without protesting against it is really cooperating with it."

Not nearly enough people gave a damn when these girls and women went missing. We did not protect them. We failed them. The police haven't solved these cases, but there are multiple perpetrators. There are those who committed these crimes, and there are all of us who stood by as it happened, and happened again, and happened again. And while we cannot undo what has been done, we can try to understand how this happened, where we went wrong. We can address the myriad factors that make Indigenous women and girls vulnerable. We can make sure it does not happen again. And we can remember them, these young women with all their dreams and troubles and hopes and cares, who should still be here today. I owe them this. We all do.

A BRIGHT LIGHT

MATILDA WILSON STOOD on a gravel road. A couple dozen people made a rough circle around her under the high, weak sun that June day in 2012. The crowd had lowered the placards they'd carried for a couple of kilometres down Highway 16 to the foot of Yelich Road, cardboard signs that read "Take back the highway" and "Killer on the loose!" They watched Matilda's bowed head in silence as cars and trucks and tractor-trailers roared past. Matilda's eldest child, Brenda, kept a hand on her back as smoke from smouldering sweetgrass, sage and other traditional medicine wafted across her face and rose westward toward the Pacific Ocean. Finally, Matilda raised weary, shining eyes and said that she was lucky; she was lucky because at least she knew.

What she knew was that her youngest child would never come home.

Ramona Lisa Wilson was born in the Bulkley Valley District Hospital in Smithers, B.C., a town of about five thousand people halfway between Prince George and Prince Rupert. It was a dreary, cold winter day, fog shrouding the wide valley in which the town lies. The hospital was drearier still, a concrete mound atop a gentle rise between the downtown business district and the Bulkley River. But Ramona was a light, even before she entered this world on February 15, 1978.

After Matilda gave birth to her fifth child seven years earlier, doctors had said she could never have another. It had been a disappointment to Matilda's eldest, Brenda, who, as the only girl in the family, desperately wanted a little sister. But Matilda accepted it: she was finished with babies. Then, in the summer of 1977, thinking she had the flu, she went to the doctor and learned she was two months pregnant. She was stunned. "Maybe it's a gift," she told Ramona's equally shocked father. She told Brenda to pray for the baby sister she'd always wanted.

On February 14, 1978, contractions started. Matilda smiled at the thought of a Valentine's Day baby, but it wasn't until about five the next morning that she needed to head for the hospital. Soon after, Ramona was born. The nurses passed her to Matilda, who felt her baby's wavy hair and kissed her tiny fingers and tiny nose and admired her eyes, so light coloured they were almost blue, though they would soon turn hazel. She said to Ramona's father, "You better go tell Brenda. Get to the phone and tell her that she's got a baby sister." It wasn't long before the family rushed into the room, Brenda in the lead.

At home, the family took turns holding Ramona, feeding her, caring for her. The house changed when the baby came in the door. It got louder, happier. Each year on her birthday, they threw a big party. As she grew, her brothers doted on her, carrying her wherever she wanted to go, treating her like a little princess. Brenda had moved out and was starting her own family, so it was her brothers Ramona cajoled into coming to her tea parties and letting her style their hair. She was a jokester. "Watch your head!" she'd shout before her foot whizzed by one of her brother's ears as she tested out her flexibility. Wherever she went, she sang in a lovely, lilting voice and a peal of delighted laughter followed her.

Thousands of years ago, the Gitxsan built a settlement on the river Xsan, which translates roughly into "river of mists," across the water from a jagged mountain that towers 1,700 metres above the valley. They called the village Temlaham, meaning "prairie town," and it grew into a large community. Perhaps 4,500 years ago, a section of the mountain perched upon a pocket of air let loose and roared down into the valley, burying Temlaham and blocking the river, which prevented the Pacific salmon, which many depended on, from making the journey upstream to spawn. It forced widespread migration across the region as people sought new food sources. Some of the people displaced by the landslide resettled at Gitanmaax, on a tongue of low-lying land at the point where the Bulkley River flows into Xsan. With its rivers and a series of overland trails, the village became a trading hub, connecting communities farther inland to the Tsimshian on the coast.

In the mid-1800s, fur traders and gold prospectors arrived, soon followed by a Western Union Telegraph Company exploration team seeking a telegraph line to connect North America to Russia. In 1866, the Hudson's Bay Company opened a post near the confluence of the rivers, and early settlers dubbed the area Hazelton. That post soon closed and plans for the telegraph line were scrapped, but Hazelton remained a bustling supply stop for surveyors, traders and hopefuls chasing gold. As Europeans moved in, the people of Gitanmaax left their village and moved uphill to a bluff overlooking the now-colonial town and rivers. The Hudson's Bay Company reopened in 1880, and during the next decade the first sternwheeler churned its way up the river, which settlers dubbed the Skeena, bringing a new wave of Europeans and transforming Hazelton into the largest town in the northwest, with three hotels, the Hudson's Bay Company warehouses, a hospital, a bank and stores, including a jeweller and a watchmaker.

Arthur Sampson, Matilda's father, grew up in Gitanmaax in the early years of the twentieth century. As a young man, he had a team of Belgian workhorses that he used for farming and logging. Sometimes, the Hudson's Bay Company hired the young man and his horses to shuttle supplies from its warehouses in Hazelton to other settlements along ancient routes known as grease trails. The corridors were named for the oily eulachon fish that First Nations people had for thousands of years carried along the trails from the coast to trade with inland communities. Settlers later widened these trails to make way for the stampedes headed for the gold fields. Bear Lake, 120 kilometres northward as the crow flies, was a traditional meeting place of Gitxsan, Dakelh and Sekani people. In the 1820s it became the site of Fort Connolly, a Hudson's Bay Company trading post, and remained a vibrant hub after the fort closed in the late 1800s. The journey to Bear Lake from Hazelton was a long, hard one; it took days to reach the community, even when conditions were good, and more often than not, they weren't. During one of these trips, Arthur and Mary met.

The two soon married and settled in Bear Lake. It was a remote place in those days; it still is. Arthur hunted and fished for food, and along with other family members served as the midwife for the births of his first six children. They kept a stainless steel container stocked with clean white sheets and cotton batting blessed by a priest, which no one was allowed to touch until the new baby came. A few years after the end of the Second World War, all the kids fell ill. Arthur and Mary managed to break the fevers of all but the youngest, Louise, who was just a toddler. There were no doctors, no medicine, and she died of pneumonia. Her parents were devastated. They packed up their surviving children and headed back to Gitanmaax. There was a hospital in Hazelton—in 1950, Matilda was the first of their children born into the hands of a doctor rather than a family member—and schools. There was also an RCMP detachment; a murder in Bear Lake had left Arthur and Mary fearing for the safety of their family. Gitanmaax would be a better place for the children.

First the government came for Matilda's older siblings. And then it came for her. Arthur and Mary tried to stop the authorities, but there was nothing they could do—the RCMP made it clear that any resistance would be met with arrest. They lost all of their children to residential schools.

Matilda was put on a train in Hazelton when she was five years old. She cried and cried. The conductor was a kindly man who tried to comfort her. He told the children that it would be okay. It wasn't. When they arrived at Lejac Residential School, an imposing, three-storey brick structure with a smattering of outbuildings on Highway 16 near the shores of Fraser Lake, staff took the kids' clothes, shaved their heads and marched them into cold showers. Matilda was assigned a number in place of her birth name. They were at Lejac to learn the white man's ways, to have the "savage" within them extinguished. They picked up English quickly—they were strapped or walloped if they were caught speaking their own language. The children were subjected to sexual abuse, beatings, starvation and neglect. Sometimes they tried to run away. One winter, four boys were found dead, frozen, out on the ice of a lake a few miles from their homes. Matilda learned what hunger and loneliness and fear were at that school.

Back in Gitanmaax, Arthur and Mary crumbled without their children. Alcohol filled the chasm left by the eastbound train. When Matilda returned home seven years later, her parents tried to put their lives back together, but it was never the same. "It did something to my mom and dad," said Matilda. "They got into alcohol really bad because they missed us so much. It did something to us, too. It just kept going from one generation to the next. Most of us just didn't really care what happened to us for a long time." Mary died of a heart attack when Matilda was twenty-four. One night five years later, a taxi dropped off her father on the road leading to Gitanmaax. A drunk ran him over, killing him.

Matilda married when she got pregnant at fifteen. By her twenty-first birthday, she had five children—Brenda, who was the eldest, and four boys. A couple of years later, she was widowed, and she moved to Smithers, about seventy-five kilometres southeast along Highway 16. It's a picturesque town, built beneath Hudson Bay Mountain in the early 1900s as a divisional headquarters for the railway where the inland hills meet the jagged, snow-capped peaks of the coastal ranges.

Main Street runs perpendicular to the highway that bisects Smithers. The stretch between the railway tracks and Highway 16 comprises seven blocks of trendy shops that sell fishing and hunting gear, mountain bikes, downhill skis, clothing and sushi. On the other side of the highway, Main Street runs uphill past the museum, the volunteer fire hall, houses and apartments and a recently closed pub, before dipping back down to the Bulkley River. Smithers is a little tidier, a little more touristy, than many of the communities strung along the highway. In the late 1980s, its town council passed a bylaw requiring storefronts on Main Street to adopt an alpine architectural theme to complement a statue of Alpine Al—the town mascot, a mountaineer blowing a horn—erected in 1973. Some merchants called the rule "monotonous, silly and a lot of trouble to conform to." One business owner, who was slapped with a stop-work order after failing to clear the replastering of an exterior wall with the alpine theme committee, erected "a pair of giant lederhosen" on the side of his building to express his displeasure. A town councillor, Doug McDonald, criticized the Alps theme for being unrepresentative of Smithers' multicultural makeup. The town itself was largely white, with only 120 people in 1991 identifying as Aboriginal. Its immigrant population was just more than 10 per cent, almost entirely from Western Europe. However, nearby communities like Hazelton had higher proportions of First Nations residents, and the Wet'suwet'en reserve of Witset, called Moricetown by settlers, was just thirty kilometres away. "Where's the longhouse at the end of Main Street?" asked McDonald. Still, the alpine theme stuck.

It was tough as a single mom with six kids to feed; there was never much money. But the family got by. They had each other. And they had Ramona. As she grew into a teenager, Ramona stayed bubbly and busy. She was well liked in her social circle, a girl always ready to lend an ear, to cheer up anyone who was feeling down. She was about twelve years old when she sat down at the kitchen table while Matilda was making bread. "Mommy," she announced, "I decided what I want to be." "And what do you want to be?" Matilda asked. "I want to be a psychologist, so I can get into people's minds and I can help them," she said. Matilda smiled. "Oh, that sounds good," she said. "That sounds like you." They made a plan: when Ramona graduated high school, she would go to the University of Victoria to study psychology. No one in her family had gone to university; none of her siblings had graduated from high school. In the district in which Smithers Secondary lies, the estimated Grade 12 completion rate for Indigenous students in 1997/98 was less than 24 per cent, almost three times lower than the overall rate. But Ramona was going to do it. "She had so much to prove by doing it," said her best friend, Kristal Grenkie.

At fourteen, Ramona took up baseball, playing outfield for the team sponsored by the Native Friendship Centre, where Brenda worked. She got a job washing dishes at Smitty's, a chain diner-style restaurant beside a car dealership on the frontage road just off Highway 16 that served enormous breakfasts, enormous burgers and unlimited coffee refills. She was a reliable employee, never missing a shift or calling in sick. She skipped school quite a bit, preferring coffee with friends to sitting through classes. A former high school administrator remembered calling her into the office to admonish her for her poor attendance record; he remembered how Ramona thanked him for caring and taking the time to talk to her.

Ramona was sneaking out of school one day, making her way down the short hallway that opened toward the smoke pit to avoid science class when she bumped into Kristal, who was doing the same thing. They'd seen each other around. It was a small town, and a relatively small high school, with about seven hundred students across four grades. Kristal and an older friend, Delphine Nikal, had hung out with Ramona's older brothers years before. "Want to go for a coffee?" Kristal asked, and Ramona agreed. The pair headed across the high school parking lot and crossed Highway 16 to the restaurant at the Aspen Inn to pass the afternoon in a smoky booth.

Kristal and Ramona were soon best friends. Kristal, who is white, started to find her way when she met Ramona. She had run pretty wild up until then. She'd spent time in youth detention—juvie, as it was called—for assault, and hung out with an older crowd that was into drinking, drugs, partying and fighting. With Ramona, it was different. Ramona wasn't much of a partier and, hanging out with her, Kristal slowed down. Once in a while, the girls would smoke a joint down on the riverbank and wander through town, talking about the big stuff: the purpose of their lives, what it all meant. Ramona was spiritual. She wanted to reconnect to the culture and traditions so nearly extinguished in her family. She wrote a lot of poetry. She believed that everything happened for a reason. Kristal's friendship with Ramona remains one of the deepest relationships she's ever had. "She was the kind of person that you couldn't not [connect with]," said Kristal. Ramona believed in kindness, in forgiveness, in understanding, with wisdom far beyond her years.

Ramona Wilson was a bright, bubbly teenager
who dreamed of becoming a psychologist.

One afternoon during the fall, when Ramona was fifteen and just starting Grade 11, Matilda was walking down Main Street, a few blocks from their home. She noticed her teenaged daughter coming up the street and, nearby, an elderly woman struggling with a bag. Matilda watched, full of pride, as Ramona approached the woman, took her bag and helped her across the street. Matilda was waiting on the other side. "Oh, God, Ramona, you are so beautiful," Matilda told her. "Thank you so much. Now I know I'm not going to be afraid to grow old." Ramona just laughed. "Mom, since when would you ever grow old?"

On Friday, June 10, 1994, Ramona burst through the door of the house on Railway Avenue. She had just found out that she'd got a summer job as a peer counsellor with Smithers Community Services Association. She was ecstatic as she discussed with her mom plans to give notice at Smitty's and the feeling that, yes, now, at sixteen, things were falling into place. It was, she told her mom, the best day of her life.

The next day was the climax of grad weekend in Smithers. The grad party was an annual tradition, a night soaked in booze when nearly everyone, even the kids who usually stayed away from raucous nights and those from ordinarily antagonistic social circles, congregated to celebrate. Teenagers piled into borrowed or beat-up vehicles and cruised up and down Main Street—the practice was referred to as "doing a Mainer," or, more pejoratively, a "Loser Lap"—or drove out on the gravel roads to bush parties at places like the water tower, the airstrip or the Twin Falls recreation site. In the days before cell phones or social media, it was this—a physical presence on Main Street—that afforded the opportunity to find friends, parties, rides, something to do for the night.

Ramona had spent Friday night in Moricetown with her boyfriend and returned to Smithers around noon. She stopped in at Mr. Mikes Steakhouse, on Main Street near the highway, to pick up a bag of clothes from a friend who was working there. Then she headed down the main drag toward her home. Along the way, her uncle pulled up beside her and offered her a ride. He planned to be a designated driver that night and asked her what she was planning to do and if she needed a lift later on. She told him she was heading to Lake Kathlyn, just across from the airport. A fellow who lived in a rundown apartment complex out there was having a party.

Ramona slept for the rest of the day, getting up at around six. Matilda ordered takeout pasta and lasagna for dinner. Ramona was in a good mood, dancing around and singing. At nine thirty, as the sun was sinking low behind Hudson Bay Mountain and shadows enveloped the town, the phone in Ramona's bedroom rang and she rushed off to answer it. Then she was getting ready to head out, packing her little overnight bag with her makeup, putting on her acid-wash jean jacket and her brand-new white and pink Reebok high-tops. Matilda didn't ask who was on the phone; she assumed it was Kristal. As far as she knew, Ramona was going to her best friend's place for the night. The two usually spent weekends together, though they weren't always where they told their mothers they would be.

After her flurry of primping, Ramona called out, "See you, Mom." Matilda didn't see her at the door, didn't watch her go, just replied over her shoulder, "See you." Ramona headed down the alley behind her house to Alfred Avenue, which would, in a few blocks, bring her to Main Street. At the first house along Alfred, an older woman was in the front yard with her son and grandson. Ramona waved to them. At the next house, there was a bit of a party going on out back. Ramona stopped to chat with people she knew and then went on her way.

Kristal lived about a dozen blocks away, in a two-storey duplex across from the civic centre where she was attending her brother's high school graduation. She had talked to Ramona earlier that day, and the two had planned to meet up that night at a dance in Hazelton, about seventy kilometres away. It wasn't uncommon to travel between towns, hitching a ride with someone headed that way. Sometimes the girls would stand out on the highway, thumb out, to find a ride—though Kristal was far more likely to do that than Ramona—but more often, it was a matter of wandering down Main Street and catching a lift with an acquaintance.

When Ramona didn't show up at the community hall in Hazelton, Kristal didn't think much of it. It wasn't all that unusual for plans to change, and there was no way to let each other know.

She figured Ramona had gone to Moricetown; her boyfriend lived there, along with a close friend of theirs. Ramona wasn't someone to worry about. She was the responsible one of the group. She was the one who took care of her friends when they got messed up on drugs and booze. She had four tough older brothers who made sure people knew not to mess with their sister. She was strong willed, sure of herself and her limits, and didn't hesitate to speak up if she felt someone was being wronged or she was getting pushed around. Ramona had her shit together. She'd be fine.

And so Saturday night became Sunday, and Matilda thought Ramona was at Kristal's, and Kristal thought Ramona was in Moricetown. Ramona's boyfriend called her house Sunday morning looking for her; Matilda told him she was with Kristal. He called Kristal and learned Ramona wasn't there, so he drove over to pick Kristal up, arriving at about eleven thirty. They decided to check if Ramona had made it home and went to Matilda's that afternoon. Kristal told him to go to the door, not wanting to get Ramona in trouble if Matilda believed the girls were together. When he climbed back into the car after talking to Matilda, he said, "Nope, she's with you." That afternoon, Kristal called Smitty's. They told her Ramona wasn't scheduled to work until after school the next afternoon.

Then Sunday became Monday and Ramona wasn't at school, but neither was their friend from Moricetown. Kristal told herself that they had probably slept in and missed the school bus. But she knew Ramona would get to town for work that afternoon, the shift when she planned to let her boss know that she would be leaving to take the job as a peer counsellor. That afternoon Kristal clocked in to her cashier job at the Petro-Canada along the highway. She told her boss she needed to make a quick phone call and went into the back office to dial Smitty's. She asked if Ramona was there. No. She asked them to double-check the schedule, to see if Ramona was supposed to be there. Yes, but she hadn't showed up. That's when Kristal knew. That's when she got scared. She picked up the phone again.

Matilda expected Ramona home after work on Monday. Instead, she got a call from Kristal, who told her Ramona hadn't been with her that weekend, hadn't been at school, and hadn't shown up for work. Matilda, she said, needed to call the RCMP— something was wrong. When Kristal got off the phone, she returned to the front of the store and a co-worker who had overheard part of her conversation teased her, saying, "What's going on? You lose your friend?" Kristal looked at him. Tears filled her eyes. "Actually, I think I did," she said.

Matilda called Smitty's and confirmed that, sure enough, her daughter had not come to work. She phoned Brenda, who came over straight away. They started calling around. They heard the story that she might have gone out to the apartments at Lake Kathlyn and drove out to check. They stopped in at Smitty's in case she had showed up or called in. Nothing. They went to the RCMP station.

The police told Matilda to give her some time. Ramona was a teenager in the heady days of early summer; it wasn't unusual for kids to take off for a few days. "What are you saying?" Matilda asked. "We've got to look for her. It's not like her. I know my daughter. I know my daughter." Matilda's sons had been in trouble; the cops knew the family and it was not a positive relationship. In a small town like Smithers, policed by fewer than a dozen officers, if you'd had a run-in with a cop, chances were you'd see that officer again. "We actually avoided any kind of contact with RCMP, so it was difficult when we had to report Ramona missing," said Brenda. "I had no faith in their ability to do anything." Matilda felt the police shrugged her off, insinuating that Ramona was unhappy at home, that Matilda, a single mom on welfare, wasn't providing a good environment for her children, that Ramona had probably run away. Ramona had sometimes stayed elsewhere for a few days, but she always, always called. She knew how much her mom worried.

Matilda Wilson knew something was wrong
when her daughter didn't show up for work in June 1994.

The Wilsons didn't wait to start searching. Brenda and Matilda worked the phones, keeping track of rumours and speculation, while Ramona's brothers, aunts and uncles combed the land around Smithers. Sometimes Matilda went along with them, afraid of finding something, afraid of not finding anything. Brenda never did go out on a search; she couldn't bear the thought of coming across her sister in the bush or in a culvert.

The first story about Ramona's disappearance to run in the local paper, a weekly published each Wednesday, was printed eleven days after she'd walked out the door of her home. It appeared on the bottom of the front page, below the fold and the other head-lines: "Japanese teacher apple of students' eyes" and "Treaty no big mystery." It read: "Smithers girl, 16, goes missing." In those eleven days, Ramona hadn't used her bank account. Her latest paycheque had sat behind the counter at Smitty's for over a week. Her things were left untouched in her bedroom.

By then, the police were on the move, too. "We're talking to absolutely everybody who's seen her or heard from her," said Const. Gerry Marshinew, a serious crimes investigator from Prince Rupert, about 350 kilometres west of Smithers, who arrived to help the resource-strapped local detachment. "So far, we've hit a bunch of dead ends. We're not treating it as foul play, but we haven't ruled that out." The family searched desperately, but they were at a loss. There was no advice to be had, no place to go for direction or support, no guide on what to do. They kept calling Ramona's friends, kept combing the highway, parks, party pits, riverbanks, following their instincts, their dreams. Everywhere they looked, there was nothing.

A week later, the police had searched the highway from Telkwa to Moricetown. A helicopter had scoured the Bulkley River. Officers had followed up on more than a hundred tips, all leading nowhere. Const. Ross Davidson, in charge of the investigation for the Smithers detachment, said the RCMP was running out of ideas. "We've run a bunch of leads into the ground and come up with nothing. We've got no place to point our finger. We can't launch a ground search because we don't know where she is."

On July 5, the Missing Children Society of Canada arrived in Smithers to help with the search. Its executive director Rhonda Morgan had dedicated her life to looking for missing kids for the past decade, since an evening in 1984 when she was an unhappy young woman, recently divorced, working as a book binder and spending too much time at the bar. On TV one night, she caught a program that profiled the cases of three missing Alberta children. It shocked her that kids could disappear and no one seemed to hear much about it. She picked up the phone and called Kathy Morgenstern, who was the founder of Child Find Alberta, a bootstraps organization run out of a basement that did its best to pitch in when children went missing. Rhonda asked Kathy what she could do to help, and Kathy told her they needed a typewriter. Rhonda found one for her the next day. And that was that. She spent so much time volunteering for Child Find that she got fired from her day job. The search for missing kids would envelop the next twenty-five years of her life.

While Rhonda threw her time into Child Find, there was always something that bothered her. The organization looked for missing kids, doing poster campaigns and drumming up media coverage. But it didn't really *look* for them. Rhonda wanted to *search*. She sent out letters to investigation agencies seeking their help on a case and received a response from a private investigator, Louw Olivier, in Calgary. She went to meet with him, and he agreed to look into it. Two days later, he called her to say he had found the missing boy in an orphanage in New York. Rhonda went to pick the boy up with a CTV news crew in tow. When she returned home to Calgary, Louw told Rhonda that he saw a great deal of potential in her. He encouraged her to start training for her private investigator licence.

Child Find didn't share her interest in conducting active investigations, so she parted ways with the organization and founded the Missing Children Society of Canada. She recruited a team of former police officers along with support staff, and, case by case, they developed and honed their processes. Rhonda, despite her lack of police experience, was accepted by law enforcement; she worked hard to prove herself to them, time and again, and usually it worked. In most cases, the society's help and resources were welcomed—they only got involved if the police approved. They could bring in forensic artists, psychologists, dog teams, psychics, ground search crews and helicopters. They conducted targeted poster distributions and media campaigns. Over the years, the society grew to have a staff of sixteen, many of them retired police detectives. It played a role in finding thousands of children.

Generally, the society wasn't called in to help for months, if not years. It was a source of endless frustration for its staff that they were always starting from behind. But when Ramona went missing from Smithers, they heard right away. They had been there before.

A BRICK WALL

IN JUNE OF 1992, Rhonda Morgan received a phone call at her office in Calgary from Judy Nikal, a Wet'suwet'en woman who lived in Telkwa, just east of Smithers. It was the day after the second anniversary of her daughter's disappearance and she was looking for help.

Delphine Nikal grew up on a hobby farm near Smithers. When she was small, the walls of her dad's bedroom were covered in pictures. Some were drawn from scratch, others torn from colouring books, some had messages scrawled in a child's hand: "To Dad, I love you, From Delphine." He saved them all. Delphine was creative, intelligent, lots of fun. She was the baby of the family, born on a chilly February day in 1975 at the same hospital as Ramona Wilson. Twelve years younger than the eldest child, Mary, Delphine spent her early years on the farm on Slack Road surrounded by chickens, goats, cattle and horses. She loved animals, especially horses, and moved around the large animals with a confidence and ease that escaped most kids. She started riding early and, with her sisters, packed up picnics and went exploring on horseback.

Other times she would wander off into the expanse of the garden and get lost among the plants. Mary, who saw her youngest sister as her baby, too, would find her sitting in the dirt eating strawberries, eyes sparkling. "There are so many good memories, but they're so short," said Mary. "I wish we had a longer time with her."

Delphine Nikal adored her nieces and nephews
and was fiercely protective of her younger friends.

Delphine's parents split up when she was still young, and in 1986, her dad died. Delphine took it really hard—they all did. She moved in with Judy and Judy's new husband in Telkwa, a village about eleven kilometres east of Smithers. Judy struggled with health problems and, like Matilda Wilson, had survived residential school at Lejac. Delphine was never happy there. She didn't like Judy's new husband, Mickey Magee, who drank heavily and tended to get "barky" when he was intoxicated.

As she reached her teens, Delphine spent a lot of time away from home, hanging out on the streets of Smithers with other girls, occasionally running afoul of the law. In 1989, she was sent away to "rehabilitation" facilities after being charged with minor offences: theft, mischief, break and enter, failure to comply. It is increasingly recognized today that incarcerating youth is harmful and counter-productive in virtually every sense, but it was far more common then, before changes to the youth criminal justice system aimed at keeping kids out of prison came into effect. At its high point in 1995, B.C. had an average of four hundred kids in custody on any given day. Then, as now, Indigenous youth were disproportionately represented in the youth criminal justice system.

While Delphine cycled through several youth facilities around the province, she stayed in close touch with her family, writing beautiful letters that ran three pages or more about how much she missed them. When she came home in May 1990, she brought them artwork and carvings she had made.

Kristal Grenkie was about twelve when she met Delphine and the two started hanging out. Delphine had stopped going to school by then. Like many Smithers teens, the girls spent a lot of time wandering up and down Main Street and lounging around an

Kristal Grenkie was close friends with Ramona Wilson and Delphine Nikal.

arcade called the Fun Centre on Second Avenue. Despite the innoc-
uous moniker, it was a rough place, a gathering point for youths to
hang out, smoke, play pool, buy drugs. It wasn't unusual for fights
to break out in the alley out behind. Youth crime and violence was
an ongoing concern in Smithers, an editorial in the local paper even
describing downtown as a "war zone" at night after a spate of van-
dalism and break and enters in the early 1990s. Around the same
time, rumours circulated of an impending gang fight between
First Nations youth and white kids. Although the fight never
materialized and police downplayed the rumours, local leaders
were concerned about racial strife among young people.

Delphine, about three years older than Kristal, was fiercely
protective of her younger friend. She made sure Kristal went to
school and was headed home by curfew. She steered Kristal away
from situations where, Kristal came to suspect years later, people
were using hard drugs. During the daytime, while Kristal was
cooped up in school, Delphine wrote her long letters. She copied
out the lyrics of her favourite song, Tom Petty's "Apartment Song,"
for her friend. She wanted to get her own place when she turned
sixteen, a spot in the world that she could call her own.

In June 1990, Judy was in the hospital in Prince George, criti-
cally ill after a surgery had gone wrong. Mickey was spending most
of his time with her at the hospital, a four-hour drive from Telkwa.
Delphine went to visit regularly. Judy would later tell a reporter
about how she grew stronger when her youngest daughter was there
with her. She would remember how Delphine promised never to
leave her, to always stay close to take care of her. While Judy fought
for her life in Prince George—she spent four months that year in
a coma—Delphine was in the care of an uncle, Frank Tompkins,
who lived in a cabin across the yard from their house in Telkwa. She
didn't complain to Kristal about her home life, but during that
period, with her mom nearly four hundred kilometres away, she
didn't seem to feel like it mattered whether she was there or not.

The afternoon of Wednesday, June 13, was warm, with temperatures in the low to mid-twenties. Around two o'clock, Delphine told her uncle that she was going to hang out with friends in town. She met up with Kristal and two other girls, and they did the usual, wandering Main Street, loitering on street corners, stopping by the Fun Centre. As evening slipped into night, Delphine, Kristal and another friend walked to the Mohawk gas station on the corner of Main Street and Highway 16. Delphine told the two girls that Judy was out of town and invited them to come back to Telkwa with her. It was unusual for Delphine to ask anyone to come to her home. Later, it would seem to her friends that she must have been afraid of something. But at the time, one girl had to work an early shift at her waitressing job and Kristal had to go to school in the morning and didn't want to risk missing the bus from Telkwa—she'd been absent too much lately. So they said their goodbyes outside the gas station. Delphine called her uncle to say she was on her way back. Then she took a few steps to the edge of the highway in the middle of town and held out her thumb.

She was fifteen years old. She never made it home.

Delphine hitchhiked frequently. So did many teenagers and adults in Smithers and all along the Highway 16 corridor. In the remote and relatively unpopulated region of northern B.C., there was no public transportation to get from one community to another. Passenger trains between Prince Rupert and Prince George only offered service a few days a week and were expensive. Greyhound buses, similarly, had limited schedules that made them impractical. For those without their own vehicles, hitchhiking was often the only option to get to work, pick up groceries, see a doctor or go to a party. In recent years, the victims along the Highway of Tears have often been described as hitchhikers—though only three of ten from the region on the RCMP task force's list were publicly confirmed to be hitchhiking when they were last seen. Various organizations have pushed hard to drill in the message that it is not a safe means of getting around, with public awareness campaigns and billboards along the road warning of its dangers. But in the 1980s and '90s, it was a fairly common practice. And it still is. There remain few options.

When Delphine's family reported her missing, the police said she had probably just taken off for a while. But it didn't make sense to those who knew her. Judy was really sick—Delphine would not abandon her mother like that and leave her to worry. All of Delphine's belongings were still at her home. She hadn't said anything to her friends or family about plans to leave. Kristal couldn't fathom why, if Delphine was planning to run away, she would have invited her friends to her house that night. Or why she wouldn't have asked them to run away with her. They had hitchhiked to other communities along the highway before; there was no reason Delphine would hide a plan like that from her friends. It just didn't make sense.

In those first days, with Judy in hospital in Prince George, the search fell to Delphine's sisters and Kristal. They heard rumours that she might have gone to Granisle, a village on the shores of Babine Lake, 150 kilometres from Smithers. They drove there and knocked on every door. They tried to get missing person posters made at the local stationery store. Kristal remembered being quoted $300 for a hundred colour pictures, far more money than they had. "We just had zero resources. Zero," said Kristal. All they could do was ask people, rely on word of mouth to spread news of Delphine's disappearance and hope that some information would come back. "There was no, literally no, support," said Mary. "The cops never really showed a whole lot of interest . . . They obviously didn't really care." Maybe it was because Delphine had a history with the police. "I think because she was in trouble, there was that discrimination against her from the police," said Mary. Maybe it was racism. "Just another native, you know."

Behind its faux-Alps facade, Smithers was fraught with racial tension during the days that Ramona and Delphine were growing up there. It had been since Europeans arrived to settle in the early twentieth century and displaced the Wet'suwet'en people who had lived in the region for at least six thousand years. "Provincial and federal policies were clearly aimed at restricting Indigenous land use and fostering northern settlement," notes the book *Shared Histories*, by geographer and former Smithers resident Tyler McCreary, detailing the history of colonial settlement on Wet'suwet'en lands around Smithers. "Pushed from their lands, First Nations peoples were forced to congregate in newly created reserves or on the fringes of the new northern settlements." When Wet'suwet'en families settled on the outskirts of town, in what came to be known as Indiantown, local officials unsuccessfully implored the military, the RCMP and Indian Affairs to remove them. In the 1920s, a public petition called for a ban on "Indians or other colored . . . folks" owning property in Smithers. Businesses refused to serve Wet'suwet'en patrons; another petition called for First Nations and people of Asian descent to be barred from starting a business on Main Street. The hospital was segregated, and Wet'suwet'en children were "either channeled into residential schools or denied an education entirely." Those officially sanctioned barriers eventually came down, but Wet'suwet'en people continued to face racism, discrimination and unequal treatment at the hospital, in schools and throughout settler society.

The early colonial economy relied heavily on First Nations people as a source of labour for building the railway, clearing land for farms, logging and mining, as well as working as cleaners, hospital aides and cooks. "Engaging in paid work, Witsuwit'en were effectively adapting to the opportunities and difficulties that the settler economy introduced," McCreary writes. But working for wages in the changing economy "fostered increasing reliance on the marketplace for items such as clothes rather than making them at home," at the same time as settlement restricted access to land. "Railways, roads, farms, fences, and sawmills interfered with Witsuwit'en territorial access, making livelihoods on the yintah increasingly difficult to practice." Government policies that restricted Indigenous people from traditional means of subsistence, such as hunting, trapping and fishing, came into force throughout the early twentieth century. By mid-century, increasing industrialization was rendering many jobs obsolete at the same time as a new wave of European settlement came to the valley. What jobs were available went to white people first. "With decreased demand for Witsuwit'en workers, post-war economic growth did not fully extend to Witsuwit'en people but instead increased their relative poverty," McCreary writes. Government restrictions did lift over the years, but the increasing number of settlers, along with commercial industry and fisheries, had reduced the amount of fish and wildlife. Many Wet'suwet'en families had endeavoured to adapt to the colonial landscape and ensure access to education—both in settler schools and through the continuation of traditional Wet'suwet'en practices—for their children. But, as McCreary notes, "settler authorities continued to blame Indigenous families for their poverty and marginalization, and then used these conditions to justify, first, removing children, and second, removing families from their homes in Indiantown. Provincial authorities targeted Indigenous children for removal from their families so they could be raised in white, middle-class homes. Municipal authorities targeted the removal of the Witsuwit'en homes in Indiantown, clearing and redeveloping the area as part of a modernizing town." The municipality cleared Indiantown. Some of its residents moved into Smithers, while "other families struggled with increased marginalization and were pushed further to the fringe."

That was in the 1970s, just as several First Nations in the northwest were mounting legal challenges to have title to their land recognized by the provincial and federal governments. Unlike most places in Canada, B.C. did not undertake a treaty process when it laid claim to the territory in the 1870s. With the exception of a few areas, the provincial government refused to recognize that First Nations had rights to the land they lived on; the Crown simply took it, without consultation or compensation. A century later, in 1973, the Nisga'a, whose territory lies west of Smithers, argued before the Supreme Court of Canada that they had never ceded title to their land. The court's decision marked the first time the Canadian legal system recognized Aboriginal title. Later, a case brought forward by the Wet'suwet'en and the Gitxsan further established Indigenous rights to the land. In 1993, the British Columbia Treaty Commission began to oversee treaty negotiations with First Nations across the province, a process that, while slow, opened the door to the reassertion of First Nations' land rights.

The treaty process amplified racism in Smithers "big time," remembered Bill Goodacre, a lifelong resident of the area whose family arrived in 1911 among the early waves of European settlers. Over the years Bill served a handful of terms on town council, decades as a board member of the local Friendship Centre, and as a member of the provincial legislative assembly for the region. Treaty negotiations and land claims dominated the news; the local paper, the *Interior News*, was full of vitriolic letters from those who feared losing their properties and businesses to First Nations, along with plenty of responses in support of the treaty process. "In those days, there was a lot of misinformation about what would happen during the treaty process—this whole idea that you're going to lose your private land," said Bill. "That was the rallying cry of the rednecks and, of course, it was a bogus issue right from the beginning. It was never in any jeopardy." First Nations block ades were commonplace, and confrontations, sometimes violent, erupted. "Tensions are growing in the Hazeltons over native Indian blockades of roads preventing loggers from working in the Kispiox

Valley," declared one newspaper story. Another recounted how a group of Kitwanga "locals" aligned with logging interests lit a First Nations blockade on fire, threw gas bombs and drove a truck into it while six people were inside.

At a packed community meeting organized to discuss local land claims, a group of twenty or so white men heckled and shouted down the Wet'suwet'en speaker as he tried to explain the treaty process. Shortly afterward, Herb George, a hereditary chief, told the *Interior News* that his people hadn't experienced such hostility since the struggle to win the right to vote in 1960. "Our people go into Smithers to do shopping and people say, 'Are you going to take my business away?' Some people won't even look us in the eyes." In a letter to the *Interior News* on October 26, 1994, Edna Dennis described how she and her family had been attacked outside a convenience store by a group of young men who hit her husband, hurled racial slurs at her and reached in the window of her vehicle, where her children sat, yelling at them. When she rushed into the store for help, the attendant refused to call the police.

Overt demonstrations of blatant racism, like the attack at the convenience store, were isolated incidents by the 1990s, said Bill, though they reflected an underlying problem that continues in the community. "The Two Solitudes is a very apt description of this town," he said, referring to the 1945 novel by Hugh MacLennan that examines the communication, or lack thereof, between French and English Canada. He offered an example: at the Christmas dinner for seniors at the Elks Lodge, which he had attended the night before, there wasn't one person out of 150 who was visibly First Nations. The next week, he planned to go to the Christmas dinner hosted by the Friendship Centre, where he predicted 90 per cent of the attendees would be First Nations. "We're both living in the same geographic spot," he said, "but we might as well be living in entirely separate communities for the amount of integration that exists." Brenda Wilson remembered going to Catholic church services in Smithers as a child, where First Nations people sat on one side and white people on the other; she sometimes went to sit on the "white" side to raise some eyebrows. "I never really understood the word racism, I only understood what I was going through," Brenda said. "Just knowing that I was always having to fight for myself and for my brothers, our family." When she eventually looked up the word, she thought, "Okay. That's what I've been [dealing with] my whole life since I was born."

The segregation, and at times hostility, made its way into the halls of the secondary school. Students from elementary schools in Smithers, as well as those from surrounding communities such as Telkwa and Moricetown, all coalesced at the high school. Social fault lines existed between geographic groups, as well as the other teenage divides: there were jocks, geeks, stoners and preppies. And there were First Nations and white kids. The barriers weren't impenetrable, but they were there. "It was quite separate," said Kristal. "There was not a lot of integration." In a public call for help to start a teen newspaper, a seventeen-year-old student called racism the biggest issue facing youth in the community. "There's a lot of fighting uptown on Friday nights and no amount of community forums or teachers saying everyone should be equal is going to do anything," he wrote. "[Racism] is the root problem that sparks so [many] other problems. A lot of the violence here stems from racism."

The *Interior News* ran a story about Delphine on October 10, four months after she disappeared. It's possible there were earlier stories, though a search on microfiche at the local museum of the issues between Delphine's disappearance and the October article didn't turn any up, and neither Mary nor Kristal remembered any coverage. The October article reported that the search for Delphine was expanding to all of British Columbia, though police were ruling out

foul play. The officer in charge of the investigation is quoted saying
hundreds of young people go missing every year in the province,
with many turning up on the streets of Vancouver. "We have no
indication of foul play. We're not considering (that) at the moment,"
he said. The RCMP and B.C.'s Ministry of Public Safety and
Solicitor General say statistics on missing people from that long ago
are not available, but figures from 2018 show nearly seven thousand reports of missing children and youths in British Columbia.
Nationally, more than 90 per cent of kids are found within a week.

   "It was really terrible because we knew," said Mary. "We knew
something was wrong." The family's efforts to find Delphine in
Vancouver had turned up nothing. Judy had searched in Granisle
and as far away as Quesnel, a hundred kilometres south of Prince
George. The following year, there was one story about Delphine in
the newspaper. Judy wanted to create a reward, but according to the
Interior News, "So far, attempts to raise money or get help have
proved unsuccessful." Judy said, "I wish some people would have the
same spirit as for the boy who went missing in Victoria," referring to
Michael Dunahee, a four-year-old whose disappearance the month
before was met with national concern.

   Rhonda wasn't sure how Judy heard about the society. It was
involved in some high-profile cases around that time, so maybe she
had seen something on the news. When Judy called in June 1992,
Rhonda did an initial interview to collect basic information about
Delphine's disappearance. She was immediately touched by the
case, by how hard Judy was trying and how little support she seemed
to have. "Judy was a sweetheart," said Rhonda, "I liked her very
much." She made arrangements to send Fred Maile to Smithers.

   Fred was a private investigator who had co-founded the
Burnaby-based firm Canpro Investigative Services after retiring
from a twenty-five-year career with the RCMP. He had worked what
was then Canada's most notorious serial killer case. In a spree that

lasted twenty months, career criminal Clifford Olson murdered at least eleven kids in B.C.'s Lower Mainland. "When distraught parents initially complained about police inaction and to speculate about the existence of a serial killer, investigators downplayed such fears. They insisted it was likely the missing teens had run away," noted a *Vancouver Sun* article about Olson's death in 2011. The RCMP was heavily criticized for its actions, as Olson, despite being a suspect, wasn't apprehended and continued to kill. When finally he did confess, it was to Fred, who soon was riding around in the back seat of a police car tape-recording Olson as the serial killer took officers to his victims' remains while recounting what he had done to them.

Fred arrived in Smithers on April 5, 1993, to look for Delphine. As was the protocol, he met with police and Delphine's family to glean all the information he could about the case. He established a timeline of the days before Delphine went missing, including a recent run-in with the law. "There were a lot of rumours in the beginning saying that Delphine had run away," said Rhonda, "and part of that came from speculating that she didn't want to face the music. We quickly ruled that out, though." They reached out to contacts in Vancouver's Downtown Eastside, where runaway youths from the north often wound up and where rumours had put Delphine, but there was no sign of her. "Plus we couldn't find any reason why—she didn't tell anybody she was leaving," said Rhonda. Aside from rumours, there was nothing to suggest she'd taken off. To be sure, when Fred returned to the Lower Mainland, he scoured the streets of the Downtown Eastside, checking in with frontline workers and service providers—needle exchanges, social services, shelters—and residents for any sign of her. It is a geographically small area, beset with grinding poverty and a population strug-gling with mental health issues and addiction, but it is a tight-knit community where people keep an eye on each other and myriad

organizations work. If Delphine had gone there, she almost certainly would have come into contact with the people who live there
and the agencies that work there. He didn't find any trace.

Fred also learned that Delphine's cousin, also from the
Smithers area, was missing. Cecilia Nikal, born in 1971, boarded a
bus in Smithers with a friend in August 1989, heading to Vancouver
to visit her mother. According to Fred's report, Cecilia called
the woman who had raised her since 1983 a few days later to say she
was okay and would be back in Smithers in a couple of weeks. But
she never returned. It's not clear whether she showed up in
Vancouver. Cecilia was never registered with the Missing Children
Society, but Fred decided to investigate her disappearance. "Cecilia,
because she disappeared so close to Delphine . . . Fred took her very
seriously," said Rhonda. "We took her on as a 'piggy back' to
Delphine's case." He looked for her in Vancouver, too, but found no
sign she'd been there. "I'm convinced she wasn't there," said
Rhonda, though Mary said a family member had seen her there.

A few months later, in July of 1993, the society returned to the
northwest to follow up on a tip that had come in shortly after
Delphine went missing. A man who drove a postal truck had found
a bloody shoe along Highway 16 about halfway between Smithers
and Prince George. "We wanted to do a search of the area to make
sure it was cleared," said Rhonda. The society flew in a pair of
cadaver dogs, trained to locate human remains, from Portland,
Oregon. But when they arrived, they found that in the time since
the discovery, road construction crews had dug up the area to
widen the highway. Rhonda recalled, "It was felt that if there
had been a body there, the construction crews would have come
across the remains, or the heavy equipment further buried her.
We put the dogs in anyway and came up with nothing." They also
brought the dogs to an area along the Bulkley River about eight
kilometres east of Smithers in response to a clue from a psychic,
but again found nothing.

One of the most promising leads, to Fred and Rhonda, came from a woman who helped Judy and the society extensively in their search efforts. She had spoken with someone who worked at the Mohawk gas station on the corner, where Delphine had parted ways with her friends, who claimed to have seen Delphine getting into a car that night. Although the woman had lost her notes and couldn't remember the name of the witness, she did remember the description of the vehicle: a red sports car. When Fred asked Judy if she knew of anyone with such a car who Delphine might have known, Judy had a name. (Rhonda said she can't disclose it—the investigation is still open.) In his report, Fred wrote, "It is evident the police have conducted a very thorough investigation and have systematically eliminated all sightings and confirmed information to date as negative." Fred has since passed away and Rhonda does not have his notes. There is no mention in her files of how, or whether, police dealt with the sports-car tip. "I don't know if it was properly looked at."

It wasn't until June 1994, in the midst of the Wilson family's comparatively high-profile campaign, that Delphine's name began to appear a little more regularly in the local paper. As Kristal said, "If you think Ramona was not reacted upon, Delphine was even worse." Fred told a reporter that he was convinced the person responsible for Delphine's disappearance was from the Smithers or Terrace area and recommended a media blitz, including a reenactment of her getting picked up along the highway. The story quoted his August 1993 report: "One cannot help but feel that someone must have witnessed her hitchhiking and possibly being picked up . . . Efforts should also be in place to have the municipality and/or native association offer a substantial reward, which should be part of the news blitz." It was the Missing Children Society of Canada that eventually coordinated a re-enactment and offered up the $10,000 reward for information on Delphine or Ramona. The RCMP sent Const. Gerry Marshinew from Prince

Rupert to help the smaller detachment with the investigation into both missing girls. In July 1994, he told the *Interior News* that police didn't know if the two disappearances were connected: "I can't say yes or no because I don't know. There's nothing linking them at the moment." By August, the increased attention seemed to be helping—police had received more than 175 tips from across the province. In the town, however, there was a ripple of acknowledgement, but no outcry, no swell of support. "I don't recall a whole lot of activity going on around it," said Bill Goodacre. "It was just a sad undercurrent."

Judy feared that the police had overlooked something early in their investigation because they had treated Delphine as a runaway rather than a missing child. If the RCMP had acted more quickly, she would later tell a reporter, "they might have found her." Rhonda's organization, under Fred's tutelage, had quickly learned that it is vital to treat every case of a missing child as a worst-case scenario. That means taking it seriously from the start and immediately getting to work on door-to-door inquiries and establishing a timeline. "When you don't take it seriously at the beginning, you lose out on too much valuable information," said Rhonda. This ran contrary to a common police practice of waiting a couple of days before starting a search, because usually missing people turned up within a day or two. But if the person didn't show up, it meant losing out on precious time and information. "We had our fair share of cases where you start to react quickly and the kid was just at a weekend party," said Rhonda, "and the resources were wasted—but not wasted. If it had turned out badly, then you're ahead of the game."

Judy looked for her daughter across B.C., all the way down to Vancouver. She sought out reporters, trying to get them and, by extension, the public to care. She went to psychics, one of whom told her Delphine had been kidnapped and was somewhere near a river. It wasn't enough information to know where to go looking. She prayed. "I was always a good mother to my kids," she said. "All

I can say is why me?" In 1995, Judy wrote a letter to the editor of the *Interior News*:

> My name is Judy Nikal, now Magee, and it's well known my youngest daughter Delphine Nikal went missing five years ago this month.
>
> It is very distressing to see all the efforts that the community has put forth on behalf of the family of Ramona Wilson to raise funds, etcetera, especially since nothing was done in efforts to find or look for my daughter.
>
> It seems that everything possible was done to find Ramona, and I don't begrudge her family that. But I do feel as if I am a different class of citizen since I have begged, written letters, made umpteen telephone calls, and tried miscellaneous avenues to get help in looking for Delphine.
>
> But I have always met with a brick wall.
>
> Why? Does no one care about my child? My heart is broken and grieving and it is hard to sit by and see nothing or no help.
>
> Financially I have nothing left; emotionally I am drained; physically I am ill. Can no one help? Please—I love my girl too.

Judy had recovered from the surgery and the coma in 1990, but she was never in a good, healthy space again, said Mary. "I think she just kind of gave up." Judy died later that year.

PART OF YOU IS MISSING

LESS THAN A MONTH after Ramona Wilson was last seen in July 1994, a Missing Children Society of Canada team consisting of Rhonda Morgan, Fred Maile, another investigator named Susan Antonello and a Louisiana psychic named Mary Martin landed at Smithers Airport. When a child goes missing and the case makes the news, psychics come out of the woodwork. With each case, the society was flooded with tips from people Rhonda had learned long before were nothing more than, in her words, "whack jobs." But she did not dismiss clairvoyants altogether; the society had worked successfully with several who had blown its investigators away. Mary Martin was one of those.

Mary had given Rhonda some clues from her home in Louisiana, and the society decided to bring her up to Smithers. They spent a lot of time in Moricetown, where Mary felt Ramona might be found somewhere between the reserve's school and the dramatic canyon where Wet'suwet'en fishers perched on the dark, slippery rocks to gaff salmon. She also had "strong feelings" about an area between the reserve and Smithers. But nothing came of it. Mary and the rest of the team soon returned home.

Mary called Rhonda as soon as she landed. She said a spirit had told her Ramona was at the end of the airport runway and she had sensed a number of clues: a white mound, the colour yellow, a pond and two waterfalls, the phrase "airport four" and a pattern of lights that she drew out and sent to Rhonda. When Rhonda returned to Smithers in August to continue the search with Susan Antonello, they headed to the airport to see if any of Mary's clues jibed with what they could find on the ground. As they approached, they noticed the signs on either side of the airport marking the distance to the turnoff: "Airport 4." They were convinced. They waited until dark and then returned to the airport to ask staff to turn on the runway lights. They wanted to see if the pattern matched Mary's drawing. It did. The man working there was intrigued. He wanted to know what the other clues were. Investigators had to be careful about what they divulged to the public, so Rhonda told him the most generic clue she had: yellow. He passed her a set of binoculars and had her train them northward, where car headlights moved slowly along a road in the distance. "That's Yelich Road," he said.

When daylight came, Rhonda and Sue drove along Yelich Road, looking on either side of the car for anything that matched the other clues Mary had provided. And then they parked the car and Rhonda looked over at Sue. "What the hell are we doing?" she asked. "She could be anywhere." They drove back to town.

Rhonda and Fred went out to the apartments at Lake Kathlyn, the same rundown motel-style strip five kilometres west of town that Brenda and Matilda had visited when they realized Ramona was missing. Rhonda said her team was warned about the young man whose apartment they were headed for, that he was a drug dealer and it was a potentially violent crowd that hung out there.

As a precaution, while she and Fred went to the door, Susan Antonello waited in the car with instructions: if they didn't emerge shortly, Susan was to drive to the RCMP detachment to get help. They would make several more trips, but the people they encountered at the apartment were not overly co-operative. No one remembered—or admitted remembering, anyway—seeing Ramona there. The team interviewed staff at stores Ramona might have passed and at a gas station that looks out onto a popular hitchhiking spot on the highway. They went door to door through the town and arranged for police dogs to search a wooded area off Alfred Avenue, near Ramona's home, where people had reported a foul smell. But they turned up nothing. Ramona Wilson went from Alfred Avenue to gone.

It is impossible to know exactly what the police did to search for Ramona or Delphine Nikal. Police files are not public documents, and officers are cautious about what they disclose about open investigations: letting the wrong information out can taint evidence, jeopardize future legal proceedings and put people in harm's way. It's a means to "protect the integrity of the information for court," said RCMP Staff Sgt. Wayne Clary, who many years later led a police task force probing a number of Highway of Tears cases. "It's important for the integrity of witnesses that get on the stand and talk about what they may or may not know, or somebody we charge, if he tells us what he did. If [the information is] already out there . . . the value becomes quite limited when you get something to tell the judge."

But Garry Kerr, a retired RCMP member who was the lead investigator in one Highway of Tears case and oversaw a file review of several others, said the RCMP often takes silence further than necessary, to the detriment of solving cases. "The RCMP cannot get the media thing right. They are so off the mark 99 per cent of the time," said Garry, who said he enjoyed a "great" relationship with media in his career, something "really frowned upon" by the RCMP brass. "It's frustrating because it could be so much more beneficial to the RCMP. You're looking for the people in that town or city or whatever to come forward, and the best way to do it is through the media." Michael Arntfield, a criminologist and former police officer, said studies show that about 90 per cent of crime is solved through some form of citizen involvement. The philosophy of "a wall of silence and keeping everything in-camera and under lockdown" is "actually antithetical to getting the case solved," he said, because it discourages public engagement. "They're not the CIA. They are a publicly funded, public-facing public service. The whole keeping everyone in the dark . . . it's a convenient way to do your job ineffectively because no one knows—nothing you do is verifiable or falsifiable. It's part of the big secret." The wall of silence, he said, can mean rumours proliferate unchecked. And it can "very quickly turn everyone, including the most important people you're working for which is the families, against you."

Lorimer Shenher, a retired Vancouver Police Department detective who investigated dozens of missing women in that city, called the secrecy "a power trip." He suggested resources might also be a reason for poor communication—typically the lead investigator would be responsible for communicating with family and the public, and many "believe that their time is better spent trying to find the loved ones than it is to try to talk to the families," said Shenher. "But there's gotta be a balance there. There's a bit of a lack of respect, honestly, for the families."

Ramona's family did not feel that police took their concerns seriously or tried very hard to find her—a sentiment echoed time and again from families and in First Nations communities along the highway with missing or murdered loved ones. The RCMP insists that they investigated thoroughly. It is difficult to assess that assertion, because, beyond newspaper reports and memories, there's no accessible record of what was done. The common perception among families, however, is clear: the police didn't care. Relations between the RCMP and many First Nations were abysmal. Rhonda Morgan saw it. "I think there was a lot of frustration on both ends," she said. She knew families perceived the police as uninterested; and in some cases, the police were too quick to write off certain people or information. "They don't trust each other."

The summer passed and stories circulated and someone arrived at the Smithers RCMP detachment with bones they'd found in the bush that seemed to resemble human feet. They turned out to be bear paws. A teenage girl's body was found near the highway just outside Burns Lake, two hundred kilometres east. It was Roxanne Thiara, a fifteen-year-old who had gone missing from Prince George a few weeks after Ramona.

Matilda didn't have money for a reward, or to photocopy enough missing posters to go around. The Gitanmaax Band Council quickly put up $1,000 for information, but Matilda knew that wasn't enough. She wanted $10,000. The family began to fundraise. Matilda made leather vests and beaded moccasins; Brenda made earrings, necklaces and bracelets. They baked. In December of 1994, as Christmas lights went up along Main Street and carols blasted from storefronts, Matilda and Brenda sat at a plastic foldout table in a small shopping centre beside the highway that housed a pharmacy, a grocery and a budget clothing store and sold cookies and raffle tickets. First prize was a vest, second prize a dream catcher. Third and fourth were sets of necklaces and earrings. Tickets went for $2 each, or three for $5.

They made $500.

Christmas came and went, and so did New Year's Eve. The lights and wreaths and ribbons that go up along Main Street each year in December were packed away for another season. Still, there was no news. The bank account set up to receive donations for the reward sat at $1,500, the money from the band council and the raffle. Public and police interest in Ramona seemed to be dwindling.

Brenda had been a social drinker up to that point in her life, but after her sister's disappearance she depended more and more on alcohol to get her through the days. "I had a good job, I was just starting out with my family, things were just starting to happen for me," she said. "It just all fell apart." Still, she pulled together a benefit dance to raise reward money. It would feature a local band, prizes and dancing. Alongside a brief story in the newspaper about the fundraiser was an open letter, titled "A part of you is missing," that Brenda had written addressing those who might know where Ramona was:

> You know how hard it is to wake up each and every day and feel that "part of you" is just not there anymore. Evenings you just can't sleep because that "part of you" keeps haunting you with dreadful thoughts of why that "part of you" is not there . . . You know there are a few people that can help you get that "part of you" back but they are just frightened to tell you how to get it back. But you know that they do not have anything to be afraid of since you are very understanding. The best thing these people can do to get that "part of you" back is to just give you a hint on where to look.

That same month, January 1995, Melanie Carpenter was kidnapped from the salon where she worked in Surrey, just outside Vancouver. At a press conference several days later, her father, Steve, produced a wad of hundred-dollar bills totalling $20,000 as an incentive for the safe return of his blonde-haired, twenty-three-year-old daughter. Soon he upped the reward to $50,000. The story was leading news across Canada, and hundreds of volunteers scoured the Lower Mainland searching for Melanie. Just over a week after she was abducted, the prime suspect, Fernand Auger, a convicted sex offender who was out on parole, was found dead of an apparent suicide in a rented car in the garage of a vacant farmhouse outside Calgary. Eleven days later, two men came across Melanie's body, wrapped in a sleeping bag, on the banks of the Fraser River near Yale, B.C., a small town along the Trans-Canada Highway north of Hope. Four thousand people attended her funeral, held at Vancouver's Pacific Coliseum. Police officers with yellow ribbons signalling their support joined the crowd, and municipal buses flashed "Remember Melanie" on their displays. Employees at BC Hydro, where Melanie's mom worked, raised $8,000 to help cover costs of the search. At the service, broadcast live on TV, Steve stood before a grieving, angry nation and said his daughter had become something more: "Today I pass her on to be Canada's daughter."

Steve launched a campaign that sought to tighten parole eligibility to keep violent offenders like Fernand Auger in prison for life. The momentum was palpable: across the country, people from all walks of life rallied to the cause. The publicity surrounding Melanie's murder was almost unprecedented—and, some warned, dangerous, a fomentation of hysteria that shouldn't inform public policy and debate. "It prepares the groundwork for demagogues," Bob Hackett, a professor of communications at Simon Fraser University, warned in a news article. The media, he said, responded to the Carpenter story not because of what her case represented but because of who she was. "Let me ask you this: Do you think Melanie Carpenter would have received this much attention if she were a native woman who was abducted?" As in communities across the country, many in Smithers threw their support behind the campaign, organizing a benefit dance to take place that spring. The event featured a popular local musician and an estimated $6,000 to $8,000 in donated

Matilda Wilson, centre, with her children.
Ramona, lower right, was a light in the household.

merchandise and gift cards from local businesses. It drew in $6,200 and hosted a "disappointing" crowd of fewer than a hundred people. As for the Wilson family's fundraiser, held not long before, hardly anyone came. Their fundraiser barely broke even.

On January 27, 1995, the RCMP got a call from a man who did not give his name. He said a friend had told him what happened to Ramona. She could be found, he said, west of Smithers. Cpl. Bob Paulson, from Prince Rupert's investigative section, said the police found "it very promising" and that it meshed with other information pointing to the same area. But investigators needed more information, he said, "to be able to act on it."

In February, a week before Ramona's seventeenth birthday, and after someone from Smithers, very upset about the lack of support for their families, had called Rhonda, the Missing Children Society of Canada announced it would cover a $10,000 reward for information about Ramona and Delphine. It wasn't standard practice for the society—usually families could scrounge up reward money on their own—but it was the right thing to do. The announcement of the reward would go along with a "saturation campaign" of posters to be sent out across northwestern B.C.

And still, nothing. Kristal Grenkie spent hours hunched over a Ouija board, asking where her friend was and who was responsible for her disappearance. Matilda wrote an open letter begging the tipster to call back with more information. She reminded the caller that he was guaranteed confidentiality. She said all they needed was a little more information about where to search. She offered up the $10,000 reward. She wrote, in part:

> I know it's hard to know or witness something you didn't want to be involved in. It will be harder for you to live with this all your life; sooner or later the truth will have to come out. You'll feel a heavy burden lifted if you can help me and my family locate Ramona—I hate to say it—dead or alive. I don't want her laying out there when someone knows where she is . . . If she has met with foul play, the family would like you to give us just the location and we'll go from there. Please do not be scared because you will never be involved in this investigation as long as you give the RCMP the main and specific details. You'll never be bothered again.

In the spring of 1995, two teenagers were four-wheeling in a muddy clearing just off Yelich Road. The narrow dirt lane angles north off the highway eleven kilometres west of Smithers, passing a few properties before brushing up against the northern edge of the airport runway and bending around old rugby fields that served as a popular party pit for local teens. It was April 9, still chilly, and green shoots would have just started emerging from the poplar groves that flank the road, the forest floor still the dull grey-brown left behind after the snow melts. The boys got stuck and headed into the woods in search of a log to use as a pry bar.

Instead, they found a body, on the edge of the woods in a thicket, where the limbs of young trees formed an archway over the remains. Beside the body was a piece of bright yellow rope and three white nylon cable ties. Clothes—leggings, a purple sweatshirt—were nearby.

The phone rang at Matilda's house on Railway Avenue. An officer told her about the remains found at the airport, told her they weren't sure yet who it was. But Matilda had a feeling then, a stirring deep in her gut. Soon, the police called back. They had identified the body through dental records.

Matilda was summoned to the police station to look at some of the items found alongside her daughter. The entire family went, not just Ramona's siblings but aunts and uncles, cousins and friends. Kristal was there, and a counsellor from the high school, all crowded into the small RCMP detachment. It was hot with all the people. Some of the family were brought into a little room where some clothing had been set out. Were these Ramona's clothes, the officer wanted to know. The family cried, held each other. Yes, those are Ramona's clothes, Matilda said. The officer marked something down on his clipboard. "Where are her shoes?" Matilda asked. "I just bought her some Reeboks. She's so proud of those because they're those high runners." Police hadn't found any shoes. Maybe an animal had dragged them off. Matilda wouldn't take no for an answer. She wanted to find the shoes. The next day,

Ramona's uncles went out to Yelich Road. They combed the bush for miles, looking for the white and pink high-tops. They never found them. Police said the murder was obviously "sexually motivated" and probably occurred at that spot on the edge of the woods ten months before.

Matilda buried her youngest daughter in the Smithers cemetery, less than two kilometres from the hospital where she was born. Matilda, standing straight and tall, told a local reporter she had something to say to the man who killed her daughter. "I want to give him a message. I want to tell him there's a God. And he will pay in the worst way. That time will come for him. He just has to wait for it. Nobody gets away with murder. Nobody."

And then Matilda fell apart. She went home and agonized over how her daughter had died, what those last moments had been like, what Ramona was thinking as she took her last breath. Matilda started drinking, and she didn't figure she would stop until she, too, was dead. She wanted to go somewhere else, to wherever Ramona was now. She didn't really make a suicide plan. She just drank and waited to die.

It was late May, or maybe early June, when Matilda received a card from her eldest daughter. Brenda wrote that she and her brothers were hurting and didn't know what to do. They needed their mom. Without her, they would die, too. She had to come back to them. And Matilda, who loves her children more than anything, did.

The second weekend of June 1995, Matilda led the Ramona Wilson memorial walk down Highway 16 to Yelich Road for the first time. She has done it every year since. It has changed over the decades. It doesn't cover the eleven kilometres from Smithers to the place Ramona was found anymore; many of the walkers, including Matilda, have grown too old to travel that distance. Other walkers, perhaps a dozen, who came every year for so many years, have passed away now. And the walk isn't just about Ramona anymore. It's about all the girls and women who have been taken from the Highway of Tears. Some, like Ramona, turned up dead. Others, like Delphine, simply gone.

Matilda marches for them all.

FALLING THROUGH THE CRACKS

THE POLICE PICKED UP Kristal Grenkie on a Monday night and brought her to the Smithers RCMP detachment just off the highway. They led her into a room. Officers laid out three photos on the table in front of her and demanded answers.

In four years, three of Kristal's friends had disappeared: Delphine Nikal in June of 1990, Ramona Wilson four years later and fifteen-year-old Roxanne Thiara, who vanished from Prince George on a long weekend in July not a month after Ramona went missing. Kristal was terrified as the police berated her: "Are you telling us that it's just circumstantial that you know all three of these people?" It was as if they believed she knew who had done this to her friends and just wasn't saying, as if they were sure she was guilty of something. She felt guilty; she had put herself in so many more vulnerable situations than Ramona ever did, "but nobody snapped up and took advantage of it," she said. "I should have had a higher probability . . . I just don't know that somebody would have wanted to take a white person off the streets, because they would have had a hell of a reaction." At one point during the interrogation, she asked if she was under arrest. "I was crying and feeling so bad and so guilty," Kristal said. "It was frickin' confusing." When Kristal finally emerged, she was overwhelmed with the feeling that somehow this was all her fault. It was devastating for the girl who had already lost her friends. And it was counterproductive.

Despite how traumatic the experience was, part of Kristal was relieved. At least the police were doing something. But looking back more than twenty years later, as a mother of four, she can hardly believe how the officers went about it. "What the hell were you guys thinking?" she said. "I hope I didn't miss anything based on how you guys made me feel, [how my] information was going to be taken." Kristal had had run-ins with the police, including a fight that had landed her in juvenile detention for six months on an assault charge. To her, and to many of the people she hung out with, cops were to be avoided and feared. They were not people to go to for help. She wanted justice for her friends, but she didn't believe the police would deliver it or that she could help them even if she did have useful information. "I don't know that I would have trusted the cops."

Roxanne Thiara was born in Manitoba. As a baby, she was put in the care of Mildred Thiara, a woman with three grown children, in Quesnel, B.C. The community of around ten thousand people, about a hundred kilometres south of Prince George, was built upon Lhtako Dene territory in the mid-nineteenth century as a mining hub that later evolved into a logging and mill town. Roxanne bounced back and forth between her biological mother's home and her foster home until she was a toddler, when Mildred was granted legal guardianship. A couple of years later, the family moved to Abbotsford, B.C., where Roxanne attended elementary school from Grade 1 to 5, before returning to Quesnel. "She was quite a good kid—a really happy, bubbly kid," Mildred told a reporter in 1994. Although Roxanne wasn't biologically related to the family, Mildred said she was "always our family. We never considered her any other way." When she was twelve, Roxanne reconnected with her biological father, Roland Twan, who described her to the *Vancouver Sun* as a beautiful girl and "a happy kid. Happy, very outgoing, friendly. A very nice person."

Roxanne began to struggle during her early teen years. "That's when she started turning. Everything changed with her. She got in with a bad bunch. She was really moody," Mildred told a reporter. She experimented with smoking pot. She stopped attending school. Things became a "constant battle" with her. Mildred tried everything, taking her to a psychiatrist and elsewhere for help. "I stepped on a lot of toes trying to get her help," she said.

When she was about twelve, Roxanne was incarcerated in the youth detention centre in Prince George, where she met Kristal Grenkie, who was serving her six-month sentence for assault. Kristal couldn't remember why Roxanne was there, but she thought it was for a relatively petty offence, stealing money or something to that effect. What Kristal recalled most clearly is how innocent Roxanne was. She was afraid to leave her cell. "She was just such a little kid, she was so young," said Kristal, who, at barely thirteen, was worldly and mature by comparison. Roxanne was naive to the ways of prison. She told on her peers, who then wanted to beat her up. "You better behave," Kristal warned her. "Keep your mouth shut." Roxanne learned quickly and was soon accepted. She made her way into a rough crowd of girls, and she remained friends with them after she left. Roxanne's former brother-in-law, Rene Beirness, said incarceration was "the worst thing that happened to her." After her release, she "went wild."

When the police showed Kristal a picture of Roxanne a few years later as they grilled her about her connection to three missing or murdered friends, she could hardly believe it was the same

innocent little kid she'd coached in prison. It looked like Roxanne
had become one of those girls who had frightened her when she
first arrived there. "In my eyes, jail became the demise of Roxanne,"
said Kristal. "This is such a fail. A young girl like that, why expose
her to this? In there, it was survival of the toughest."

Roxanne Thiara was an outgoing, friendly girl
who wanted to become a fashion designer.

In B.C., youths who are taken into care before their first birthday
have a nearly 50 per cent chance of ending up involved in the youth
criminal justice system, a percentage that remains fairly consistent
until the age of seventeen. Authorities remove children from their
homes when there is reason to believe they face abuse, neglect or
are "otherwise in need of protection." There is much criticism
about how child welfare authorities reach their decisions and
widespread accusations of arbitrariness and racism. According to
a report by B.C.'s Representative for Children and Youth, an officer
tasked with providing independent oversight of the child welfare

system in the province, children who have been abused or neglected "suffer disproportionately from neurodevelopmental disabilities, mental health concerns and behaviour issues related to past victimization and neglect." They are at least 25 per cent more likely to develop problem behaviours such as violence, substance abuse and low academic achievement. "They are generally members of families where there are disproportionately high levels of substance use, domestic violence, untreated mental health issues and multiple stresses related to poverty."

The child welfare system, which ostensibly removes children from their families to protect them, often fails at that goal. Children, particularly those who are the most troubled and thus difficult to deal with, are frequently shuffled through the system, bounced from foster home to group home, sometimes housed in hotels with little adult supervision, sometimes fleeing to the streets to escape the system supposed to care for them. In just a three-year period, from 2011 to 2014, B.C.'s Representative for Children and Youth documented 145 incidents of sexualized violence against 121 kids in care. Over the following two years, sexual violence was the most common critical injury suffered by children in care, accounting for 21 per cent of injuries. The true total, the report noted, is "likely far higher as reporting is often delayed by these young, traumatized victims or never completed at all." It is well established that many victims of childhood sexual abuse don't disclose it until adulthood, if at all. B.C. does not track whether children who have been in its care later report abuse.

The system's failures are reflected not only in the experiences of children in care but also in the outcomes of their lives. A child in care is more likely to become entangled with the youth criminal justice system than they are to graduate high school. Those who leave the system because they reach adulthood are five times more likely to die than others in their age group.

Across the country, child welfare systems affect First Nations,

Metis and Inuit children at staggeringly disproportionate rates. Nationally, nearly half the children younger than fifteen living in care are Indigenous, though they make up only 7 per cent of the population. In B.C., Indigenous children account for less than 10 per cent of the population but more than half of those in care. One in five Indigenous children has encountered the child welfare system in the province, compared to fewer than one in thirty non-Indigenous kids. Research suggests the outcomes and experiences of Indigenous children in care are particularly dreadful.

A survey of Indigenous youth who used drugs in Vancouver and Prince George found two-thirds had been involved with the child welfare system. Those who had been involved were more than twice as likely to have a parent who had attended a residential school and to have been sexually abused. They were more likely to have harmed themselves, thought about suicide and tried to kill themselves. They were more likely to overdose and contract HIV. "Indigenous scholars have described the intense psychological distress, cultural dislocation, identity confusion and emotional emptiness of young Indigenous people apprehended from their families and moved from home to home as wards of the state," the survey noted.

The B.C. study of sexual violence against kids in care found that 61 per cent of the victims were Indigenous girls, though they only make up a quarter of the total population. They are at heightened risk of sexual abuse because of poverty, intergenerational trauma, isolation and social attitudes toward them. The report noted, "Perpetrators of this violence may also believe that they will not risk detention or prosecution since society is less concerned with the welfare of Indigenous than that of non-Indigenous children and youth."

Kids who have been in the care of the state are more likely to wind up in the youth criminal justice system, and once there, to be incarcerated. Most commonly, they are there because of petty crimes: property offences, assault and administrative offences like breaching bail or probation conditions. Indigenous children in care are even more vulnerable; they are five times more likely than youths in the general population to be incarcerated. Once kids in care land in custody, they have a graduation rate between zero and 6 per cent. The province is a poor parent, often subjecting vulnerable young people to the same abuse and neglect it is supposed to be protecting them from and failing to help them with the aftermath of trauma. Instead, it funnels them into a justice system that in turn harms them further.

On a map of British Columbia, two highways cross paths in what is roughly the centre of the province. Highway 16 runs southeast from Prince Rupert until it traverses the Rocky Mountains and carries on across the Prairies. Highway 97 cuts a line across the northeast of the province from the Yukon to Dawson Creek, then southwest through the Okanagan to the U.S. border. Prince George sits at the crossroads of Highways 16 and 97.

Most of the province's population lives in the Vancouver area. A few densely populated areas lie on Vancouver Island and in the Okanagan. Outside those regions, communities tend to be small and far apart, separated by vast stretches of largely uninhabited land. Prince George is, for all intents and purposes, the capital—the only city—of the north. The closest comparably large urban centre is Kamloops, more than five hundred kilometres to the south. North of Prince George, there is only one community with more than twenty thousand people, and three with populations around twelve thousand.

The city has had a reputation for drugs, violence and crime since its early days around the turn of the twentieth century, when its corruption made headlines in national publications, with the 1913 Toronto *Globe* quoting a local priest who referred to it as "the very gates of Hell." In a CBC article, crime historian Jonathan

Swainger noted that the early 1900s in Prince George were a chaotic time "marked by bootlegging and moonshine, including a popular mixture of opium, tobacco juice, water and rubbing alcohol," the streets replete with "gambling, brothels, illegal liquor and petty crime." The situation was not helped by a police force that was, "without any pretence at all, awful."

That reputation carried on through the decades. As a young recruit at the RCMP training academy in Regina, Saskatchewan, in the late 1960s, Ray Michalko recalled the city being known as "the toughest place for cops anywhere in Canada." "At that time, RCMP members seemed to be getting beat up at a high rate in Prince George, so they were taking the biggest, toughest recruits and sending them to Prince George," he said. Decades later, when Ray worked in the area as a private investigator probing some of the Highway of Tears cases, he figured "the north attracts the weirdest troublemakers and it seems to me that the whole Prince George area has got more of those than any other place I've worked." Another RCMP officer stationed there from 1986 to 1988 remembered it as a "crazy" place, with lots of robbery, violence and homicide. "If you had had a hundred bucks in your pocket in the back alley, somebody would rip you off, it would be gone."

In the mid-1990s, heroin emerged as the drug of choice across British Columbia, and Prince George was not immune. One police officer estimated the number of users in the city had ballooned from about seventy a decade earlier to as many as five hundred. Overdose deaths in B.C. leapt from 39 in 1988 to 331 in 1993. In the Prince George area, 21 people died from overdosing in 1993. The needle exchange, opened in 1991, had registered 855 users in its short lifespan.

Lying as it does where the two highways connect B.C.'s north to everywhere else, Prince George draws people from across a huge geographic area. Some travel there to shop at Costco or the Pine Centre Mall, others to attend the University of Northern British

Columbia, others to see a medical specialist. And for decades, it has been a place where people from across the north go in search of a better life. Some are drawn by the promise of excitement, the "bright city lights," and more opportunities; others are fleeing desperate circumstances or seeking the kind of services, like shelters, needle exchanges or counselling, that aren't available in smaller places.

In the early and mid-1990s, Prince George hosted a substantial number of young people who headed for the city and found themselves on its streets. A program for homeless kids had more than two hundred clients, many of whom had run away from abuse, violence and poverty. A later study of street kids in B.C. suggested that about two-thirds had witnessed family violence and a similar number had been physically abused themselves at home. It noted, "Many young people leave home to escape abuse only to find themselves experiencing violence outside their family as well." By the age of eighteen, nearly two-thirds of girls had been abused sexually, about three times the average for B.C. girls as a whole. Nearly a third of girls reported being raped by an adult. Four out of five girls living on the street were Indigenous.

In Prince George, many kids, especially girls, who wound up on the streets were sexually exploited, performing sex acts in exchange for money, drugs, a place to sleep or something to eat. George Street, in the heart of downtown, was the public face of street prostitution in those days. Children as young as nine were out there. Dealers and pimps lured kids with free drugs, and once they were hooked, they'd do just about anything to pay for their habit, whether it was peddling drugs or their bodies. A seventeen-year-old interviewed by the *Prince George Citizen*, who'd spent her earlier teens homeless, addicted and sexually exploited, said kids took drugs to kill their feelings. "Numb," she said. "You have to be numb." At a 1994 speakout on violence in Prince George, attendees complained about violence on the streets and a recent rise in street prostitution and drug dealing. "I'm hard on Prince George. Downtown is an ugly place," said one man. "Now I see kids selling themselves on the street. That's no good at all." Another said there had been an influx of people to the downtown streets in January and February that year, and "there are people trying to sell or obtain drugs on virtually every downtown street corner." Another spoke of dozens of people descending on someone and beating them to near death because of their race or suspected sexual orientation.

Roxanne Thiara got into cocaine, another common drug in northern B.C. at the time, and by 1993, she was rarely home in Quesnel, spending her time with a friend she met in youth detention in Prince George and Williams Lake, a town about a hundred kilometres south of Quesnel. "She just got out of control," said Rene Beirness, her former brother-in-law. "It was a never-ending story. She needed someone to take her in and care for her, but you know, nobody ever did. It's sad, but it happens all the time. These young girls, they feel nobody cares about them and they just go wild. They fall through all the cracks." People would later remember Roxanne showing up on the streets of Prince George in early 1994, around the same time locals noticed a precipitous hike in the number of people on the streets downtown. She only survived a few months.

On the streets, Roxanne was sexually exploited. Despite her difficult existence, she kept in touch with her family. "She still came home," said Mildred. "She used to come home, or phone, every two or three days. We were just waiting to see if Roxanne would change, and would want to go and get help. I hoped to the very end she was going to change." And she did want to change. In late June of 1994, Roxanne told Mildred she would enter a drug treatment program. "She wanted to stop it," Mildred said. "She had dreams. She wanted to go to school to become a fashion designer." Roxanne made the appointment. Then she left Mildred's home in Quesnel on June 27 to collect her things in Prince George.

She said she'd be back the next day. "That was the last time we seen her," said Mildred. On a long weekend in July, Roxanne was in downtown Prince George. She told a friend she was going out with a customer. Her friend watched her walk around the corner of a building. And then she was gone.

Throughout July, Mildred searched for her, phoning around, checking in with her probation officer. Rene Beirness handed out photos of her in Vancouver, Kamloops and Prince George. At some point, they reported her missing, though newspaper articles give conflicting accounts of the date, with one reporting July 5, another August 11.

Her body was found on August 17, 1994, about six weeks after she was last seen. Someone had murdered her and dumped her in the bush along Highway 16, just east of Burns Lake. "When she did want to change, she wasn't given the chance," Mildred said. She was fifteen years old.

The phrase "over-policed and under-protected" is often, and aptly, used to describe Indigenous people's relationship to Canadian law enforcement. Examples of over-policing abound: in cities across the country, Indigenous people are far more likely to be stopped and questioned by police conducting "street checks." In Smithers, where Ramona Wilson and Delphine Nikal grew up, Indigenous youths were targeted and harassed by police so much that they took to hanging out in an area covered by video surveillance to ensure there was a record of how police treated them, according to a 2011 report. The same report, gleaned from a series of workshops surveying participants in small towns in B.C., quoted Indigenous people in Terrace, west of Smithers, saying police "treat me like a dog, worse than a dog," and "I wasn't even resisting, they slam me around, hog tie me, they say . . . even if you don't do wrong, I'll find a way to charge you." The Cedar Project, which studied Indigenous youth who used drugs in Vancouver and Prince George, found that nearly three-quarters had been stopped by police and more than a quarter had an officer use physical force on them. Fourteen per cent had been assaulted by the police. In Prince George, 4 per cent of youths reported non-consensual sex—rape, in other words—with a member of the criminal justice system.

Across Canada, Indigenous adults account for more than a quarter of the prison population, despite making up about 4 per cent of the overall populace. Youths account for about 37 per cent of those in custody, a rate about five times that of their representation in the population. Girls and women are particularly overrepresented. Indigenous women account for more than 35 per cent of those in federal and provincial prisons, while half the girls in youth facilities are Indigenous.

The disproportionate rate at which Indigenous youth are incarcerated is due, in part, to how they are disproportionately affected by factors that make a person more likely to get in trouble: poverty, involvement with the child welfare system, abuse, addiction and homelessness. But there is something else at play in the equation: racism. One advocacy group observed that "the courts tend to respond to Indigenous girls as though it is inevitable that they will become criminal, drug/alcohol addicted, or seriously ill on the street, and that their lives may only be salvaged through the harsh treatment of the criminal law." The Native Women's Association of Canada noted that it is common for Indigenous girls to enter the youth criminal justice system for minor offences—public disturbance, shoplifting, a "minor aggression"—and end up in prison for subsequent administrative offences: breaching bail or probation conditions or failing to appear in court. "The terms of probation are often so unrealistic that they set girls up to fail. There have been cases where girls went into custody on one charge at 13, only to be released on impossible conditions, and picked up time and time again for breaches," noted one report that highlighted how one young girl was in custody for her entire youth due to breaching probation terms that resulted from a single, "fairly insignificant" charge.

A study published in 2015 sought to separate the chances of a young Indigenous person being incarcerated from risk factors in order to determine if race alone had something to do with the high number of Indigenous kids in prison. "Two plausible scenarios present themselves: one, that Aboriginal peoples are committing a disproportionate number of crimes, or two, they are subjected to a discriminatory criminal justice system," it notes. The study found that, after controlling for many risk factors, "Aboriginal ancestry remained independently associated with incarceration, suggesting that policing practices or other aspects of the current criminal justice system may be partly responsible." It goes on to note, "Today, Canadian police officers are accorded substantial discretionary power in how best to maintain peace and order on the street and research suggests that the viewpoint that Aboriginal peoples are criminal, violent or dangerous is prevalent among, at least, a minority of officers."

Particularly when it comes to youth running afoul of the law, police have a great deal of latitude in their response, which can range from a warning to arrest and recommending a formal charge. In B.C., where criminal charges are laid by the Crown prosecutor instead of the police—one of the few jurisdictions in Canada where this is the case—prosecutors, too, use their discretion in deciding whether a formal charge is warranted. Minors in the criminal justice system will go on to encounter judges, probation officers, prison guards, a whole swath of adults whose day-to-day encounters and decisions add up to have enormous sway over the trajectory of their lives. To suggest that the racism and bias apparent across our society does not trickle down into this system would be naive.

Clearly, though not surprisingly, the relationship between police and vulnerable Indigenous youths is often a poor one, and it has far-reaching repercussions for those kids most in need of protection. Many are hesitant to go to the police with information, or for help when they are in danger. And they are right to be; in some cases, members of the law enforcement community are the perpetrators.

The girl was sixteen when the man picked her up from the streets of Prince George. He drove her out of town to an isolated road near the prison, where he agreed to pay her $150 for sex. But when she reached for a condom after removing her clothes, he got angry. He smashed her head into the dashboard, cutting it open. She fought her way out of the truck and ran, but he chased her, and when he caught her, raped her. Then he tossed her clothes out of the truck and drove away. Another girl was twelve; he paid her eighty dollars for sex. A few months later, she appeared in his courtroom. Shortly afterward, he picked her up from the street again and offered $150 for "aggressive sex," which led to a "confrontation." She managed to escape; he told her that if she reported him, no one would believe her.

He paid for sex numerous times over several years with another girl, from the time she was fourteen until she was seventeen, years during which she appeared before him in court hearings that made clear her "fragile mental state, low self-esteem, limited education and her past with abusive adults," noted a later court judgment. He drove another girl, fifteen, out on the same isolated road, offered sixty dollars for oral sex, then as she began, attacked her to get the money back. She escaped from his vehicle. He said he'd have her killed if she told anyone, then drove away with her clothes, leaving her to hitchhike back to the city.

The man was David William Ramsay, a provincial court judge in Prince George, who also worked a circuit throughout northern British Columbia. The girls he abused were without homes, sexually exploited, from "disadvantaged backgrounds" and "not strangers to abuse, be it physical or mental." They were all Indigenous. They were all addicted to drugs. Presiding over their court appearances, he knew how vulnerable they were.

Born in Nova Scotia in 1943, Ramsay grew up on Vancouver Island, working as an elementary school teacher before returning to university to become a lawyer. He moved north to Prince George, where he established the city's first legal aid office. Over his decades in the city, he was widely lauded for his community service, sitting on boards of a halfway house, a home for troubled youth and a shelter for women fleeing domestic violence. He was appointed a judge in 1991.

The abuses for which he was convicted took place over the next nine years. Rumours circulated during that time. A girl on the street in Prince George told a reporter that everyone knew about Ramsay picking up young girls, taking them out of town and assaulting them. A health worker from the Native Friendship Centre said it was "whispered about in legal circles and among people who work with prostitutes." The worker said she had seen the judge with a girl in his car talking to a police officer and reported it to the RCMP, to no avail. By 1999, the police had heard the rumblings and started an investigation, but the girls were too afraid to come forward. "We didn't have any substance. We had rumours only," the lead investigator would later explain. It wasn't until 2002 that one of the girls spoke out, after learning that Ramsay was to preside over a custody hearing involving her son.

Ramsay was removed from his duties in July 2002 and resigned that October when the province appointed a special prosecutor to investigate the allegations. The following spring, he was indicted on ten charges. However, in a surprise move on the first day of a scheduled three-week trial, Ramsay pleaded guilty to five of the charges; the rest were stayed. He was sentenced to seven years, a term longer than that recommended by the prosecution, and died in a Nova Scotia penitentiary in 2008.

But it didn't end with Ramsay. Police continued to investigate allegations of misconduct, including paying girls for sex, made by Ramsay's victims and others against Prince George RCMP officers. Ultimately, the Crown concluded there wasn't enough evidence to lay criminal charges. As the *Globe and Mail* reported, a subsequent RCMP disciplinary hearing against one officer was scrapped because his supervisor took too long to inform superiors of the allegations. Gary Bass, the RCMP deputy commissioner for the province, told the disciplinary panel that he first heard the accusations in 2002 but didn't believe them. Even when Ramsay was charged—suggesting a certain level of veracity to the girls' stories—Bass did not take them seriously. Sex workers in Prince George, he said, had implicated as many as nine officers during the investigation into Ramsay. "With the number of members and our officers mentioned, it was a concern in terms of believing that that amount of activity could go on in a small town," he said. "We weren't going to rush to judgment in terms of anyone involved." It was only when Ramsay pleaded guilty, thus verifying the girls' stories about the judge, that the deputy commissioner believed them. When Ramsay told one of his victims that no one would believe her if she told, he was right. Lee Lakeman, of the Canadian Association of Sexual Assault Centres, told a reporter at the time, "I don't think his capacity to abuse those young women was sustained by him alone. It was sustained by other people's silence, by other people's tolerance for prostitution and other people's racism." An appeal to have the misconduct hearing proceed fizzled out when the main witness died. First Nations leaders and advocates called for an inquiry, to no avail. And so, while the allegations are uncorroborated and no charges were ever laid, questions and doubts have long remained. Years later, "reports continue to circulate in Prince George about connections linking the law enforcement and legal establishments with use of children in sex work and other forms of child sexual

exploitation," Human Rights Watch wrote in 2013, in a scathing
report on abusive police practices against Indigenous women and
girls along the Highway of Tears. "For many indigenous women
and girls interviewed for this report, abuses and other indignities
visited on them by the police have come to define their relationship
with law enforcement," the report noted. "At times the physical
abuse was accompanied by verbal, racist or sexist abuse." The
researchers heard allegations of rape or sexual assault by police
officers in five of ten towns they visited; they were "struck when
carrying out this research by the high levels of fear of police among
the women interviewed, levels of fear that Human Rights Watch
normally finds in communities in post-conflict or post-transition
countries such as Iraq . . . The palpable fear of the police was accompanied with a notable matter of fact manner when mentioning
mistreatment by police, reflecting a normalized expectation that if
one was an indigenous woman or girl police mistreatment is to be
anticipated." As researcher Meghan Rhoad later said, "I just kept
thinking, 'But this is Canada.'"

Shortly after Roxanne was found, police released a photo, hoping
people might recognize her face, if not her name. "We're trying to
find as many people who may have had contact with her, trying
to determine her circumstances just before her disappearance,"
RCMP Staff Sgt. Bruce Wylie told the *Prince George Citizen*. "We're
hopeful someone saw her going with the person we're looking for."
By September, police had forty tips to investigate. Police came to
believe someone had killed her elsewhere and dumped her body
near Burns Lake. "It's a good possibility the person knew the area
very well—somebody familiar with Highway 16 West," Const.
Dieter Poschmann said. Mildred Thiara, Roxanne's guardian, said
police called from time to time but did not provide details on

the progress of the investigation. "We're still having a hard time coming to terms with everything. She was a well-loved little girl; she was well-adored." Her funeral was held December 8, 1994.

The next day, it happened again.

Alishia Germaine, who sometimes went by Leah Germaine and Leah Cunningham, was born in Prince George. Her aunt, Connie Menton, described her to the *Vancouver Sun* as an affectionate little girl who loved to sing and act. She began to rebel in adolescence, especially after her parents separated, and fled a "tumultuous home life" at twelve. She was small—five feet two and a hundred pounds—and not afraid of anything. A Prince George youth worker told a reporter that she was tough, independent and didn't fit in well at group homes or with foster families and wound up on the streets. She was a regular at the Urban Coffeehouse downtown, an all-ages performance space, and wrote poetry. Her mom, Debra Germaine, would later tell a reporter that she had worked hard to straighten out her own life in order to be there for her daughter. "She was independent. She got a taste of a little bit of freedom and she got in with the wrong crowd. I didn't know what the solution was, to get her off the streets. I tried but I didn't know what to do to help her," Debra said. "She was really very sensitive. Her feelings were hurt often. She would just cry her little heart out. When she got older she put on a hard face but deep inside she was soft." Like Roxanne— the two girls in the close-knit community of street youth knew each other— Alishia became addicted to drugs. Like Roxanne, she was sexually exploited. And like Roxanne, she was trying to change her life. In the later months of 1994, though homeless, Alishia was working hard to stay off drugs and planning to return to high school to finish Grade 10. She wanted to get her life on track. It wasn't easy when she also had to figure out where to sleep every night.

Friday, December 9, was the evening of an annual Christmas party for street kids at the Native Friendship Centre in Prince George.

The police took part in the dinner every year, a brief moment when young people might see cops as something other than the bad guys, and cops, too, might catch a glimpse of the youngsters in a different context. About 150 youths showed up to the event where, for one night of the year, they were treated to the kind of comfort many take for granted. RCMP officers served turkey dinners and staff distributed presents donated by local businesses. Alishia got a plate and lined up for the buffet. When she reached the end of the line, Supt. Ric Hall was in his traditional position at the gravy, ladle in hand. He would recall in a newspaper article published the next year that she dumped her plate on him; it wasn't clear whether or not it was an accident.

Alishia had dinner and then, as the dancing was about to start, told a youth worker she was leaving for a moment with her cousin. She said she'd be right back and asked them to save a present for her. The youth worker set aside a ghetto blaster, some tapes and a sweater.

Alishia Germaine was artistic, a regular at performances at Prince George's Urban Coffeehouse and fiercely independent.

Alishia never came back.

The Haldi Road Elementary School sat on Leslie Road in a semi-rural area on the outskirts of Prince George, about thirteen kilometres west of downtown. It has since closed down, but in 1994 it was a small school on a large lot in a mostly wooded area off the highway. At about eleven that same night, three young people were walking across the field behind it. There, they found Alishia, stabbed to death. She had celebrated her fifteenth birthday six days earlier. "She had potential," her aunt, Connie, told a reporter years later. "We all make mistakes, but it didn't mean that mistake would be carried into her adult years."

In the fall of 1994, not long after Roxanne's body was found, a sixteen-year-old boy had been shot dead, making Alishia Prince George's third teenaged homicide victim in less than six months. The violence was enough to shake the small city. At a council meeting a few days after Alishia was murdered, a city councillor complained about the local media painting Prince George as a murder city.

Others were worried about the murders, too, for different reasons. In an eloquent response to the city councillor, a resident wrote that she didn't "give a damn if the coverage of the murder puts us in a bad light."

If a 16-year-old daughter of a member of city council had been snatched off the street and stabbed to death the city would be in an uproar. But Ms. Germaine was different—she was a prostitute. Does anyone really think that because of her life-style she deserved to die or that her death doesn't matter? Ms. Germaine was a child, apparently victimized by a long line of adults that she came into contact with . . . The fact is that our community allows troubled girls to sell their bodies on our streets, contains men who are willing to pay for sex

with minors, and contains a predator who has killed . . .
Perhaps if the media was a little more outspoken about the
plight of the most vulnerable members of our community we
wouldn't have to worry about the embarrassment of having
teenaged girls murdered on our streets.

The Northern Society of Musicians and Artists, which ran the
Urban Coffeehouse where Alishia had gone to music and art shows,
cancelled plans for a Christmas event and in its place announced a
town hall–style discussion about violence in the city. "We're concerned that the victims are being vilified—not so much by the
press but by society," said Barry Keibel, the society's president.
"The feeling among some people is, 'She was a hooker, so it's OK.'
We've got to stop thinking that way, and take care of each other."

At the event a few days later, police said they were following up
on 150 tips about the murder of Alishia and 90 about Roxanne.
Investigators released a composite sketch of someone they believed
might have information, but it was a dead end. They asked for the
public's help to find a truck seen downtown, near the spot where
some of Alishia's things had been found, in hopes the driver had
witnessed something useful to the investigation.

But, in the public eye, the issue quickly faded from view. In the
spring of 1995, Roxanne's brother-in-law, Rene Beirness, conducted a poster campaign across communities in northwestern
and central B.C., trying to stir up new information. "There hasn't
been anything about Roxanne in the press for a while," he said.
"And maybe people will take notice and think of something when
they see the poster. After time people tend to talk a bit and maybe
somebody heard something." He said he was thinking of getting in
touch with the father of Melanie Carpenter, the young woman
found murdered in the Lower Mainland a few months before
whose disappearance had generated nationwide fervour and whose
death had united many across Canada to call for harsher penalties

for offenders. Rene had hung posters for Steve Carpenter and thought perhaps the grieving father could marshal some of the publicity for Melanie to aid in the search for the person who killed Roxanne. "One thing I do know, though—this case is never going to be closed until we find out what happened," Rene vowed. A few months later, on the anniversary of Roxanne's disappearance, he was still handing out pictures of her everywhere from Vancouver to Prince George. He was certain a serial killer was responsible for the murders of Roxanne and the others. So was Mildred Thiara.

The police weren't ruling it out, either. In four years, Delphine disappeared and Ramona, Roxanne and Alishia were murdered. And there was Cindy Burk, a twenty-one-year-old from Carmacks First Nation in the Yukon, who was murdered, her body found near Dawson Creek, northeast of Prince George, in 1990.

Early in 1995, a team of a half-dozen investigators from across Canada convened in Prince George. Organized by Bob Paulson, then a corporal who would work his way up through the ranks to eventually serve as commissioner of the RCMP, the detectives were to bring a fresh perspective to the cases, which had a disturbing number of similarities. All the women were young: three were fifteen, one was sixteen, and the fifth was twenty-one. They were all First Nations. "Obviously, we're concerned that there is [a serial killer]," said Paulson. Fred Maile, the retired RCMP member and private investigator who'd worked with the Missing Children Society of Canada on the Delphine and Ramona cases, was there, along with two detectives trained in behavioural profiling by the FBI. The Ontario Provincial Police sent a couple of people. Insp. Ron MacKay, the head of the RCMP Violent Crime Analysis Branch, in Ottawa, led the group as it re-examined leads and compiled lists of likely characteristics and traits of an offender or offenders. They were looking for a common thread.

And then it happened again.

THE NOT KNOWING

THE CITY OF TERRACE lies in a low valley surrounded by smooth-shouldered mountains looming more than two thousand metres overhead in places. Close to the coast, the region is in a temperate rainforest, where the summers and winters are cool and wet. Nearly six hundred kilometres northwest of Prince George, Highway 16 leads into the eastern outskirts of Thornhill, a suburb of sorts across the river from downtown Terrace. A Petro-Canada gas station sits on a frontage road on the south side of the highway, its windowless back wall set against the drone of passing vehicles. This is where Lana Derrick was last seen, in October of 1995. She was nineteen years old, home from college for the Thanksgiving long weekend. She may have climbed into the back seat of a blue car. The rest of her story, no one knows.

North of Terrace lies the Nass Valley, named for the river that flows through it. The Nass is the territory of the Nisga'a, who have lived for thousands of years along the river they call Lisims. "Ours is a

world of teeming inlets, dense forests, and sleeping volcanoes,"
notes the Nisga'a Lisims government website. "It is a land that is as
much a part of us as our own flesh and blood." Europeans reached
the Nass in 1793, when George Vancouver sailed up the west coast
in search of sea otter pelts and met the Nisga'a at the river mouth.
Soon the region was a trading hub between Europeans and First
Nations. Like elsewhere on the continent, European diseases like
smallpox and influenza decimated the Nisga'a, just as further
intrusions were underway: gold was discovered, bringing the gold
rush and its disruption and disorder to the valley. Missionaries
soon followed. In 1871, the Nisga'a territory along with the rest of
British Columbia was declared property of the Crown. Then
came the Indian Act and reserves, which left a minuscule portion
of land to Nisga'a people. For more than a hundred years they
would fight to get it back. In 2000, the first modern-day treaty in
B.C., the Nisga'a Final Agreement, went into effect, legally returning to the Nisga'a control over their land and people.

Lana's mother, Marge, grew up in the Nisga'a community of
Gitwinksihlkw in the days when it was commonly referred to by its
colonial name, Canyon City. The village of about 250 people lies on
the north bank of the Nass River, about a hundred kilometres north
of Terrace.

In the days Marge was growing up, the fishing industry in the
northwest employed thousands. Each summer when the season
began, people flocked to the coast from inland communities. There
was big money to be made pulling fish from the sea and packaging
it to be sent around the world. The men trawled the dark waters
of the North Pacific; the women worked in the canneries. At the
industry's height, in the early 1900s, nearly forty canneries oper-
ated in Prince Rupert and along the Nass and Skeena Rivers. The
work brought together First Nations people from across the region
to toil alongside migrant workers from Japan, China, India and
Europe. Labourers were segregated by ethnicity and housed in

bunkhouses or shacks built on pilings over the water, connected by rain-slicked boardwalks. Canneries were like small towns, with doctors, general stores, blacksmiths, net menders, cookhouses and staff housing all on site. While the boom began to dwindle in the 1920s, the industry continued to draw seasonal workers for the rest of the century.

As Marge grew older, she joined the flows of people to and from the Pacific coast who worked at the Cassiar Cannery at the mouth of the Skeena River. There she met John Derrick, who came from Gitanyow each summer to work as a fisherman out of Prince Rupert. Both had older children, so when Lana was born in the Prince Rupert hospital, she was the baby of both families. Marge and John chose Gitanyow as a home base, bringing newborn Lana back to grow up with her grandmother and a large, loving extended family. She was a rambunctious, inquisitive little girl. Wanda Good, her older cousin, remembered the toddler tearing around the home, reaching for china, precious memorabilia, what have you, and their grandmother a few steps behind, forever telling her, "Lana, no!"

Gitanyow is a small community of a few hundred people. It lies about twenty kilometres north of the Yellowhead Highway, along a narrow dirt road that winds down a gentle hill under the limbs of cottonwoods before crossing a creek and opening up into the village. Houses are spread out along four streets that run roughly parallel to the Kitwanga River in the shape of a teardrop. First Avenue is closest to the river, separated by a grassy expanse that holds the cemetery, totem poles and a gas bar that provides the village's only commercial services—fuel, lottery tickets, potato chips, cigarettes. The cedar poles, designated as a Canadian National Historic Site, draw visitors en route to Alaska each summer, whose motorhomes and fifth wheels line the rough street during the height of tourist season. The poles date back to at least 1850; Emily Carr made one of the oldest, Hole in the Ice, famous when she painted it in 1928. While

Gitanyow's traditional territory, where they lived for at least seven thousand years, covers about seventeen thousand square kilometres, the reserve system allotted to the people less than nine square kilometres. Colonial policies cut off the people of Gitanyow from their traditional means of survival, yet allowed them few alternatives. Jobs were, and remain, hard to come by in the community. The unemployment rate in 2016 was over 44 per cent, more than six times the provincial average. The average income was $18,245, less than half the B.C. average. More than half the population had an income of less than $10,000. "You have to leave here if you want to work," said Sally Gibson, Lana's aunt.

Each spring, Lana's family migrated from the peaceful village beside the river to the Cassiar Cannery on the coast—the last cannery in operation along the Skeena by the 1980s. Each spring was a reunion with family and friends from the previous seasons, the women working all day in the cannery while the men went out on the boats and the older children took care of younger siblings. The bustling cannery was like a wonderland to the kids from Gitanyow. All summer, the children played and explored, carefree and happy. "It was a different time, it seemed so much more relaxed," said Lana's cousin Wanda. "It all seemed to just work. It was a really cohesive community." It was, to Wanda, a time of innocence. It was a time when she and Lana weren't afraid of strangers. It was a time when they weren't afraid of being hurt.

Lana's parents split up, and Marge moved with her youngest daughter to Terrace, setting up a new home in an apartment just outside downtown. Another daughter soon came to live with them. It wasn't long, though, before Marge began to consider moving back to Gitwinksihlkw. There was a house there for them, and her mother lived close by. Marge asked her daughters what they thought of the idea of moving up the Nass. "You should have seen both of them: 'Yes!'" Marge remembered. Before she could even call their grandmother to discuss the idea, the girls were packing.

The power to their house in Gitwinksihlkw had been cut off, but people stopped by to lend Marge a propane stove and kerosene lamps. It might have been rustic to some, but the girls loved it. The household would never see so many young visitors as when they didn't have electricity. When Marge got the power turned back on, she noticed her daughters' friends weren't coming around so often. She asked them at dinner one night why, wondering if there had been a falling-out. They shrugged a little sadly and said, "We got power. It's not the same."

Darvin Haugan met Marge in Terrace in the mid-1980s. Soon after they began dating, Darvin invited Marge and Lana to move to his place, an acreage about forty kilometres east of Terrace cinched between the Skeena River and steep, forested hills. There was no phone—the telephone wires stopped halfway from Terrace—though he kept a radio phone for emergencies. There was a large garden, and wild berries and mushrooms were plentiful on the hills behind the house. It was a bustling place—family and friends who would stop by for bonfires, music jams and parties had nick-named the place Haugeyville.

It was a rainy evening in late October when they pulled into the driveway at Haugeyville, the back of Darvin's pickup piled with Marge and Lana's belongings. The leaves of the poplars and cot-tonwoods along the Skeena had turned yellow and brown by then, and a damp chill had crept down the mountains. Darvin ushered in the new members of the Haugeyville family, then headed down-stairs to the basement's large wood furnace. As he hunched down and prepared to light the crumpled-up newspaper and kindling, he sensed movement and looked up. There were those big, dark eyes, that beautiful round face, peering out at him from behind the furnace. Lana looked straight at him and said, "Can I call you Dad?" He felt his heart lurch, and thought, "Uh-oh, what am I up against?" But he tried to remain composed as he thought of what to say. He told her they would have to work together on things. There would be chores, meals to help prepare and discipline, if needed. He wanted her to know that it wasn't going to be a picnic. Lana wasn't at all fazed; she agreed to the arrangement, giving him "the eyes" all the while. He told her, "If you're going to call me Dad, you're going to be my daughter." And so she was.

Darvin built an addition on the house so that Lana could have her own room, but she was usually headed outside—she could never stand being cooped up indoors. The family trained their dog, Randy, to lead Lana and other members of the family home if they got lost. All you had to say was, "Randy, take us home," and he'd show the way. Lana loved roaming the hills around the property—a woman who came to Haugeyville with her guitar wrote a song about little Lana picking berries. Every summer, the family went to Babine Lake, a four-hour drive away, where they would rent a boat and fish for a few days. One summer, Lana figured out she could purchase items at the lakeside shop on her family's account. She came back from the store with loads of candy; when Marge asked her where she got the money, she hedged. Eventually Marge realized Lana was charging it all to their bill. Lana memorized the number on their calling card in one glance and racked up over a hundred dollars in long-distance charges. They put her to work to pay that off. When Lana fell behind during a crib game with a boarder at Haugeyville, she simply turned the board around when he wasn't looking. He didn't notice; she won the game. Twenty years later, her pranks were still the stuff that makes a dining room table erupt in laughter.

During her years in Gitwinksihlkw and at Haugeyville, Lana kept in close touch with her family back in Gitanyow, returning on many weekends to visit. Her father, John, had a new partner with a daughter, Clarice Dessert, almost the exact same age as Lana; Clarice and Lana spent many weekends when Lana was visiting running around the village, "bein' kids" and "gettin' in trouble." In the evenings, a slew of youngsters gathered at the old community hall to play go-go, a game that's kind of a cross between hide-and-seek and tag. As they grew into teenagers, the girls drifted apart. Clarice's mom and John split up, and Clarice moved to Kitwanga, about twenty kilometres away along Highway 16. "We wouldn't see each other as often," said Clarice. "We'd run into each other in Terrace, or I remember picking her up off the highway hitchhiking once or twice. We had different crowds and we lived in different towns."

That was the age when Lana's energy and independence were beginning to drive her in directions that worried her mom and Darvin. She was strong willed and independent. She was hanging around with friends her parents felt were bad influences and hitch-hiking. "She wanted to spread her wings," said Darvin. "Things kind of deteriorated and we couldn't keep control." While Lana went through some teenage rebellion, she continued to do well at school and remained a hard worker. She spent months vole-guarding, installing mesh protectors around seedling trees to prevent rodents

(Left) Lana Derrick, pictured in 1988 at Haugeyville, loved playing tricks on her family. (Right) Lana Derrick with Marge and Darvin Haugan at Haugeyville on New Years Eve, 1990.

from eating them. It was tough physical work, slogging through mud and brush in pouring rain and burning sunshine, the air thick with bugs. But she took to it. As her graduation neared, and she mulled her options with family, it was clear pretty quickly that she wanted a career that would keep her outside. She often told her auntie Sally in Gitanyow, "If I have to work my butt off, I would rather do it outside. I can't see me inside all day." She was eager to get a college education. "Lana was so bound and determined to do something with her life," said Sally.

In 1995, she graduated and was accepted into a forestry program at Northwest Community College (since renamed Coast Mountain College), which has campuses in many communities along the northwest stretch of Highway 16. Her classes were in Houston, a town of fewer than three thousand a three-hour drive from Terrace. Lana took her studies seriously; she loved the program and made friends quickly. But she remained attached to home, travelling back most weekends to see her family. On October 6, 1995, she caught a ride back with a classmate. Darvin and Marge had a forestry contract they had to finish before the snow came, so they were planning to work through the Thanksgiving weekend. Lana dropped off her weekend bag at Haugeyville and headed into town.

Clarice had moved from Kitwanga into Terrace earlier that year, working at the Kmart and living in her own apartment, a tiny bachelor unit in a converted motel downtown near the bars and alongside the railway tracks. That Friday before Thanksgiving, she had gone out earlier in the evening, driving around with Lana's cousin. There was little in the way of organized entertainment for teenagers in many of northwestern B.C.'s small communities; it was a common pastime to cruise the streets looking for friends, parties, gossip—anything to fill the hours. Lana's cousin had some cash at her home that John had given her to pass along to Lana. So when they happened on Lana walking, they pulled over to let her know. Lana asked Clarice to pick up the money and take it to her apartment downtown, where it would be easier for Lana to collect later. They said goodbye, never thinking to ask where Lana was going.

The night was still young when Clarice headed home. Her younger sister was spending the night, and they went to bed early. Hours later, Clarice awoke to knocking at the door. It was the wee hours, sometime after bars closed. This was not unusual. Clarice was well accustomed to late-night knocking on the door or tapping on the window. She laughed, remembering hearing the phone ring in the middle of the night when she was an adolescent and racing to answer it before her mother woke up, the inevitably drunk friend on the other end.

On this night, it was Lana at the door, coming to collect her money. Clarice was groggy with sleep and doesn't remember exactly what the conversation was, but suspects she gave Lana shit for being "drunk as a skunk"—she was swaying in the doorway. They chatted for a minute, Clarice gave Lana her money, and they said good night. Clarice didn't notice any vehicle waiting for Lana or see any headlights. There was no one around. Lana wasn't upset or distressed. There was nothing unusual. Clarice went back to bed.

On Saturday morning, Darvin and Marge noticed Lana's bag at home. They figured she had stayed in town with friends—it was a long way back to Haugeyville. Working hard to finish their contract, they were hardly home over the weekend. But on Monday, there was still no sign of Lana, and the belongings she'd left at Haugeyville were untouched. They were getting worried. Tuesday morning, she didn't show up when classes resumed in Houston. She never missed school. They called around to her friends, including the young women they'd assumed Lana had stayed with in Terrace over the weekend. No one had seen her for days. No one had any idea where she was. That's when they knew something wasn't right. They called the police.

It had been three days since anyone had seen Lana, but initially, the family felt the RCMP brushed them off, suggesting she was probably out on a bender or shacked up with a boyfriend for a few days. Her family knew that wasn't the case. "The initial police response was very slow, almost non-existent," Wanda said. Lana always called to let them know where she was; she didn't just vanish for a few days. There was no way no one would have seen or heard from her. "I think it was Friday before anything really happened," Darvin said. Friday was nearly a week after Clarice saw Lana for the last time.

First Nations communities from across the region came together to search. Marge's family travelled down from the Nass and joined the family from Gitanyow to look for her. Friends and relatives came from across British Columbia. They scoured Terrace looking for clues. They combed the dense rainforest beside the highway, back roads and logging roads along a three-hundred-kilometre stretch from the coast inland to Hazelton. Nothing. The police helped search for a few days, then told the family it was time to call it off. Sally recalled, "They had put in their seventy-two hours. 'Everybody go home now, we'll let you know what we find out.' And we said, 'You go home. We're not done.'"

The first article to appear in the local weekly paper, the *Terrace Standard*, was on October 18, 1995—eleven days after Lana was last seen—and fewer than a hundred words. It simply said the RCMP were asking for assistance and included a description: "Lana Patricia Derrick, 19, was last seen in Terrace Saturday, Oct. 7 at about 3 a.m. Derrick is described as five-foot-seven, 150 lbs. with shoulder-length black hair, brown eyes and eye glasses."

The next mention of her was three weeks later, describing the search efforts underway. Gitwinksihlkw's search-and-rescue group, coordinated by Clifford Azak, was leading a volunteer team of about twenty-five people who had been working since November 1, focusing on the area between Terrace and Lana's home. "We feel that's where she was heading. We're looking for any clues that can help," he said. "She's family to our community and that's why we're here." The volunteers worked out of a room at the Northern Native Broadcasting offices on the Queensway, where they'd put up maps and a photo of Lana on the walls. But already, time was running out. "The pressing issue for us is snow," Clifford Azak said. "There's a lot of ground to cover and very little time in which to do it."

The paper was in the meantime awash in stories about a contentious plan for the city to borrow upward of $20 million to build a second hockey arena. The story was front-page news and took up considerable real estate within the paper, including, in the November 15 edition, a full page of letters to the editor about the project. That same edition noted the havoc caused by a huge snowfall the preceding weekend, a near-record 63.2 centimetres that fell between Friday night and Monday morning. Though the story doesn't mention it, in addition to car accidents and road closures, the snowfall essentially ground the search for Lana to a halt. In a story the following week—the first time Lana's disappearance appeared on the front page—the search coordinator described intentions to launch a widespread information campaign, targeting hospitals and large media outlets across the province, since they were no longer able to comb the land. "We said we would go until the snow fell," Azak said. "Unfortunately it came two or three weeks sooner than we had wanted."

The disappearance of Melanie Carpenter from Surrey was fresh in the minds of Lana's family. It had been less than a year. They'd seen the enormous search on the news, the police officers and helicopters and hundreds of volunteers who kept at it for weeks, until Melanie was found. "That just broke our hearts," said Sally, "because we thought, 'Yup, if Lana was white, maybe she would be getting the same attention.'"

About a month after Lana disappeared, a witness reported seeing her at the Petro-Canada station in Thornhill at about three thirty on the morning of her disappearance. Police brought in a hypnotist who spent an hour with the witness trying to refresh her memory; a police artist then worked with her to prepare a composite drawing of someone who had apparently been with Lana. RCMP Cpl. Rob MacKay said police didn't intend to release the sketch until they'd done all they could to find the person themselves. "Are we looking at a witness? Are we looking at a suspect? We don't know at this point in time," he said.

Early in 1996, police reached a dead end and put out a call to the public seeking help. Contrary to the earlier report, the police artist had drawn sketches of two men. Information gleaned from the witness, who had been in a car parked nearby that morning, suggested Lana had got out of the back seat of a car, gone into the store, come back out and climbed back into the car, which then headed north toward the Northern Motor Inn. Along with the sketches, police released detailed descriptions of the men said to be in the front of the car, and of the vehicle itself. Police checked the store's security camera footage, but it had been recorded over and they couldn't restore the previous images. Nothing ever came of it—police later said neither man was relevant to the case, though they did not explain how they'd reached their conclusion.

It was, for Gitanyow, the cold, hard end of the innocence the village had once known. "It was a rude awakening," said Wanda. "We realized, 'Okay, you're on your own.' We can't count on the justice system to advocate or to protect First Nations women or the interests of the communities. We've only got ourselves."

As the months dragged on, Lana's family didn't know what to do. They heard rumours, so many stories about what might have happened to her. They wracked their minds thinking of what to do next. That's something people might not understand, said Darvin, the way families "hammer at that stuff in our brains" when we don't have any answers. Otherwise banal occurrences take on new, frightening significance. Sitting at the kitchen table and hearing a cougar scream off in the distance—is that her, out there, needing help? The man who lived nearby, who was always a bit of a weird fellow—was it him? A piece of women's clothing lying in the bush where Darvin was working—was it hers? A girl calling out "Mom" in the mall—was it Lana? Marge would wheel around and search for her in the crowd. It was a thousand imaginings, a thousand stories, crashing around at once. "The loss of Lana, bad enough that we didn't have her anymore just to hold her in our arms and talk to her. All these other things that come at you—oh, it's tough," said Darvin.

They searched, and they searched. The rumours came in fast, the stories about where she had been, who she had been with, what had happened to her. Each one brought a surge of hope. Each one the family passed along to police and checked out themselves as best they could. One by one, the stories proved false. Except for two loose ends that some of Lana's family members and friends still wonder about.

The morning after she saw Lana, Clarice woke up to the phone ringing. A young man she knew from Kitwanga had killed himself. Clarice had dated him a couple of years earlier until one night, after he got really drunk and became rough with her, she split with him. Recently she'd heard that Lana was seeing him. "The police came out and tried to find the connection between the two happenings," said Sally, "but I guess they didn't, because that's as far as I know. That one just went by the wayside, too." Police never told the family how they ruled out any link. There is another thread forever hanging in Sally's mind. A couple from Kitwanga were driving home from Prince Rupert early the morning Lana vanished and noticed a red van pulling out of a deactivated logging road. When they got home and heard that Lana was

missing, they reported it to the RCMP. Officers promised to be in
touch, but that was the last anyone heard until many years later,
after British Columbia launched an RCMP task force to investigate
eighteen unsolved murders and disappearances across the province, including Lana's. Sally said she told investigators about the
tip, wondering what had become of it. They told her there was no
record of the report in the old file; the man who'd seen the van
passed away before he could provide a location. "There were so
many little things that the police could have checked out, because
we heard so many stories," said Sally. "You get so many stories, you
just go nuts. You get so many people saying, 'I know what happened.' And you go running because you want the truth. And you
run your feet off. For nothing."

Clarice Dessert crumpled when she got the phone call telling her
Lana was missing. She went numb. The days that followed passed
in a blur, her mind spinning with scenarios of what could have happened to Lana, of what she should have done that night when Lana
came to her door. Clarice's mom had recently moved to Fort
Nelson, a small town in B.C.'s northeast corner. By road, it was
1,400 kilometres away. Clarice followed her. She couldn't stand to
be in Terrace. The guilt was too heavy there. It screwed her up for
a long time; it was years before she could go back. Twenty years
later, she couldn't remember that time very clearly. She wondered
if it was a defence mechanism, her brain still needing to protect
her from the trauma. "I don't know if I've dealt with things or . . .
I've just shoved them all under the carpet."

For years, Sally tried to believe that Lana would come back.
She researched human trafficking, hoping that Lana was the victim of a criminal organization and still alive. She was such a strong
girl; if someone had her, she would eventually escape and find her
way home. But after so many years, hope fades. Sally sobbed when

she gestured from her living room, adorned with photos of her grandchildren and adages about love and family, across the overgrown yard to John Derrick's place. Lana's dad never really figured out how to live, or even feign living, these decades since his daughter disappeared. He could not speak of her. His pain was a daily reminder to everyone in the family of what had happened. "He doesn't know very many sober days," said Sally. "They didn't just victimize those kids. They victimized whole families."

Not quite two months after Lana disappeared, a story appeared on the front page of the *Vancouver Sun*'s B section. Headlined "Highway 16 road of death for Indian teenagers: A serial killer is considered a possibility in three slayings and two disappearances," the 1,400-word article echoed a fear that was rumbling across the northwest. Families told reporter Lindsay Kines—who would go on to be one of the first journalists to document the women

"You get so many people saying, 'I know what happened.' And you go running because you want the truth. And you run your feet off. For nothing," said Sally Gibson, who lost two nieces along the Highway of Tears.

missing from Vancouver's Downtown Eastside—that the story hadn't received much attention because the girls were First Nations.

The RCMP was tight-lipped about the findings of the meeting earlier that year, when behavioural profilers met in Prince George to try to determine whether any of the cases were linked. The day after the *Vancouver Sun* story appeared, a Prince George officer told the local newspaper that investigators did not believe the same person had killed Roxanne Thiara and Alishia Germaine. In Terrace, Sgt. Randy Beck called it "an awful leap" to suggest a serial killer was targeting girls in the north. "It's a bit irresponsible if you ask me," he said.

AN INCH SHY OF A MILE

GARRY KERR WAS a relatively new detective when he investigated what would become one of the Highway of Tears cases, though it was many years before that moniker was coined and even longer before the RCMP launched a concerted effort to solve the rash of disappearances and murders in northwestern B.C. He had grown up in Foam Lake, Saskatchewan, a small town along Highway 16 about 250 kilometres east of Saskatoon. With a present-day population of about 1,200, the town's motto is "best place in the world to live," though it is based on a questionable, if endearing, methodology. (As the town website explains, the United Nations in 1996 declared Canada the best place to live; subsequently, a research company determined Saskatchewan the best province in the country; and, finally, a CBC Radio search determined Foam Lake the best place within the province.) It was, and still is, the sort of place that, as the saying goes, if you blink, you miss it. At eighteen, Garry found himself working at a John Deere dealership and dreaming of bigger, better things. Like many young guys growing up in an isolated prairie town, he looked up to the cops. And the RCMP offered a ticket out of a small-town life. On a frigid day in early January 1981, shortly after he turned nineteen, he walked into the local detachment and filled out the forms.

He moved to Regina for the requisite six months of basic training. The provincial capital seemed exotic to the kid who had never been anywhere. When the time came for his cohort to request their first postings—RCMP members were not allowed to serve in their home provinces—Garry put British Columbia as his top choice. He didn't know it from Newfoundland, only that it was where most of the guys wanted to go. Known as E Division, it had a reputation as the wild west, the place where the big, bad things happened. The last thing Garry wanted was to end up in another sleepy small town, cruising around all night waiting for a call. E Division seemed a surefire way to avoid that fate.

Garry's first posting was in Powell River, a town of about twelve thousand on the Pacific coast, 120 kilometres north of Vancouver. Despite the relatively short distance, it's a half-day trip from the city even today, via two ferries and narrow, snaking roads through the rainforest. After graduation day, Garry had three days to report for duty. He packed his car and headed west with a map folded up in his pocket.

Everyone who completes basic training in the RCMP starts out in uniform. As members gain experience, some branch out into specializations: traffic, forensics, narcotics. "I knew I certainly didn't want to write traffic tickets or do general-duty policing," Garry said. He wanted to solve murders and rapes, the serious stuff, of which there was precious little in Powell River. The town had what was called a General Investigation Section, GIS for short, consisting of two plainclothes officers who handled serious crime. To Garry, they were like gods. Even more divine were the officers from E Division headquarters' Serious Crime Unit, in Surrey, who were occasionally called in to assist with a difficult investigation. "These guys were the closest thing to God I'd ever met in my life," said Garry, who "whined and snivelled and grovelled" to hang out and learn from them when they arrived in town to help with a homicide case a few years after he'd joined. The detectives told him to call next time he was in Vancouver, to wear a suit, and they would introduce him to the boss, who surely would hire him on the spot. He headed to the city a few weeks later and sure enough, a couple of investigators took him to the office of the staff sergeant in charge of major crime. There was a conversation for fifteen or twenty minutes; it was going so well that Garry was already imagining what his office would look like. Then the staff sergeant said, "There is a place for you on E Division Serious Crime." Long pause. "In about fifteen years."

Garry worked his way into plainclothes in Powell River, and then in 1987 he transferred to Prince Rupert. The city just south of the tip of the Alaska Panhandle was founded around the turn of the twentieth century by Charles Melville Hays, the driving force behind the Grand Trunk Pacific Railway, who saw in its harbour—third deepest in the world and ice-free year-round—an opportunity to overshadow the far larger city of Vancouver in the rivalry for cruise ships, marine transport, fishing and tourism. Hays went down with the *Titanic* in 1912, but the city he dreamed of lived on as the terminus of the railway and a major fishing port.

By the 1980s, the fishing industry was slowing down. In a few short decades, European settlers had decimated stocks that had remained healthy and stable for millennia under First Nations' stewardship. But Prince Rupert was still a boom town, a rough-and-tumble hub of fishermen and loggers and sailors clawing a living out of the northwest coast. Its streets were unusually diverse for the region, with immigrants from South Asia, China and Europe mingling with members of First Nations from across the northwest, along with the Tsimshian, upon whose territory the city lies, and settlers largely of British origin. And there was a lot of money kicking around. The average annual income of almost $40,000 was 15 per cent higher than that of the province; nearly 30 per cent of households reported earning more than $50,000 a year. It was almost impossible to find a place to rent, and house prices were higher than Vancouver's.

Prince Rupert was a place where men landed after months at sea or in logging camps, with a lust for booze and women and pockets thick with cash. The Department of Fisheries and Oceans would notify the local RCMP detachment when boats were bound for town so they could ready for the onslaught. Especially when there were fishing closures, hundreds or thousands poured into the downtown, and it was "just a big whisky show," according to Garry. Deckhands would not even blink at a $600 bar tab, and it wasn't unusual for the police to pick up someone passed out in an alley with $10,000 in their pocket.

The city would erupt with drunks and drugs, fighting and sexual assaults. Violent crime incidents were two and a half times higher than in Powell River. On weekend nights, the RCMP "bun wagon" prowled the downtown streets, manned by the detachment's meanest, toughest guys, "because you know you're going to get into some physical altercations, that's just the way it was," Garry said. Third Avenue West was known as "Apache Pass," its centre line dividing a couple of bar-strewn blocks between those frequented by First Nations people and those where the white people went. The Empress, on one side of the street, was referred to as the "Indian bar," while the Belmont across from it was the "white guys' bar." The police wagon cruised between them picking up drunks. "They might fill it up with thirty people, and I can guarantee you twenty-nine of them would be native," Garry remembered. The detachment was the only one in Canada serving a town that size to have full-time, dedicated police dogs. They were used for crowd control when the bars let out. "Everybody would spew out of the bars and the fights would start, and [we'd] get the dogs down there, they'd chew on a few people and they'd run home until the next night," said Garry. The drunk tank at the local detachment would fill every Friday and Saturday night, with forty-five or more people packed into a cell that measured about ten-by-twelve feet. In the morning, they'd be released, leaving behind cells full of vomit and urine. And then the next night, do it all over again.

The RCMP detachment had a force of nearly forty officers, almost all white men. Prince Rupert, like other small northern communities, was not considered a plum post, so officers sent there were required to serve a limited duration of "three to five years," a term that sounded an awful lot like a prison sentence. Within a few months, Garry was assigned to the General Investigation Section, which consisted of two plainclothes detectives who handled serious crime in the city and on a handful of reserves in the area, some only accessible by air or boat. Their cases included everything from fraud to arson to murder, under the oversight of a sergeant who also supervised a two-person narcotics unit. As the most junior member of the section, Garry was the grunt, a constable working alongside then corporal Rick Ross, another small-town prairie kid who'd joined up in 1973 and worked his way up the ladder in plainclothes on Vancouver Island and then Prince George. It was a busy section; a couple of guys had to divide their time between all manner of cases, often within the same shift. They did a lot of overtime, much of it unpaid, trying to keep up. If serious offences, like murders, happened back to back—and they did—things got really hectic.

Garry had been in Prince Rupert for a couple of years when a report came in that Alberta Williams was missing. The case would be one that stayed with him throughout his career, thirty years investigating cases like it, including other missing and murdered women and girls across northwestern B.C.

———

August 25, 1989, was the kind of glorious day that doesn't often come to the Pacific Northwest: warm enough to wear a T-shirt outside, the sky blue and clear. The rugged peaks that surround Prince Rupert and the dark green islands that dot its waterfront emerged from behind the grey, billowing shroud that so frequently blankets this part of the world. On a rare sunny day, the northern coast is a glistening, magical place.

It was the Friday before Labour Day weekend. For sisters Claudia and Alberta Williams, it was the last day of a summer's hard work. They had tickets to return to Vancouver that weekend. They had moved south to the big city years before, but they made the eight-hundred-kilometre trip north every summer to work in the fish canneries that surrounded Prince Rupert. The Williams family was from Gitanyow and, like so many others across the northwest, made a yearly pilgrimage to the coast for work, which they'd been doing since Claudia and Alberta were babies. The sisters' dad, Lawrence, was from Gitanyow; he met Rena in Gitsegukla, a reserve about fifty kilometres away. They married and, in the early years, lived in a tiny two-bedroom house, their growing brood of kids sleeping in bunk beds lining the walls of one bedroom while he and Rena stayed in the other. Later, Lawrence built a house for the family, the first on the reserve to have running water and electricity, even a backup generator.

Gitanyow was a quiet place when the Williams kids were growing up, largely removed from the booming economy of the northwest and the troubles it wrought. Lawrence and Rena worked hard year-round, Lawrence driving logging trucks during the winter months while Rena grew a large garden, put up food, sewed clothes and tended the house and the children. Everyone in the family had their chores, and Rena and Lawrence saw to it that everyone played their part.

Each spring, the family went to the coast, where Lawrence worked as a gillnet fisherman and Rena worked in the canneries.

Eventually, in the 1970s, they moved to Port Edward, just outside the city, and then into Prince Rupert itself, though they still returned often to Gitanyow. Claudia moved to Vancouver when she was old enough, and Alberta followed not too long afterward to carry on high school in the city. Lawrence and Rena wanted their children to get good educations, to get out of the confines of the northwest and see some of what the world had to offer, and so had sent their younger daughters down in succession to stay with

Alberta Williams was raised in Gitanyow in a large, loving family where the kids were taught to always do the right thing.

Claudia in Vancouver and finish high school. Alberta had gone back and forth between Vancouver and Prince Rupert for years.

That summer of 1989, Alberta and Claudia returned to seasonal jobs at the B.C. Packers plant in Prince Rupert, a sprawling operation built over the Pacific on the edge of town in 1973 to replace an older facility razed by fire the year before. It was capable of producing ten thousand cases a day; in its banner year, 1985, more than half a million cases of salmon came off the cannery's lines. One had only to show up at the front gate in the morning to get a job, although it was tough work: twelve-hour shifts six days a week filling cans of fish by hand. But it paid well, upward of $200 a day, and the young women would return home to Vancouver flush with cash after a couple of months of work.

The two sisters were close. They had been taught to take care of family, to stand up for each other, to be kind. You did the right thing—that was the expectation. Alberta had absorbed those lessons, as had all the Williams kids. She was shy, remembers Sally Gibson, who is an aunt of both Alberta and Lana Derrick. She was really, really nice. When, a few years before, the heat stopped working in Claudia's apartment and she was scrambling to try to find somewhere for herself and her son to stay, Alberta didn't bat an eye. She just said, "You move into my place for now." It was a small one-bedroom that Alberta already shared with her boyfriend, but no matter. They piled Claudia's stuff in the middle of the living room.

Alberta loved life and she was satisfied with what came her way. She trusted people, too much sometimes, her siblings thought. She believed the world was a gentle, virtuous place, a larger version of the world in which she'd grown up. Her older siblings always felt a little extra protective of her.

Alberta was twenty-four years old and happy the season was coming to an end. It had been a long summer, and she was ready to go back to Vancouver, where she had a fiancé, a job lined up waitressing at a diner and plans to go to college. When the siren wailed late on the afternoon of August 25 to signal the end of shift, Alberta collected her paycheque and made plans to celebrate. Bogey's Cabaret sat in the bowels of the Prince Rupert Hotel, downstairs from Popeye's Pub. The hotel was a landmark, the oldest in the city, built in 1914 and rebuilt in 1977 after a fire razed the building. The basement bar was a dingy room with booze-soaked carpet and a sticky dance floor that was the go-to spot to let loose on a weekend night.

Francis Williams was already in bed when his phone rang. It was Alberta, his little sister, calling from the payphone outside the bar. "Come on down to Bogey's," she cajoled him, "there's lots of people down here." Alberta wasn't much of a partier. She didn't touch drugs and rarely drank. But she was excited to go out that night, to see her Prince Rupert family and friends one last time before going back to Vancouver. She sounded happy and carefree. Francis told her he couldn't go. He was headed out fishing early the next morning with their dad. "But it's my last night in town," she persisted. But Francis, who was a drinker in those days, knew that if he went, he wouldn't make it to work. So he held his ground. He had to be down at the boat at dawn.

When Claudia arrived at Bogey's, Alberta was with a big group of friends, laughing and chatting. They had pushed two tables together to make room for everyone. There weren't any free chairs at the table, so Claudia said hello and then roamed the cabaret, watching the band, talking with people she knew, checking in on her sister every once in a while.

At closing time, more than a hundred people poured out of the nightclub onto the sidewalk along Second Avenue West, the route Highway 16 takes through downtown Prince Rupert on the way to the terminal, where ferries depart for Vancouver Island, Alaska and Haida Gwaii, an archipelago that is Canada's westernmost point. Claudia wound her way through the crowd until she found Alberta, laughing with her friends in the warm, damp air of late summer. "Claudia, Claudia, come with me," Alberta said. "We're going to a house party." Claudia was considering when an ex-boyfriend interrupted, wanting to talk. "Just wait," she said to her sister, before telling the man she didn't want anything to do with him. She turned back to her sister. But Alberta was gone.

Claudia waited on the sidewalk for a few minutes as the crowd thinned out and people climbed into taxis or trucks or staggered off down the street. She looked down Sixth Street toward the water. No sign of Alberta or her friends. She checked the hotel lobby and then the ladies' washroom, calling out Alberta's name and peering under the doors of the toilet stalls. She went back out and stood on the corner of Highway 16 and Sixth Street so she could see down both dark thoroughfares. Claudia waited about half an hour. Then she went home. There was no reason to worry. Alberta was with family and friends; she would be safe.

Early in the morning of August 26, 1989, just a few hours after Claudia headed home, Francis got up and went down to the docks. He met Lawrence at the gillnetter, and father and son headed out to sea.

Not long after, Rena woke up and saw that Alberta had not come home. Worried, she phoned Claudia to check if Alberta was with her. Claudia told her it was fine, Alberta had headed for a party the night before and probably stayed over. Later that day, Rena called Claudia again. Alberta still hadn't turned up. Claudia told her maybe they went a bit overboard, just kept partying.

Out on the fishing boat, Lawrence and Francis had gone up the Skeena River to the fishing grounds, where they set the net and drifted across the rippling grey waters where the tides of the Pacific thrust up against the Skeena's currents, bringing seals, crabs and other marine life dozens of kilometres upriver. The mountains around them were topped with snow, heavy forest giving way to jagged peaks—gothic, primordial forms silhouetted against a fading sky. Around dusk they had drifted around a bend in the river and outside the fishing ground. It was around then that the radio phone rang. It was Rena, calling to tell them Alberta wasn't home. She had already phoned Alberta's friends, but no one knew where she was. Lawrence and Francis didn't think too much of it. They suggested Rena keep asking around, maybe give the police a shout, but mostly they reassured her; Alberta would be home soon.

The Williams men didn't want to travel by night—those waters are dangerous in the dark and they had drifted into unfamiliar territory—so they dropped anchor and settled down, planning to head back to Prince Rupert at first light. Francis had spent many nights on the boat; it was a comfortable place for him. But that night he couldn't sleep. He was sweating buckets, lying there in his bunk. He wondered if perhaps he was getting sick. Something felt wrong.

Dawn that Sunday morning came with the dull lightening of the vast landscape around the gillnetter. The mist had risen from the Skeena and the forests, and the river flickered silver under a low, churning sky. In daylight, Lawrence and Francis saw how far they'd drifted off course, all the way around the river bend to the Tyee overpass. They had never come this far up. They headed back toward Prince Rupert. When they arrived home, Alberta was still nowhere to be found. No one had seen her. No one had heard from her. She had never, ever disappeared like this, not even for a night. Rena and Lawrence looked and looked, and then they went to the police.

On Sunday, Lawrence and Rena filed a missing person report, probably with a uniformed officer who would have been working the front counter at the RCMP detachment. From there, the report went to the General Investigation Section. The first entry in Garry's notebook reads: "Missing person, Alberta Williams . . . 24 years old. Was in Popeye's pub Friday night until closing." There was nothing to suggest foul play. People are reported missing all the time, and in the vast majority of cases—upward of 90 per cent— they turn up unharmed within a day or two. But it wasn't long before Garry felt that something didn't add up. Same went for Rick Ross, who, as a corporal with the GIS, was Garry's senior and a more seasoned detective. It was totally out of character for Alberta to vanish. She was a responsible young woman. She wasn't a partier or the type to go on a bender for a few days. She had never run away. She had a ticket to go home to Vancouver. And yet she didn't turn up.

By the next day, Garry was interviewing staff at the bar and those who had been out with Alberta. Rick started looking for her, too. The first entry about Alberta in his notebook was made on Wednesday, August 30, 1989: at 6:30 P.M. he perused the missing person file. Twenty minutes later, he headed out to start asking questions. That first night, he took statements from Claudia and one of Alberta's best friends. Then he went to talk to a relative who'd been at the bar and apparently hosted a party afterward. Rick found him evasive and uncooperative. It struck him as odd— you would think a family member would do everything he could to help. "There were some red flags there for us right away," said Rick. "We felt that he was certainly a person of interest."

The Williams family had started searching Saturday when Alberta didn't come home. They wouldn't stop until autumn. By the end of that first week, Francis and Lawrence had combed Prince Rupert and every community along the highway as far away as Smithers, more than three hundred kilometres inland. Back in Prince Rupert, they tried to figure out their next move. The family was out of ideas, but they couldn't just stay home, couldn't just wait. Lawrence had a four-wheel-drive truck, and he and Francis decided to search all the side roads between Prince Rupert and the Tyee overpass. The two men climbed into the pickup, and Lawrence looked over at his son. "Where do you want to start?" he asked. "I don't know, I guess start anywhere," said Francis. So they left Prince Rupert and worked their way inland, turning down every logging road that veered off the highway and careened up to cut-block after cutblock. They followed dozens of roads to their ends, high on the shoulders of the dark mountains. It took all day. By nightfall, they were a couple of kilometres from Tyee. But it was dark. They went home.

Francis Williams searched dozens of forestry roads between Prince Rupert and Terrace when his sister was missing.

The Tyee overpass is not quite forty kilometres east of Prince Rupert. The Skeena is vast here, and depending on the tides, it might be fresh water or salt. The mountains rise steep from the water, in places blanketed in dark old-growth trees, and in others bearing the scars of the clear-cuts that decimated these ancient forests in years past. The morning of September 25, 1989, was foggy, but by noon, temperatures had risen to the double digits and it had cleared off somewhat. There is a pullout on Highway 16 a little west of the overpass on a promontory that looks over the railway tracks to the great expanse of the Skeena. Just below is a rugged, muddy access road that runs from the highway and follows the railway a short distance before it fades into the forest. Some hikers crossed the tracks to a trail that led to the water. And there beside the trail and a pile of railway ties, a young woman lay face down in a ditch, surrounded by metre-high reeds, rubble and debris piled on top of her. In the dirt and mud around her body, signs of a violent struggle were obvious. She had fought hard for her life. But here she was, in the bush beside the railway tracks, below the highway, out of sight of the river and the mountains and the shimmering light.

Rick made a note when he got a call at 2:50 that afternoon. Garry remembered being notified that someone had found what could be human remains; the person wasn't sure. Rick and Garry met up and drove out to Tyee together, arriving at 3:39. There was no doubt it was a human body in the ditch, though they weren't certain who it was. It was a miracle that she was spotted; had there been more rain in the preceding days, or had the hiker who spotted her been walking a couple of feet farther away, it's unlikely she ever would have been found. The officers went to work, taping off the scene and methodically combing the area for evidence. Rick made sketches that show the twin set of railway tracks and the gravel crush upon which they're laid, the pile of rail ties, the path, the ditch, the reeds, the trees. The area around the body was divided into quadrants to keep track of any evidence that was found. Police pumped out the ditch in which she lay and pored over the ground with a metal detector. They took photographs. Uniformed officers stayed overnight to guard the scene while Rick and Garry headed back to the city. They returned early the next morning and called in a forensic entomologist, an expert who can use insect activity to determine when someone died. Then came time to move her.

As soon as they turned her over and saw her face, they knew it was Alberta. Garry went with her to the morgue at the Prince Rupert hospital and made arrangements to take her to Vancouver the following day for an autopsy. Meanwhile, Rick went to tell her family. Often, police would wait to do the notification until irrefutable evidence—dental records or the like—confirmed the identity. But Rick discussed it with his superiors and they all felt they were so close to certain, and the family was running themselves into the ground with their own search efforts, that they had to let them know right away. He arrived at the house at 7:30 P.M. Lawrence and Rena weren't in; Rick told Francis and Alberta's sisters what police had found. He was gone by 7:45.

On Monday, Garry went to Vancouver with Alberta for the autopsy. Rick returned to Tyee to continue looking for evidence. Over the next few days, the investigators did more interviews with people who'd been with Alberta. Garry and Rick walked the highway for hundreds of kilometres looking for Alberta's belongings— she had only a blouse and bra on when she was found—in garbage cans and ditches. They worked sixteen, eighteen hours a day. At the end of the fifth day, at 11 P.M., Rick wrote in his notebook: "Feeling tired."

The police heard a lot of conflicting information and ran down a lot of tips that amounted to nothing. This isn't unusual, especially as time passes. "After these cases drag on for a while, a lot of people want to help and stuff gets fabricated, stuff gets embellished," Rick said. "What happens from a police perspective is, you've got these five or six different stories that people are telling you, and you've got to try and sort all of this out." Forensics in 1989 were far less advanced than today; technology to use DNA as evidence was years in the future. Rick and Garry felt they had a strong suspect, but they didn't have enough to get a search warrant for his house or to arrest him. The investigation was, in Garry's words, an inch shy of a mile.

Rena turned inward. Alberta was the second daughter she lost—another had been killed by a drunk driver in 1986. She drank more, and when she did, she broke down. Lawrence did not speak of it. He was always a quiet man, but he was quieter after Alberta was killed. Fellow fishermen noticed a cloud that seemed to move with him, an air of tragedy so palpable they could almost see it.

Looking back, Garry said there might have been a lot of things the police didn't know, things that could have changed the investigation, could have been that last inch. But there were barriers. The relationship between the RCMP and First Nations was, as he put it, "the shits." People did not trust the police; it was a near-daily occurrence for First Nations people to accuse the police of racism, brutality, apathy. "You constantly got that thrown in your face," Garry said. "I can only speak for myself, but when it came to the serious crimes, we didn't care if you were purple, pink." Rick said the same: that race had nothing to do with how a serious crime like murder was investigated. "A murder was a murder. Colour, sex, religion had no play in it," he said. "It's a human body."

Numerous reports over the years document troubling allegations of police violence against First Nations people in northwestern

B.C., not to mention the RCMP's role in enforcing federal government policies such as the reserve system and residential schools. In
Carrier, the word for police translates into "those who take us away."
Scott Whyte, who served twenty-three years in the RCMP, was posted
in Aklavik, in the Northwest Territories, in the early 1980s, when the
police force launched an initiative to include on its detachment signs
local dialect translations of "Royal Canadian Mounted Police." "We
noticed little old ladies in their parkas and stuff would be walking
along past the detachment office and they'd stop and they'd look
and point, and they'd giggle," Scott said. Officers asked around and
learned that the local name for the RCMP, which the force had just
posted on its sign, was "war makers." The RCMP took down the
sign. Later, when he was working in northwestern B.C., locals from
Witset, near Smithers, explained to him that the police were considered the enemy and anyone providing information to the RCMP was
like a traitor. For an officer who had always seen himself as one of the
good guys, it was a surprise. "I had always envisioned my role as
being someone who was there to help people." Garry recalled that
people were often wary of the officers, reluctant to talk. "I think if the
relationship had been better, we'd have probably got a lot more
co-operation," he said. While he didn't believe race was a factor in
how hard he tried to solve the murder of Alberta Williams, it was
"certainly a factor" in why he failed.

Michael Arntfield, a criminologist and former police officer,
said the RCMP's practice of moving its members frequently is one
of "the fundamental issues facing them." The force might, for
example, recruit a longshoreman in Newfoundland who lost his
job when the fishing industry tanked. He'll get six months of training at depot and then he's a cop, working wherever he's posted—
a frigate in the North Atlantic, a two-member post in Nunavut, a
First Nations reserve in B.C.—regardless of whether he has any
particular aptitude, training or experience for it. "They're moved
around as though they're drillers on a job, and the job is so much

more complex than that," said Arntfield. Police officers need to cultivate informers within the communities where they work. "It takes years to build those kinds of surreptitious but very important mutual-trust relationships, and if people are constantly on the move or constantly being transferred or looking to get out of the area, and [they're] not from that area, don't understand the culture, those relationships will not be forged." While Arntfield credited the RCMP for its efforts in recent years to diversify its force and do further training, "you see a lot of these departments that are still old boys' clubs, overwhelmingly white rural hockey players, that just don't have the experience or the empathy required for the job, very much less to deal with people of other cultures." In other words, it's not that members are necessarily overtly racist— though some certainly are, which then RCMP commissioner Bob Paulson acknowledged in 2013—but more that they are unequipped, untrained and incompetent when it comes to dealing with people different from themselves.

Lawrence and Rena went to the RCMP detachment looking for updates and to answer questions. Garry remembered them entering the little GIS office. "They were heartbroken," that he could tell. But they were very quiet. They didn't pound on the desk or demand that the RCMP—an organization where "the squeaky wheel gets the grease"—not rest until they found Alberta's killer. They didn't say much at all. Garry had found that was common in cases involving First Nations people. Sometimes police were met with open hostility; always, with caution. "A lot of it had to do, I think, with that mistrust of police, and [the feeling that] 'we're native so they're not going to do anything,'" he said. People are unlikely to demand help when they do not expect to get it. At the time, Claudia felt the police should have acted more quickly once Alberta was reported missing. "I think their timing should have been a lot better. Don't wait until she's gone a long time," Claudia said. "You've given a person a lot of time to clean up their act."

As the weeks and then months passed, other cases increasingly took up Garry's and Rick's time. In 1990, Prince Rupert police dealt with more than five hundred violent crimes. There were eighty-five sexual offences and more than four hundred assaults. The city had one of the highest crime rates in the province.

Garry wasn't there much longer—the year after Alberta's murder, he was transferred. Rick left in 1992. Members rarely stayed long in isolated postings like Prince Rupert. "Things very quickly lose continuity," Garry said. "'There was a murder two years ago? Who gives a shit, I wasn't here when it happened.'" They took with them their knowledge of the case, along with a sense of ownership over it, what Garry called "that fire in the belly." The investigation fizzled. Garry would go on to work dozens of homicides, more than he can count. But Alberta always stayed with him. With Rick, too. Garry believes that he and Rick investigated thoroughly, that they did everything they could. "We truly did give a shit," he said. But he knew that Lawrence and Rena probably went to their graves thinking the officers didn't.

The family took Alberta home to Gitanyow, to bury her in the cemetery on the grassy expanse between First Avenue and the Kitwanga River. She was laid to rest beside her sister Pamela. It was a closed-casket funeral. It had to be. Francis always wondered what might have happened if he had gone to Bogey's that night when Alberta asked him to come. He was her big brother; if he had been there, he could have protected her. He should have protected her. He wondered whether that sweat, that awful feeling he had on the boat that night, was the moment that his sister was fighting for her life and losing, whether he was that close when someone was hurting her so badly. He wondered if, that day he and Lawrence searched all the back roads, they had gone a little further, they might have found her, at least before the forest and the water had all those days to tear her apart. The same guilt that gnawed at Claudia—if only she hadn't turned away for that moment—chewed on him. He lost many years to alcohol after Alberta was murdered. It took a long time for him to find his way home to Gitanyow, where sometimes he went down to the cemetery on the banks of the river, the whisper of leaves on the cottonwoods overhead and the mist wrapping around the hills across the river, to be near her.

BLATANT FAILURES

IT WOULD BE MANY YEARS before Alberta Williams's name began to appear on lists of women and girls killed on the Highway of Tears, but Garry Kerr's career took him, by the late 1990s, to Prince George, as the RCMP grappled with what to do about the cluster of cases along Highway 16. While criticism from families mounted about the lack of attention and interest police showed their lost loved ones, local officers were struggling to find time and resources to pursue the cases. As one Terrace newspaper story noted, "If an answer does exist to Lana's 1995 disappearance, it's likely buried in one of two battered green filing cabinets bearing the girl's name in the Terrace detachment's serious crime bunker. They're full of tips—which the police get to when they've got time."

The city's population was growing, and with it the number of violent crimes. Sgt. Anders Udsen, the head of the detachment's two-person general investigation division, said his hair had turned grey in the three years he'd worked in Terrace. Officers were working huge amounts of overtime and were at risk of burnout; investigators struggled to keep on top of new crimes while trying to continue investigating older cases like that of Lana Derrick. "What are we doing about it now? We're doing what we can—when we get the opportunity," he said. "The fact of the matter is that we just aren't in a position right now to provide what is needed to get the job done." It wore on the investigators. Const. Liz Douglas kept a photo of Lana on her desk and said she was confident the case could be solved, if she had the time to devote to it. "It's frustrating. It's very frustrating for the family," she said. "I never knew her, but she becomes somebody that you think about. Like a sister. Each of these girls, they had something to offer—but something happened to them."

In late 1995, police had searched a house in Telkwa in connection with the murder of Ramona Wilson. Six months later, the Prince Rupert officer in charge of the investigation said objects seized during that search were still under examination. "We always like to think we are close to solving it but it's a very frustrating investigation," said Sgt. Randy Beck. Families joined police calls for more resources. In Smithers, Matilda Wilson said the officer in charge of Ramona's case was trying to get assistance from Prince George. "He can't follow up everything on his own," she said. "He needs help." In Prince George, media officer Const. Mike Herchuk said that if the local RCMP had the resources, it would "throw them into these investigations," but "in many cases, we just don't have the manpower or the money available to take it that extra step."

Const. Scott Whyte arrived in Prince Rupert in the mid-1990s, and was one of four officers working out of the RCMP subdivision's General Investigation Section. The subdivision GIS was separate from the city's, where Garry Kerr had worked; its investigators were responsible for serious crimes across an enormous swath of the northwest. "It's a big chunk of cake to bite off," said Scott. "It's a huge area to cover." Smithers fell within the northwest subdivision, and Scott was assigned to look into the disappearance of Delphine Nikal, in 1990, and the murder of Ramona Wilson, in

1994. He said he cannot discuss the investigations publicly—upon leaving the police force he was given explicit "thou shalt not" instructions—but he was willing to explain some of the factors that made it difficult to investigate them.

Scott estimated that, during the about four years he spent in Prince Rupert, he was home perhaps four or five months in total. The rest of his time was spent on the road, driving or flying to remote communities and staying in crappy motels while investigating serious crimes. "It's difficult living that kind of a lifestyle," he said. In the late 1990s, the RCMP was preparing to restructure its operations in B.C. The investigative unit in Prince Rupert was going to be shuttered; a "super section" in Prince George would be handling cases for the entire north of the province. When the other constable in the section left, management decided not to fill the position. The same thing happened when the sergeant departed, and then the corporal. So Scott was left trying to handle what had been the workload of four members by himself. He worked weeks on end without a day off. He was hardly ever home. He was, increasingly, struggling with mental health. "It created a huge amount of stress, because the work wasn't slowing down," he said. Office politics and infighting compounded the situation. "There was a lot of frustration," said Scott. The impact of the tumult on investigations, he said, was that "not much got done on them." He did the best he could, though "using hindsight, one person can't do all of [what] needed to be done."

Scott, who had worked in the RCMP for more than two decades by that time, suffered an acute mental health breakdown; he left the force not long afterward, and has since worked as a mental health advocate and in training police officers in dealing with mental health issues—in those they encounter as well as their own. Asked how much he felt the lack of resources and the weight of the Highway of Tears cases contributed to his breakdown, Scott replied: "It was solely responsible for the breakdown, that's what I believe. It contributed to a sense of desperation, that something needs to be done. I remember feeling very passionate doing this on behalf of the families that were involved. I still do. I still feel strongly that the families deserved more."

Policing is a constitutional responsibility of the provinces and territories. Quebec and Ontario alone have their own police forces—the Sûreté du Québec and the Ontario Provincial Police. The other provinces and the three territories, along with many municipalities, contract the RCMP to provide police services. The practice of contract policing began in 1928 as a means to repurpose the national police force. Formed six years after Confederation and tasked with settling the west, the North-West Mounted Police, as it was then known, was a paramilitary organization that more closely resembled an army unit than a police force. As Peter German wrote in a 1990 paper, "To settle the west meant dispossessing the aboriginal people of their traditional hunting grounds, stopping American expansionist sentiment at the forty-ninth parallel and constructing a transcontinental railway. Each required either a military or a police presence, or both." Prime Minister John A. Macdonald "sought the amalgam of an army and a police presence: the equivalent of the frontier marshal, the cavalry and the town constable rolled up into one." By the beginning of the twentieth century, the goals of the colonial government—taking land from Indigenous people and forcing them onto reserves, holding off the Americans and building the railway—were complete. Contracting the RCMP, with the federal government covering a portion of the cost, to the nascent provinces gave the Mounties a new lease on life.

Today, the Mounties are a national police force, the law enforcement agency tasked with policing areas such as commercial and organized crime, terrorism and national security. As its website notes, "Our mandate is multi-faceted. We prevent and investigate crime, maintain order, enforce laws on matters as diverse as health and the protection of government revenues, contribute to national security, ensure the safety of state officials, visiting dignitaries and foreign missions, and provide vital operational support services to other police and law enforcement agencies." But its foremost function is municipal policing. Nearly two-thirds of the roughly twenty thousand police officers in the RCMP work as municipal officers under contract. A third of the force is in British Columbia, or E Division, where the RCMP has jurisdiction over more than 80 per cent of the province. The paramilitary culture of the RCMP hasn't adapted along with its evolving role. Numerous reviews, reports and inquiries over the years have singled out the force's culture— called "horribly broken," "dysfunctional" and "toxic," among other descriptors—as a major factor in a litany of scandals that have enveloped the once-iconic force, from cover-ups to investigative failures to endemic sexual harassment to a rash of suicides among members. An investigation by Global News published in January 2019 found more than $220 million has been spent in the past twenty years paying for lawsuits and legal settlements, inquiries and reports, and employee claims. Ken Hansen, a defence and security analyst, argued in a January 2018 opinion piece in *Maclean's* magazine that a huge problem arises when a military-style force takes on such a role. "The key problem—one that has bled into the RCMP's culture—is that the organization's central purpose is as a federal defensive force, and not a municipal protective force. In their minds, RCMP officers do not 'serve and protect' as many municipal force mottos assert," writes Hansen, who goes on: "This dichotomy sets up a problem of organizational schizophrenia, a state in which the federal police are directed to conduct municipal missions and tasks for which they are inherently unsuited. The RCMP has the culture of a military force, and the expectations of a policing one—a hard collision of identity and perception that was meant to be a seamless blend of both when it took on those contract-policing duties."

Garry Kerr arrived in Prince George just as the RCMP rearranged its operations in B.C., going from seven subdivisions to four districts:

the Island District, which covers Vancouver Island and the smaller islands that dot its coast; the Lower Mainland District, responsible for the region surrounding Vancouver; the Southeast District, which polices the Okanagan, Kootenays and as far north as Williams Lake in the Cariboo; and the North District, which covers a geographic area more than twice the size of the other three districts combined. From Williams Lake its jurisdiction stretches all the way north to the borders of Alaska and the Yukon, and east to the Alberta border.

Garry worked in the North District Major Crime Unit. When he arrived, he was a sergeant, working under a staff sergeant who oversaw the unit with about ten corporals and constables. Those dozen or so officers were responsible for investigating homicides, suspicious deaths, sexual assaults and other cases deemed too complicated or sensitive for local detachments to handle on their own. The only exception was Prince George itself, which has its own autonomous RCMP detachment, though North District investigators assisted the city force at times. During those years, Garry and the other investigators lived out of their suitcases, crisscrossing the province's small towns, remote work camps and reserves. "It was insane, it truly was," said Garry. "It was just murder after murder after murder after murder."

Newspaper articles in the early 2000s noted the Mounties planned to launch a task force into the Highway of Tears cases in 1997, but it was put on hold because of budget constraints. An RCMP spokesperson, Sgt. Janelle Shoihet, wrote in a 2018 email that she had no information about a potential task force in the '90s, noting that when a 2002 article was published the RCMP was "full into" Project Evenhanded, a joint probe with the Vancouver Police Department investigating women missing from the Downtown Eastside. After Project Evenhanded was designated a task force, "everyone called for a Task Force for everything," she wrote. It is not clear whether the RCMP had concrete plans for a large-scale investigation along the

Highway of Tears. Whatever the case, according to several former police officers and criminologists, it should have. "The real annoying thing is, they should have thrown these resources at this case in '94, '95, '96 at the latest," said Kim Rossmo, a former Vancouver Police Department detective who unsuccessfully raised the alarm about a possible serial killer at work in the city years before Robert Pickton was eventually apprehended in 2002.

Fred Maile was worried about the possibility of a serial killer in the northwest. The retired RCMP officer turned private investigator, who had worked with the Missing Children Society of Canada on the disappearance of Delphine and Ramona, publicly contradicted the RCMP, which continued to assert that there was nothing to suggest a link between the cases. He had been at the 1995 meeting when investigators and profilers sat down in Prince George to look for signs of a serial killer along Highway 16. He said that after reviewing five cases—Delphine Nikal, Ramona Wilson, Roxanne Thiara, Alishia Germaine and Cindy Burk—the group felt the same perpetrator was probably responsible for three murders: those of Ramona, Roxanne and Alishia. Fred was convinced Delphine's disappearance was connected, too. Ron MacKay, an RCMP behavioural analyst who'd led the group, backed up Fred's assertion, saying the investigators had thought there were "enough similarities at that time to show that two, and possibly three, of the girls could have the same offender."

Fred Maile has since passed away. Rhonda Morgan, the founder and then executive director of the Missing Children Society of Canada, worked closely with him for years. She surmised that he spoke out because he was long haunted by the length of time it took authorities to determine that a serial killer was behind the disappearances and deaths of the eleven kids Clifford Olson had murdered. And Fred was haunted—and frustrated—watching a similar scenario play out in Vancouver not two decades later. He was concerned that the same thing—authorities failing to grasp that they were dealing with a serial killer—might be happening along the Highway of Tears. He was not the only one.

"I find it very frustrating," Kim Rossmo said. B.C. police agencies had dealt with Olson; in Ontario, Paul Bernardo had gone on a five-year spree of rape and sexual assault before escalating to the murder of a fourteen-year-old girl in June 1991 and a fifteen-year-old girl the following year. He was finally arrested in 1993. An investigation review released in 1996 by Justice Archie Campbell noted that the mistakes of the Bernardo investigation mirrored virtually every "interjurisdictional serial killer case," including Ted Bundy, Clifford Olson and the Green River Killer. "The Bernardo case, like every similar investigation, had its share of human error. But this is not a story of human error or lack of dedication or investigative skill. It is a story of systemic failure." That report was read across the country, said Rossmo. "There were multiple opportunities to learn and prevent mistakes. But the mistakes keep happening."

In 2018, Rossmo was the University Endowed Chair in Criminology and director of the Center for Geospatial Intelligence and Investigation at Texas State University, in Austin. In the preceding twenty-five years, he had earned renown as the first street cop in Canada to earn a PhD and as the developer of geographic profiling, an investigative technique that uses a computer algorithm to determine the most likely area of residence of a serial offender. It has since been used to study the hunting patterns of sharks, to track terrorists, and even to attempt to identify the elusive street artist Banksy. But while the method was embraced by law enforcement around the world, many of Rossmo's colleagues at the Vancouver Police Department, where from 1995 to 2000 he headed the newly minted geographic profiling unit, derisively referred to it as "voodoo."

It was the mid- to late 1990s, and Vancouver was seeing a marked increase in the number of missing women. As investigative journalist Stevie Cameron documents in her 2010 book *On the Farm*, the *Vancouver Sun* reporter Lindsay Kines had recently published a series of articles about the rise in missing women cases from the city's Downtown Eastside, and public attention was increasing. A couple of worried officers went to Rossmo looking for help. "He completed a statistical analysis to see if the disappearances were simply standard events and to determine if there was any possibility that the missing women would be found," Cameron writes. "He met with [the officers] two days later. Yes, he told them, they were right to be so concerned. Yes, statistically there is something here. There is a good chance a serial killer is at work." With Rossmo's backing, the officers pitched their case for an investigation into a possible serial killer. Although they got some support, the recommendation was shunted around and eventually quashed by what Cameron refers to as an old boys' club that despised Rossmo and argued that "without bodies—the physical evidence—there were no cases. Then they argued that the force had only limited resources available. What they didn't say was that ignoring these victims was possible because they were only addicted prostitutes from Canada's poorest neighbourhood."

The same year, 1998, police received two tips that a pig farmer named Robert Pickton had killed a woman on his farm. A working group established to look at the increasing number of missing women was soon disbanded, as was surveillance of Pickton after nothing suspicious turned up over the course of a few days. Over the following years, Pickton reappeared on the police radar, only to fall off again amid what was later determined to be bureaucratic bungling, poor case management and a lack of coordination between police forces—many of the same problems identified in previous investigations, like Olson and Bernardo. Meanwhile, women continued to disappear. Ultimately, it was a tip about Pickton having illegal firearms—"chance and luck," said Rossmo— that brought officers to his farm in 2002, where they found items belonging to several of the missing women, sparking what would become the largest forensic search in Canadian history. Police found evidence of thirty-three missing women on the property. Pickton was charged with twenty-six murders, though convicted of only six—the Crown decided to stay the remainder of the charges to save resources. He bragged to an undercover officer posing as a cellmate that he had killed forty-nine women. Cameron quotes a former officer: "If they had followed [Rossmo's] analysis and put the best and brightest onto it, they would have saved lives. But they just paid lip service. We had an opportunity to save lives and we blew it."

Years later, Rossmo analyzed a number of Highway of Tears cases for the *Vancouver Sun* and concluded that there was a "reasonably high" probability of links between the murders and disappearances in the mid-1990s. The cluster in 1994 and 1995 in particular should have set off alarm bells. Rossmo brushed off the RCMP's insistence that there was no definitive evidence of connections as "irrelevant." Only if you have physical evidence, like DNA or fingerprints, can you establish links with certainty. "If you don't have that, then you're guessing, you're dealing with probabilities. But the two most important variables are proximity in time and place," said Rossmo. "By the end of '95, it was damn clear that something was going on."

Rossmo said that when a potential serial killer is at large, "it has to be treated with a high priority, which actually causes the police sometimes to want to deny the existence of a serial killer because that means that they realize they're going to have to step up and start putting some resources into it." A proper response requires a lot of people and it requires a lot of money. It requires police to pull out all the stops. The RCMP is a national police force that touts its ability to muster resources when needed—it can summon members, expertise and funds from across the country—but doing so requires a higher-up taking the risk. If they are wrong and call in the cavalry for what ends up being nothing, their credibility and career can be hurt. "Sometimes, politically, they're reluctant to do that," said Rossmo. "The reality is that governments are horrible at what are called low-probability, high-impact problems. You sit there and go, well, maybe it's a serial killer but most likely it's not . . . we've only got so much money and if we do this, we can't do something else."

How fast, or slow, police are to act is influenced by many factors, one of which, Rossmo argued, is the nature of the victim: "if the victim is seen as a true innocent." Lorimer Shenher, a retired Vancouver Police Department detective who worked on the missing women cases in Vancouver in the late 1990s, said officers harboured stereotypes that clouded their ability to recognize what they were dealing with. In Vancouver, many of the missing women lived in poverty, suffered from addictions and mental health issues, and worked in the sex trade. Many were Indigenous. Shenher's colleagues sometimes didn't believe the women were actually even missing. "People would say to me, 'Oh, well, she's not really missing. She's taken off before, this isn't unusual,'" he said. In fact it was unusual, as anyone who understood their lives well knew. Women were not picking up social assistance cheques. They were not calling family or friends, or visiting their children, as they usually did. Many were tightly bound to the ready supply of heroin in the Downtown Eastside—they couldn't just up and leave without facing debilitating withdrawal. But most police officers "had no conception of their lives or what it would actually take for them to disappear," Shenher said. "Those stereotypes were a huge problem."

By the mid-1990s, the RCMP developed what is known as the Major Case Management system, which Shenher likened to "the amber alert of serious crime." Once it's triggered, "it works terrifically well." The problem, he said, is how the decision to trigger it is reached. He recalled "sitting there at the height [of the missing women in Vancouver] with thirty-four piles on my desk of missing women who had not talked to anybody and picked up money in years and yet I could not ring that bell loud enough to get anybody to say, 'You know what? Yeah, this is a major case.'" He likened the national police force to the medical system, where, if you go into an emergency department with a sliced finger that needs a few stitches, you will likely wait hours for service. If, however, you show up with something serious, the medical system will respond with the best treatment possible. "If you have something serious going on . . . like a murder, they're excellent," he said. "But a lot of things have to be in place: that's assuming you have a victim that people sort of care about. It assumes that there's . . . a little public attention around the case." He said discrepancies in how police respond depend on who the victim is. "You see it all the time, the twelve-year-old white girl who goes missing and ends up murdered, you will see the earth moved for that investigation. Rightfully so—I would say rightfully so if I felt like eleven- or twelve-year-old Indigenous girls were getting the same courtesy. You'll see heaven and earth moved because you'll see the white, straight, middle-class nuclear family, and they will tell you that those RCMP officers were like the best people they've ever dealt with and just were tireless in their investigation and worked so hard and did such a great job.

"They don't apply the same standards to other people."

Steve Pranzl, a long-time homicide detective with the Vancouver Police Department who later worked on a Highway of Tears task force, explained that certain factors seem to influence how cases are prioritized, "often in subtle and difficult to articulate or measure ways—ways even the police services themselves may not totally recognize are occurring." It typically starts with a victim's family showing interest: "'squeaky wheels'—that show they care and want action—tend to engender a more active and persistent investigation," said Steve. That, in turn, ignites further interest in the immediate community that intensifies the pressure on police. And sometimes that spreads to a whole city, province or country, the flame fanned by the media keeping a wrenching story in the public eye. "This often leads to outrage and demands for 'everything to be done' . . . In my experience, these factors may sometimes influence the doggedness, resolve and willingness to use limited resources manifested by the police pursuing a case."

From a public safety perspective, Rossmo said a "cluster" like that of the Highway of Tears in the 1990s warranted a major response: "If you're only right one time out of five, the four times you're wrong is more than compensated for by the one time you're right." But that's not often how these matters were viewed within the culture of the RCMP. Rossmo stressed that there are many "great RCMP officers, but as a whole, the organization seems much more concerned about itself than what it's supposed to be doing, because it's paramount to protect the reputation of the force and less important to actually make sure the force is doing what we want it to do in the first place." Rossmo noted revelations during the inquiry into the bungled investigation of missing women from Vancouver and Robert Pickton, when documents were disclosed showing that in April 2000, two years before Pickton was arrested, police had him at the top of their suspect list. According to a *National Post* story, "Major crimes investigators were already aware, for example, that Pickton had a predilection for prostitutes. They knew of his episodic, sadistic violence. They had sources who claimed he was murdering women and chopping them to pieces . . . Perhaps most telling, on April 25, 2000, RCMP officers were already discussing the possibility that bungled efforts would lead to a public inquiry. On that date, a staff sergeant named Brad Zalys had a conversation with a superior officer, RCMP Inspector Earl Moulton. Staff Sgt. Zalys made the following observation in his notebook: 'Also discussed Pickton again→if he turns out to be responsible→inquiry!→Deal with that if the time comes!'"

"It's just so egregious," said Rossmo. "Their concern is organizational, bureaucratic. Not about, if the time comes, how many more victims are there going to be?"

Twenty-three more women went missing before Pickton was arrested.

Garry Kerr recalled that the North District Major Crime Unit did undertake what's termed, in police parlance, a "file review." In those days, police investigational files were stored in bankers boxes; the review consisted of a couple of officers poring over the standardized forms and documents of the unsolved cases along Highway 16, thousands of pages in cardboard boxes. The officers didn't do any interviews or further investigation. The material they had to work with, Garry remembered, was in some cases "garbage": pages were missing, or notes were unsigned or illegible, rendering them nearly useless. In some of the investigations, he recalled, the basics were done "and then it was just kind of like, okay, throw everything into a box." In some cases the reviewers had to spend an inordinate amount of time just figuring out who had written something, essentially having to do an investigation of the investigation. "It was just boxes of crap," he said. "That was one of the biggest problems we had." As forensic technology evolves, what is potentially valuable as evidence does, too. But some exhibits had been lost or had never been collected in the first place.

At the end of the review, the investigators didn't feel anything pointed to a serial killer. There were, of course, the obvious similarities: the victims were all young First Nations females who went missing along Highway 16. "The feeling was that there definitely was not a serial killer," Garry said. "That was the opinion we came to and I stand by that to this day . . . We couldn't say, 'I think these three are connected.' There was just nothing."

In 1998, then head of major crimes for the North District, Sgt. Howard Goodridge, denied that either resources or racism had anything to do with the failure to solve the cases, but instead owed it to not getting any good breaks. "Funding isn't an issue at all," he told the *Terrace Standard* that year. The article noted, "He explained that race never comes into consideration when working on a murder investigation. He said RCMP forces aren't just made up of white officers. People from various ethnic backgrounds work on these cases, so racism can't be an issue."

A later inquiry that focused on Vancouver's missing women found that police—both Vancouver's municipal force and the RCMP—failed to act on the missing women or, in some cases, even take proper reports on them. Officers didn't connect the dots to realize a serial killer was at work, or take steps to protect women in the neighbourhood. Investigations mismanaged sources, disregarded tips and faced delays; there was weak coordination between various police departments. Inquiry commissioner Wally Oppal found the investigations to be "blatant failures." For all the failures of police, however, Oppal made an important point in his final report, writing:

> Sir Robert Peel coined the phrase: "the police are the public and the public is the police." I keep this phrase at the forefront of my analysis. The police failures in this case mirror the general public and political indifference to the missing women. While the police have a legal duty to overcome systemic biases and ensure equal protection of the law, they cannot do it alone. The lack of prioritization of the missing women investigations never became a matter of public importance. At some level, we all share the responsibility for the unchecked tragedy of the failed missing women investigations.

IT DEPENDS WHO'S BLEEDING

NICOLE HOAR'S CREATIONS are full of whimsy, replete with reused, seemingly random items. She was a scavenger, collecting things everywhere she went to make into art: a couple of mini-cassette tapes from when she was experimenting with audio sculpture; cloth and bead-covered notebooks, using recycled paper as the pages; a poster calendar advertisement for a Chilean chicken restaurant, depicting a scantily clad woman, which she used to write a letter to her older sister, Michelle. Many of her letters arrived this way, scrawled on funny, odd things she found in her travels. Laughter rings out through the handwritten words. A green and blue dragon sewn on an orange cloth square that Nicole used as part of a lampshade—that lamp was a little testy, because Nicole was definitely not an electrician. Only recently did Michelle dismantle the lamp and mount the dragon on one of Nicole's favourite paint-splattered sweatshirts. That was hard. Nicole had the mirror image of that patch—orange dragon on a green and blue background—sewn onto the bag she was carrying when she went missing.

Nicole Hoar was born in Toronto, the middle of Barb and Jack Hoar's three children. Michelle is the eldest, three years Nicole's senior.

John is two years younger. The three of them were always close, but Nicole acted as the peacemaker. "She was always kind of Switzerland," Michelle said, laughing. Nicole was drawn to offbeat things, places and people: the outsiders and eccentrics and weirdos, the people who were misunderstood by everyone else. She had this way of figuring out and appreciating what made each person special, of accepting people as they were and delighting in their oddities and uniqueness. People were an adventure. "She loved interesting characters and was naturally curious about the world. She found things to like about a much wider range of people than most do," said Michelle.

Barb and Jack were originally from Edmonton, where Jack worked for the Hudson's Bay Company. They had moved east when Jack took a transfer, just before their first child was born. They lived in Toronto for many years, but when Nicole was sixteen, Barb and Jack felt it was time to go back to Alberta. Jack got a placement in Red Deer. The kids had never heard of the place and took out an encyclopedia to read up on it. A small town on a big prairie halfway between Calgary and Edmonton, the city seemed a world away from what they knew.

Michelle was nineteen, just finishing high school and about to head to university, but Nicole and John went with their parents to Red Deer. It was an adjustment, but they settled into life in the small Alberta city. Nicole finished high school and stayed on for another two years to do an arts program at Red Deer College, then moved to Halifax to finish her fine arts degree at the Nova Scotia College of Art and Design. During the summers in between, she would travel north to the far reaches of British Columbia and into the Yukon to work. She made her first trip north in the spring of 1996, driving up to Dawson City with Michelle after school had let out. They worked crappy jobs and lived in an old canvas tent in the informal municipal campground known as Tent City, and they had a blast. That summer gave Nicole an itch for the north, the outdoors, the vast landscapes and colourful characters.

Nicole started tree planting when she graduated from university. She got hired on at Celtic Reforestation, a silviculture company based in Prince George. Celtic's planters worked in crews of about fifteen people, living in camps near the cutblocks, often hours away along dirt roads from the nearest towns. The planters worked for ten or more hours a day, trudging through mud, bog, brush, inserting seedlings into the earth stripped of forest. The going rate around that time was fourteen cents a tree. An average planter might do 1,500 or 1,600 trees a day, earning about $200. A good planter, known as a highballer, could do 2,000 or more trees a day. Planters often aimed to work sixty or seventy days a season; that could earn them enough to cover university tuition and residence for the coming year. Nicole told her sister, Michelle, and Dave Gowans, Michelle's partner, how she went into "machine mode," became an "automaton" and just planted and planted and planted, repeating the same process thousands of times a day: stab the spade into the ground, bend over while pulling a seedling from a waist bag, ease it into the slot, then backfill the hole. She became a highballer, a designation that was hard-earned

Nicole Hoar was a talented artist, forever collecting
odds and ends during her travels to fashion into unique creations.

and rare, especially for women. She made good money and returned the next summer, and the next, to plant for Celtic.

Every year on the weekend closest to summer solstice, there is a festival in Smithers, B.C. The Midsummer Music Festival brings people from across the northwest to hear bands from around the province.

Dave Gowans was the frontman in a rock group, the Buttless Chaps, which was performing at the festival in 2002. In late June, he and Michelle packed up the band van to drive north to Smithers. Nicole had visited them in Vancouver, where they were living, before heading to Prince George to plant, and she told Michelle that if the break between spring and summer planting seasons fell on the weekend of the festival, she would meet them in Smithers. "It wasn't a plan," said Michelle. "It was like, we're going to be up there, if it works, awesome."

Tree planting attracts a certain kind of person; it has a certain culture. There is a strong countercultural milieu, a sort of modern-day hippie mentality that's against materialism and corporate control and wasting money on comforts like hotels. The work draws people who want freedom and flexibility: travellers and adventurers and those who aren't satisfied sitting behind a desk. Hitchhiking was a standard means of getting around for many of the youths working in Celtic's camps. Nicole was no different. An intrepid traveller, she'd hitched around western Canada and South America.

On Friday, June 21, 2002, three of Nicole's friends from camp dropped her off on the outskirts of Prince George in the afternoon. It was a warm day, clear skies occasionally masked by clouds rolling in and out, temperatures in the low twenties. The western edge of the city by a gas station, just past Gauthier Road, was a common spot to hitch a ride. The crew had a week off before the next round of planting began. Nicole was headed to Smithers, carrying a sixty-litre black and purple Mountain Equipment Co-op backpack and a green shoulder bag. On it was the green and blue patch with an orange dragon, the mirror image of the one she'd given her big sister. Her friends were concerned about her hitchhiking, but she was determined. She told them she took precautions: she wouldn't get in a car where men outnumbered her or if she felt uncomfortable. They trusted her judgment. "All she kept talking about was how excited she was to see her sister," one of her friends later told a reporter. "She was just so happy and focused." They drove away.

All these years later, a lot of memories are fuzzy for Michelle. She doesn't know the extent to which some were shaped by what happened afterward. That weekend was a bit of a blur—they drove the 1,150 kilometres north to Smithers, spent a day or so at the festival, and drove home—but Michelle remembered feeling weird, unsettled. Dave remembered, too, that Michelle was restless because she hadn't heard from Nicole, even though it was never a firm plan that they'd meet up. He remembered reassuring her that Nicole was working, far away from a phone or any way to get in touch.

Nicole's crew was due to meet up after their break on June 27, six days after she'd set off for Smithers. But she never showed up. It was completely out of character for her. Celtic contacted her family, wondering if there had been an emergency. When it became clear that no one knew where she was, the forestry company reported her missing to the local RCMP. The response was immediate and intense.

Barb and Jack travelled from Red Deer to Prince George. John flew in from Nelson, B.C., and Michelle and Dave came from Vancouver. Aunts, uncles, cousins, other extended family joined them, along with many friends. They spent the first couple of nights in a hotel until a local businessman offered two side-by-side vacant houses for the searchers to stay. A ground and air search was launched, with the police and search-and-rescue teams working alongside Nicole's family and friends and dozens of her tree-planting colleagues. Celtic shut down operations so that everyone could assist in scouring an enormous swath of land. That week, hundreds of people searched the ground while a police helicopter combed the land from above. In four days, searchers covered more than eight thousand kilometres of highway, logging roads and trails. The search area was more than twenty-four thousand square kilometres.

On Friday, July 5, Nicole's family held a press conference begging for information. "We need our daughter home, we need to have her back," Barb said, bursting into tears. "Anything that anybody can do to help us, just absolutely anything, any article of clothing that you find, if you could report. We just need to find a place to get started. We want our precious daughter home." A subsequent Canadian Press story was picked up and published in newspapers across the country, including Canada's two national newspapers, the *Globe and Mail* and the *National Post*. It ran on an American wire service, the Associated Press, too. Local media was saturated. RCMP Const. Mike Herchuk said the heavy coverage "sparked a tremendous amount of recollection," generating about a hundred tips in five days. Almost overnight, Nicole was known across the continent. In the coming days, the story continued to make its way into newspapers and broadcasts Canada-wide and internationally.

That initial search for Nicole was one of the largest in northern British Columbia, with the number of searchers swelling to three hundred. And yet they found no trace of her. On Sunday, July 7, the RCMP said it was time to scale back. Police said they would shift their focus toward the "investigative aspect," such as following up on tips that came from as far away as Barrie, Ontario, adding, "We will not stop searching for Nicole." By then, RCMP investigators had traversed Highway 16 "talking to anyone who had a view of the highway." Investigators had collected hundreds of hours of security videos from gas stations, banks and convenience stores from Prince George to Smithers to look for any sign of Nicole. Search teams with volunteers from thirteen communities were working their way outward along the highway corridor, walking shoulder to shoulder along ditches for seventy-kilometre stretches on either side of Prince George, Burns Lake and Smithers. "They are covering every metre of every forestry road. They are going up trails, they are looking in every small camping site. They are prodding under every bush, every tree," Const. Herchuk said. Detectives even travelled to the Yukon to follow up on leads. The flood of tips, police said, seemed to indicate that Nicole had made it to at least Burns Lake, about 225 kilometres west of Prince George. But nothing was certain.

While the RCMP shifted gears, Nicole's family and friends continued the ground search. Each day they blocked out an area, divided into groups and combed the wilderness. Every morning they left at dawn and searched for as long as they could, until dusk set in and they had to head back to Prince George, where they would regroup, decompress and plan the next day's search. It was like a crisis camp, everyone going full tilt, set on the same objective: finding Nicole.

Help and support came from across the country. Barb's running group set up a trust fund to help cover costs of the search and to establish a reward. Olympic speed skater Steven Elm, Nicole's prom date and long-time friend, vowed to skate for her at Calgary's Olympic Oval, covering a metre for every dollar raised to contribute to the effort. "I'm doing this to get as much publicity and get people talking about her so she becomes a household name," he said. "I want everybody to know who she is." Many others in Red Deer held fundraisers; donations came in from B.C., Alberta and beyond. The Hudson's Bay Company, Jack's employer, put up a $25,000 reward. The branch where Jack worked set up a journal for people to write well wishes and encouragement to the family.

By July 10, three days after the search was called off, the RCMP had twelve officers on the case, investigating more than two hundred tips. At the homes in Prince George housing the searchers, locals dropped off groceries and offered help with tasks like photocopying posters. The Rotary Club of Red Deer East announced a second reward of $5,000 to add to the amount already posted. Musicians in Red Deer organized a benefit concert to raise money for the trust fund. A search-and-rescue member, Gary Bratton, wrote a letter to the local newspaper commending the efforts of Celtic and its planters in searching for Nicole. "What you did for the search was admirable . . . I've never seen such a thing. Look at it this way, each person came here to work, but instead are searching, and the company they work for is in the business to make money planting trees, but aren't because they all stopped what they were doing to come and search. Words can't express how impressed I am."

Michelle couldn't bring herself to search. Instead, she helped deal with the media, plastered the northwest with posters bearing a photo of her grinning sister, and worked on logistics like feeding and housing the dozens of volunteers. For a couple more weeks the family and supporters continued to scour communities along Highway 16 between Prince George and Smithers.

The RCMP was quick to distance Nicole from the girls and women who had gone missing or been found murdered throughout the 1990s, cases that, by 2002, media referred to as the Highway 16 murders. Const. Mike Herchuk, the Prince George detachment's spokesperson, was paraphrased as saying Nicole did not fit the same profile—those victims were young Indigenous females who were hitchhiking at night. Michelle can't remember how the family learned about the girls who had vanished along the highway in the preceding years—it was not something they'd heard about before Nicole went missing—but it was shortly after they arrived in Prince George. In their first days in the city, she went with her brother, John, to the RCMP detachment to drop off missing posters. "There were no posters up for the other women, and we knew at this point that there were a number of other women," Michelle said.

"We were like, 'Where the hell are their posters? Why do we get to put up a poster and there's no posters for these other women?' I remember we were both really angry about that."

The outpouring was overwhelming and brought some light to unspeakably difficult days for the family. But they realized very quickly that the response to Nicole, to them, was different. "I think it was pretty clear right away that we were getting more attention, not just from the media but from the police," Michelle said. "We felt a pretty big responsibility to use that wisely, and discomfort around it, too. There's a certain amount of guilt that goes along with that." Nicole had a strong sense of justice; she would have been appalled. From the outset, in interviews, the family endeavoured to raise the spectre of the other girls missing along the highway, stressing that they, too, should get the same kind of response. It marked the first time many of the girls' names appeared in major publications. "We were aware, we did feel a responsibility because we knew we were getting so much media attention." The family had a great deal of support, resources and skills at their disposal. Michelle worked in communications and knew how to deal with media and the public. So did Jack, as a manager of the Bay. And media cared about their story—reporters clamoured for it. With donated housing and the many contributions to Nicole's fund, the family was able to manage the costs of the extended search and donate leftover money to local search and rescue and Crime Stoppers. "It was still incredibly hard," Michelle said. "I can't imagine, if you don't have all that support."

Media coverage is vital when someone goes missing and, more generally, in solving crimes. As much as some police officers detest reporters, most will agree that they must work with them to do their jobs effectively. News stories generate much-needed tips.

Press coverage also influences the resources allotted to investigations. "The more media attention on a case, the more pressure is going to be on police," said Kim Rossmo, the criminologist formerly with the Vancouver Police Department. He credited the dogged, accurate reporting of several *Vancouver Sun* journalists—Lindsay Kines, Neal Hall, Kim Bolan—for hauling into the light the story of women missing from the Downtown Eastside. "I'll bet you we would have had different results if they weren't paying attention," he said. Dave Aitken, a twenty-five-year veteran of the Vancouver Police Department, including about a decade investigating homicides, agrees—media attention leads to political motivation. "A lot of these things [task forces] are brought on by thorough reporting . . . that [brings] people's attention to the fact that all these things are going on," he said. "Nobody really gave a shit about what was going on on the Downtown Eastside . . . until the press jumped on it and the cops had no alternative but to jump on it themselves." Michael Arntfield, a former London police officer and criminologist, said media and public attention has a significant impact. "Police bureaucrats are fundamentally concerned about their own well-being and advancement, and at the end of the day, the altar upon which their reputation for promotional purposes is measured is in the public, in the media," he said. "As soon as there's negative publicity that may impact them personally, versus the victim, that ultimately is the prime mover."

The media also carries the story to the public. If that story captures people's hearts and minds, it coalesces to provide much-needed support for families and search efforts. In Nicole's case, and that of Melanie Carpenter seven years earlier, public support led to hundreds of search volunteers, reward funds and other financial and logistical support. Whether the media covers a story, and how it covers that story, makes a difference.

Indigenous women and girls in Canada, although far more likely to be victims of violence, sexual assault and abuse, and homicide, have received less media coverage—and less sympathetic coverage. In a 2010 paper titled "'Newsworthy' Victims?: Exploring differences in

Canadian local press coverage of missing/murdered Aboriginal and White women," sociologist Kristen Gilchrist noted that previous research showed severe violence, especially murder, was considered newsworthy and that crime against young and elderly white females was particularly so. Within news coverage, a "hierarchy of female victims" was evident, with a divide between those deemed good, innocent and worth saving and those considered bad, unworthy victims beyond redemption. "Like social relations in general, this binary is deeply tied to race and class," wrote Gilchrist.

She analyzed news coverage of six cases of women who disappeared between 2003 and 2005. Three were Indigenous and three were white. Otherwise, they were of similar backgrounds: all attended school or were working, all maintained close connections with friends and family, and none had connections to sex work or were believed to be runaways. The discrepancy in local newspaper coverage was stark. The white women were mentioned in 511 articles, whereas the Indigenous women were mentioned in only 82 articles. When broken down to only count articles focused on the cases, the three white women accounted for 187 stories, versus 53 stories about the Indigenous women. The articles about the white women were longer and more likely to appear on the front page. And there were marked differences in how the victims were portrayed. In headlines, the Indigenous women were usually described "impersonally and rarely by name," whereas the white women were referred to by their names in headlines "written as heartfelt personal messages from the victims' friends and family to the women."

Within the articles, Gilchrist's analysis showed that the white women were discussed "in glowing ways, using potent adjectives and imagery." Stories about the Indigenous women, while describing them positively, lacked the same kind of personal stories, anecdotes and memories. "Beyond superficial details, readers did not get the same sense of who the Aboriginal women were or what they meant to their loved ones or communities," she noted. "The lack of coverage to missing/murdered Aboriginal women appears to suggest that their stories are not dramatic or worthy enough to tell, that Aboriginal women's victimization is too routine or ordinary, and/or irrelevant to (White) readers. The common news adage 'if it bleeds it leads' is not an accurate one as 'it really depends on who is bleeding.'"

In the "hierarchy of victims" in the pages of the nation's press, Indigenous women and girls have long been squarely at the bottom, regardless of their occupations, achievements, appearance or circumstances. This hierarchy of victims, Gilchrist and others have noted, might suggest to offenders that Indigenous women can be targeted without repercussion because they are dismissed by society and receive considerably less attention from the public and police.

That the disappearance of Nicole Hoar garnered far more attention than those of the girls who went missing in the 1990s was not just clear to her family; it was clear to all the families. "It was blowing up the newspaper," said the sister of a girl later murdered in Prince George. "That was the big talk, about Nicole and how she went missing on that road and her parents were looking for her. When it comes to Indigenous women, there's no big stories about that, and there's so many that go missing." Leoni Rivers, the executive director of the BC Native Women's Society, told a reporter: "When our families first went to police reporting our girls missing, they were told they were only runaways who'd gone to [the] bright lights of Vancouver . . . Maybe some of the publicity for Nicole might help everyone remember there were six missing women and girls before her."

Indigenous leaders pointed out similarities between the disappearances along the Highway of Tears and those in Vancouver's Downtown Eastside, where, for years, police denied there was anything unusual going on. Matilda Wilson hoped police and the public in northwestern B.C. would remember the other daughters who went missing and were murdered before Nicole. "I don't want to say that now this girl is missing maybe they will do more, but maybe there will be more of a focus on these cases. Now people are talking about these girls again," she said.

Although Nicole's disappearance bolstered media interest in all the cases, the content of many stories demonstrated the same kind of bias that Gilchrist found in her analysis. While glowing and personal stories about Nicole abounded, painting a vivid image of the kind, intelligent young woman she was and examining the impact of her disappearance on her family, co-workers and friends, articles about the previous victims tended to describe them briefly, often with language that assigned blame to them. Roxanne Thiara and Alishia Germaine were routinely described as prostitutes, rather than sexually exploited teens, with no context or details about who they were or any examination of how young people in our midst could be left so vulnerable. Most stories referred to them as missing and murdered women, when in fact only two, Lana Derrick and Alberta Williams, were technically adults, and barely at that. (It's worth noting that the judgment against David Ramsay, the Prince George judge convicted of an array of sexual assaults and other crimes, referred to the victims throughout as "young women." At the time of Ramsay's first offences against the victims, their respective ages were twelve, fourteen, fifteen and sixteen.) Children are generally considered innocent victims, and as such, tend to elicit more public concern. The widespread propensity to refer to marginalized teenagers who are victims as "women" perhaps belies, however unintentionally, the deep-seated tendency in our society to judge victims rather than perpetrators, to find reasons not to care.

All the girls were routinely lumped together as "high risk" and hitchhikers, including by the police. One story quoted a police spokesperson drawing a line between Nicole's disappearance and that of the earlier victims and paraphrased him thus: "One of the main reasons is lifestyle differences: Two of the girls were known prostitutes. Four were native or part-native," as if race were a poor lifestyle choice made by the teenagers. In another article, Const. Mike Herchuk is quoted saying, "It would be very, very easy, given the history of the other cases, to say that Nicole has come into harm's way as some of the others did. But she falls outside the mould of so many other disappearances we've had." It goes on to paraphrase him saying most of the women in the other cases were native, known to engage in high-risk behaviour—including prostitution—and others were chronic runaways known to police. "Nicole is a university-educated, 25-year-old Caucasian woman who has not so much as had a parking ticket," he said.

More than fifteen years later, Michelle looked through some of the articles from that time and was struck, again, by the tone that blamed the other victims for their fates and focused on their so-called high-risk activities. "Nicky never got any of that," said Michelle.

People were, as Matilda had hoped, talking about the highway again. The names and photos of the other girls missing along it had finally been vaulted into the national news. But that didn't lead to a task force. Instead, another case in the south of the province was sapping resources that otherwise might have been dedicated to the Highway of Tears. On February 5, 2002, police raided Robert Pickton's pig farm in Coquitlam, and soon a massive search was underway that would balloon into one of the largest forensic excavations in history, with hundreds of people, including police, forensic experts and archaeologists, combing through acre after acre. Investigators took 200,000 DNA samples and sifted through more than 290,000 cubic metres of dirt. The RCMP's Historical Homicide Unit had looked into the Highway 16 murders in the years before Nicole went missing, but after the gruesome discoveries at Pickton's farm, fourteen of its nineteen investigators were seconded to assist in that investigation. "Our unit got gutted and sent to the pig farm," said one of its officers.

Nicole's family and friends carried on their search for weeks. But there was nothing, not a trace of her, no clues to help focus their efforts. Eventually, they had to go home. Barb and Jack urged Nicole's friends and tree-planting colleagues to return to work. At the camp where Nicole had lived while tree planting, her friends and co-workers reeled upon their return. It was like a bomb had gone off; it felt surreal. No one laughed anymore. An air of sadness sat heavy on the young people in the bush. Of her three friends who had dropped her off that June afternoon, one did not go back to work, instead returning home to grieve. "Every time we dig a hole and plant a tree, she's in our thoughts," Katherine Foxcroft said. "So in a way, this whole part of the forest is a memorial to her."

In late July, the family and remaining friends packed up the duplex that had served as their operations centre. "We have to ease our way back into our real world if there is any such thing anymore," Jack told a press conference. Their last night in Prince George, they went down to a gravel bar beside the river and lit a bonfire. The gathering was a way to thank those who had put weeks of their time into searching for Nicole; it was a way to remember her and honour her. It was, Michelle remembered, a "rough night." Emotions were raw; everyone was devastated. Some got ripping drunk. "There's a feeling of real guilt," said Michelle's partner, Dave. Michelle said, "Everybody felt really horrible about leaving."

Michelle and Dave went back to Vancouver and tried to live their lives again. Michelle, twenty-eight at the time, couldn't talk to most of her friends about it. They hadn't experienced that kind of loss; they didn't understand. "It was a rare person in their late twenties who had had an intense experience of grief and knew how to talk to you," she said. People avoided them; they felt like pariahs. "We couldn't go to a party," said Dave. "We'd go in and the room would go silent."

The first Christmas after Nicole went missing, the family gathered in Golden, a mountain town near British Columbia's eastern border. They rented a big house, and extended family and friends travelled from around the country to get through it together. Sometime around then, maybe earlier, the idea of an art show came up. The rituals to say goodbye when someone dies don't apply when someone is missing. "It's not like normal grief with the different phases of it. You don't get to progress through them," Michelle said. Nicole had friends across the country, from all the phases of her life, who were grieving and in need of a way to honour her, to remember her, to do something.

The family and Nicole's close friends planned the exhibition to fundraise for a scholarship for art students at Red Deer College. They reached out across the country to those who knew Nicole, inviting them to contribute art to either sell or exhibit. Pieces came from all over, from the Nova Scotia College of Art and Design, in Halifax, and from friends in Toronto and B.C. Some came from people who had never met her or her family but wanted to contribute. Michelle, who had so far only dabbled in ceramics, found an artist to help her make the piece she wanted to create for her sister. The show ended up with about a hundred pieces. Many of them were Nicole's. "We all needed something that felt positive to focus on in those early months," Michelle said. "We all needed to stay connected, too, because we were the only ones that understood what each other was going through. Everybody who knew Nicky well or was part of the search was feeling pretty traumatized."

Michelle spent the next year going through the motions. There were days at work when she just stared at her computer screen for hours, catatonic. But she knew she couldn't fall apart; Nicole wouldn't have wanted that. "She would want us to survive and thrive. Losing Nicky and not knowing what happened is bad enough, but if we had all fallen apart, we just all felt like that would be a dishonour to her," said Michelle. "So we all worked really hard to keep it together." For Michelle, that largely meant burying it. "I found that if I didn't after a certain amount of time just keep pushing it back and burying it to some degree, I couldn't function," she said. "And that feels terrible, too, you feel guilty about that. You feel guilty about prioritizing your own survival and happiness and not spending every moment of your life trying to figure out what happened . . . There's a lot that goes on in your head that you feel pretty shitty about." Without closure, without knowing what happened, there's no end to the wondering, said Dave. "Your brain doesn't get the opportunity to not keep replaying it over and over and over and over and over."

In the first years after Nicole went missing, there were near-constant reminders. Pseudo-psychics called repeatedly with bold theories about what had happened. Reporters did, too. Some were horrifically insensitive and deployed cruel, manipulative tactics in search of quotes from the family. There was a tip that a young woman hitchhiker had gotten into an orange-yellow vehicle on the afternoon of June 21 at the place where Nicole was last seen. There were calls from the RCMP with questions, suspicions—the police chased down 1,400 tips in the first year. Once those were exhausted, the reward was doubled to try bringing another surge of tips. There were days when Michelle or Dave would stroll down the street to get a coffee in the morning and see Nicole's face on the front pages of newspapers in the boxes on the corner; they never knew when to expect it. It was always hard. "You're always kind of bracing yourself for the next thing, because for the first number of years, there was always something," Michelle said. Each time, it would bring up a swell of emotions again. Each time, it would amount to nothing.

RISING TIDES

WITH NICOLE HOAR'S DISAPPEARANCE, communities not just in northern B.C. but across Canada and, to some extent, the world became aware of what was happening along Highway 16. In October 2004, Amnesty International released a report, *Stolen Sisters*, that estimated the number of victims on the Highway of Tears could be more than thirty, and insisted the Canadian government should have done more to protect Indigenous women and girls. The report made note of the systemic, deeply ingrained nature of the violence toward Indigenous females wrought by inadequate policing, social and economic marginalization, and historical and present-day government policy.

With the passage of the British North America Act in 1867, the Canadian government unilaterally declared authority over Indigenous people and their land. "This, despite the fact that First Nations people did not knowingly enter into any such arrangement to forfeit their inherent rights to their land and resources, much less their autonomy as the first people of what became Canada," wrote Lynda Gray, a member of the Tsimshian Nation and author of *First Nations 101*. "Canada was formed under the false pretenses that it had the cooperation and assent of the many individual First Nations—Nations that had already been here for a very long time. And so began the wholesale implementation of laws and policies that would govern the day-to-day lives of First Nations people."

The government's policy and practice viewed Indigenous people as inferior and sought to absorb them into European ways or, failing that, annihilate them. *Stolen Sisters* noted that the Royal Commission on Aboriginal Peoples, tasked in 1991 with investigating the relationship between Indigenous people, the government and the public, described legislation as "conceived and implemented in part as an overt attack on Indian nationhood and individual identity, a conscious and sustained attempt by non-Aboriginal missionaries, politicians, and bureaucrats—albeit at times well intentioned—to impose rules to determine who is and is not 'Indian.'" The Indian Act imposed federal government control over virtually every aspect of Indigenous people's existence. It defined who was "Indian" and quashed traditional governance and social structures, replacing them with band councils consisting, in patriarchal European fashion, of only men, and gave the federal government the power to veto any decisions councils made. It restricted the work and economic activity Indigenous people could perform; any aberrance—earning a university degree or becoming a lawyer, for example—resulted in the loss of one's Indian status.

As the power of Indigenous nations waned, subsequent amendments to the Indian Act tightened the noose further: a ban on cultural ceremonies such as the potlatch; legalization of forced relocation and, in some cases, seizure of reserve land; and the appointment of Indian agents—federal bureaucrats dispersed to administer the Indian Act—to chair band meetings and cast votes. A 1906 amendment expressly stated that those registered under the act were "non-persons." Indian agents implemented a pass system under which Indigenous people had to get written permission to leave their reserves; they faced jail or forcible return to their community if caught without the documentation. Even the North-West Mounted Police protested that such a practice was illegal. The Department of Indian Affairs continued it nonetheless. In short, the Indian Act was "a piece of colonial legislation by which, in the name of 'protection,' one group of people ruled and controlled another," noted the Truth and Reconciliation Commission.

The Indian Act, and the wider forces of colonization, took particular aim at women. "It was absolutely part of a larger project to assimilate and eliminate," said Dawn Lavell-Harvard, former president of the Native Women's Association of Canada, "but also just completely reflective of a misogynistic, patriarchal world view. Women were property." In most Indigenous societies, men and women played complementary roles that were seen as equally valuable. Indigenous women were independent and powerful, with control over their property, sexuality, marital choices and resources. They were leaders in their communities, responsible for major decisions. They were revered and respected as the givers of life. The prevailing view of women is reflected in an oft-quoted Cheyenne proverb: "A nation is not conquered until the hearts of its women are on the ground. Then it is done, no matter how brave its warriors or strong its weapons."

Colonial legislation and policy deliberately set out to dismantle the long-held power of Indigenous women. Matriarchal and matrilineal traditions were swallowed up in patriarchal laws. The Indian Act, which already defined those registered under it as less than human, left women out entirely by classifying an Indian as a "male person" with "Indian blood." It forbade women from voting in band elections, holding leadership positions or even speaking at public meetings. It dictated that any Indigenous woman who married a man from another community—even if he was also Indigenous— lost her status. Children born to an Indigenous mother and a non-Indigenous father were denied status. This assimilatory provision, which sought to reduce the number of "Indians" in Canada, had the added effect of making Indigenous women who married outside their communities extremely vulnerable by cutting off family ties and support systems.

These laws remained in place until 1985; the discrimination has persisted long beyond that, despite various changes meant to address it. As recently as January 2019, the United Nations Human Rights Committee found the Indian Act continued to discriminate against Indigenous women and their descendants.

Colonization slashed Indigenous women's power directly, but also implicitly. Stereotypes of Indigenous women as promiscuous abounded: settler society and the church frowned upon inter-marriage between European men and Indigenous women; women were viewed as the "culprits" behind such arrangements. As Indigenous gender roles changed, Indigenous men absorbed the pervading colonial attitudes, becoming "acculturated into believing they had to think like white men." This meant a need to control women, a lack of respect for them and, often, violence toward them. In the power structures of Canada, Indigenous people were legislated to the bottom of the heap, and even below that were Indigenous women. As Amnesty International noted, "The resulting vulnerability of Indigenous women has been exploited by Indigenous and non-Indigenous men to carry out acts of extreme brutality against them. These acts of violence may be motivated by racism, or may be carried out in the expectation that societal indifference to the welfare and safety of Indigenous women will allow the perpetrators to escape justice."

In September 2005, a crowd of about seventy people gathered on the west side of Terrace, B.C., near the sprawling lumberyards nestled against the river. They drummed, sang and prayed, and then began to walk eastward. The march, dubbed Take Back the Highway, was an offshoot of Take Back the Night, an annual event marked in countries around the world aimed at ending violence against women. Communities all along Highway 16 banded together to organize their marches around a common theme: the Highway of Tears.

Four days later, Tamara Chipman disappeared.

Tamara was born in Prince Rupert. Her parents, Tom Chipman and Cory Millwater, lived on the top floor of a duplex on Ninth Avenue. Tamara had her mom's hair, extraordinarily thick and curly— beautiful hair, except that it grew really, really slowly. Tamara was pretty much bald until she was about four years old. As a toddler, she hated getting dressed. There was a family gathering when Tamara was about two, where she soaked up attention from her relatives, bouncing around the living room butt naked. Her uncle had bought a chunk of plastic poop at a novelty shop in Vancouver and, when Cory was out of the room, dropped it in the middle of the floor. Cory came back in, saw the lump of poop, and exclaimed, "Tamara!" While the room exploded in laughter, Tamara looked around trying to figure out what she'd done wrong. Her uncle picked up the fake poop to show her the joke. "Oh, you asshole!" Tamara said. Everyone in the room went into hysterics again.

Tamara adored her grandfather, Jack, a heavy-duty mechanic. Nicknamed "Jack's shadow," she spent hours with him in the shop, playing, chatting, helping, as he worked on big machines. They went everywhere together, an old man with hands permanently stained black from engine grease and a little girl with bouncing curls and a mischievous grin. Tamara was devastated when Jack died in 1987 from lung cancer. The family moved to Terrace where, as Tamara grew into her teens, she got into some trouble—she was feisty and fiery and didn't take crap from anyone. "She wasn't afraid of anything," said Gladys Radek, Tamara's aunt. "She never was afraid of anything."

Gladys had moved back to Terrace from Vancouver in June

2001. Born into the Laksilyu, or Small Frog, clan of the Wet'suwet'en in Moricetown, Gladys spent the first years of her life in a hospital in Prince Rupert with tuberculosis. Shortly afterward, she was apprehended by child welfare authorities and moved through a series of foster homes and group homes, before being sent to a reform school in Burnaby. She hadn't spent a lot of time in Terrace after leaving the northwest as a teenager; it was difficult to return to the small city where she had been abused as a child in foster care, where she risked running into her abuser on the street. But by her mid-forties, she had earned her Grade 12 diploma and began to feel she had control over her life. She went to the police in 1999 about the abuse, and by the spring of 2001, a trial date was set in Terrace. She moved north to see the case through, renting a house less than a block from the courthouse downtown.

Gladys hadn't seen her niece in years. But shortly after she arrived in Terrace, Tamara, eighteen now, burst through her front door early one morning, singing out, "Hi, Auntie!" with an enormous Rottweiler in tow.

Tamara visited Gladys nearly every day. The two of them would make a pot of coffee and chat for hours, with Tamara often talking about her dreams of one day getting married and having kids. But Tamara also knew her aunt was hurting. She knew how hard the trial was. On days when Gladys would be at court, Tamara arrived in the morning to give her aunt a supportive hug, and would be back, waiting with a fresh pot of coffee, when Gladys returned home at the end of the day. When the man who had abused Gladys was convicted, and she returned to Vancouver, she never imagined it would be the last time she saw her niece.

Tamara gave birth to her son, Jaden, when she was nineteen. She loved him fiercely. But in the years that followed, her family noticed that she was looking rough; they worried she was getting into the drug scene. She didn't come around as often. Her mom, Cory, would later tell the *Vancouver Sun* that Tamara's life was troubled and she was hanging out with a "not very nice" crowd. "She was just going through a really hard time at that point," Cory said.

Prince Rupert clings to the northwest edge of Kaien Island, a rugged, steep piece of land separated from the mainland by a narrow waterway. Highway 16 runs along the northern shoreline at the base of the mountain that forms the island's centre, wedged against the jagged inlet. From downtown Prince Rupert, the road climbs steeply and the city abruptly disappears into towering cedar forests and damp, mossy cliffs. About five kilometres from downtown, beside the highway, lies the industrial park, an expanse of warehouses and heavy trucks and parking areas for machinery with a gas station at the area's edge. This is the last place Tamara was seen.

September 21, 2005, was a chilly day, and it rained on and off throughout the afternoon. Tamara had been in Prince Rupert for a couple of days. She frequently travelled between there and Terrace; her parents had split up years before and her mom had moved back to Prince Rupert, while Tom remained in Terrace. She visited both frequently. Tamara had her own car—a Mustang—but it had broken down a few weeks earlier and was parked in Terrace until she could get it repaired. A long-time friend of Tom's saw Tamara hitchhiking east toward Terrace the next afternoon at about four thirty. And then, nothing.

It was a long time before anyone realized she was gone. Tom saw his daughter regularly when he was home, but during the fishing season, he was gone for long stretches of time. When he was away, Tamara called every so often to check in and make sure he was safe. She knew fishing was a dangerous job, and she worried about her dad. But they didn't have any set schedule to touch base. October ticked by and he still hadn't heard from her. And while family

Tamara Chipman adored her father, Tom. He realized
she was missing after returning from a fishing trip.

and friends in Terrace assumed she was in Prince Rupert, family and
friends in Prince Rupert figured she was in Terrace. Tamara was
facing several assault charges, and warrants for her arrest had been
issued. When she failed to show up in court, some people suspected
she was trying to avoid the law.

When Tom returned home in early November, he phoned
around, and it was quickly apparent that no one had heard from
Tamara in weeks. He reported her missing, and RCMP in Terrace
and Prince Rupert launched a joint investigation on November 15.

Unlike so many families previously, Tom found the police co-
operative from the outset. There was also support from the public,
in the form of searchers, donations and media coverage. But it was
difficult, after so much time had passed, to piece together Tamara's
last movements, to figure out where she might be. A week after Tom
reported her missing, the RCMP put out a call to the public for information. "It's definitely out of character for her," Tom told reporters.
"At first it wasn't so bad, we figured she's going to call, she's going to

call." But she hadn't paid the rent on her apartment. She hadn't touched her bank account.

Ten investigators were assigned to find Tamara. The story published in Prince Rupert's daily newspaper was picked up by the Canadian Press newswire and published in papers around the province, including the *Times Colonist* in Victoria and the *Vancouver Sun*. *The Province*, Vancouver's other daily, had a staff reporter do its own story about Tamara that noted her "colourful wigs or short-cropped hair, tall stature and fiery personality." Two days later, the *Vancouver Sun* followed suit with a 2,200-word feature about the murders and disappearances along the highway. A Prince George businessman launched a website to help raise awareness about Tamara and the other missing women and girls.

Tom walked the highway from Prince Rupert to Terrace and back again, checking the shoulders of the road, the ditches, the culverts for his daughter's body. The Kitsumkalum fire hall at the edge of Terrace was converted into a search headquarters. Volunteers congregated at seven each morning to divide the rugged terrain surrounding them into search areas. The B.C. Forest Service donated maps. The searchers covered fifteen to twenty kilometres a day, helped by local search and rescue, volunteer firefighters and fishermen who came up from Prince Rupert—many dropped their work when the call came across the radio that Tom's daughter was missing. They combed every logging road snaking off Highway 16 between the two cities. But it is tough land to search, vast and steep and heavily forested. A human body is nothing in this place.

In early December, volunteer searchers erected a Christmas tree beside the highway in Terrace, decorated with ribbons from September's Take Back the Highway march, to honour Tamara and the others. The weather by then was making things difficult. Snow began to fall, sometimes shutting down the search for a day or two. As soon as they could, the searchers went out again. But eventually, winter hit in earnest. An average of more than three metres of snow falls in Terrace during the winter months, with some storms bringing a metre or more at a time. "We were forced to stop searching only because the weather, because of the snow," Tom told a national inquiry many years later, his voice cracking. "We searched for, what was it, over two months. Every day. We had a huge team at first but people have lives and jobs and responsibilities and at the end our search team got smaller and smaller. But we kept going."

Lorna Brown, Tamara's aunt, called Gladys in early December to warn her that there would be a story about Tamara on the news that night. After hanging up the phone, Gladys started thinking about where someone would go if they wanted to vanish from northern British Columbia. She thought of her own history. The natural thing would be to hitchhike down to Prince George or Vancouver. Gladys had been living in the Downtown Eastside on and off for thirty years by then; she intimately knew the area where so many girls from the north wind up. She knew that if Tamara was there, she could find her. Gladys began scouring the Internet for any sign of her niece. She checked online forums, web sleuth groups, Facebook pages. A couple of days later, she got a tip claiming Tamara had been seen in front of the Balmoral Hotel, a nine-storey building near the corner of East Hastings and Main in the heart of the Downtown Eastside. It boasts a pub on the main floor and a slew of bug- and vermin-infested rooms above. In 2014, residents of the Downtown Eastside voted the Balmoral the worst of the neighbourhood's single-room-occupancy hotels.

Gladys printed a hundred photos of Tamara off her computer and headed to the Balmoral. She handed out pictures and asked everyone: Have you seen this girl? When she got home that night there was a message from Tom. He was heading up to Fort St. John, about a thousand kilometres from his home in Terrace, for a job. Money was running out and he had to work.

As Tom pulled into the northern town after a fourteen-hour drive, he heard the tip that Tamara was in Vancouver. He called his wife, Christine, in Terrace and told her to jump on the bus and meet him partway. They arrived in Vancouver the next day. For the next few weeks, Tom, Christine, Gladys and other family members got up early every morning, printed off piles of posters, then walked the city block by block, putting up pictures, asking questions and combing the streets until two or three in the morning. Each day, they had to put up the same posters in the same places—for some reason, people take missing posters constantly. They spent hundreds printing out posters, and money was getting tight, so they went to the police detachment on Main Street to ask if the cops could help out by photocopying some more. The officer at the front desk refused, telling them, "There's nothing we can do."

"Assholes," Gladys said.

Late one night when they were cruising the Downtown Eastside in Gladys's old van, they passed a girl who looked and walked just like Tamara. They circled around, Tom ready to jump out as Gladys slowed down for a closer look. "Tom, that's not her," said Gladys. The girl wasn't tall enough.

That's the closest they came to finding her.

The day after Gladys heard the tip about Tamara being seen at the Balmoral Hotel, she had gone into the Downtown Eastside Women's Centre, on the corner of Columbia and East Cordova. In operation since 1978, the centre provides basic necessities such as showers, a mailing address, breakfast, medical treatment and counselling from its drab storefront in the heart of the neighbourhood. Gladys was studying the bulletin board in the reception area when she sensed movement behind her. Expecting to find a staff member, she turned, asking, "Is it okay if I put this picture up?" There stood Bernie Williams.

Bernie had two decades as a frontline worker in the neighbourhood under her belt. She snatched the picture and pinned it on the bulletin board, while Gladys began telling her what had happened. Bernie had searched for missing women before, including many of those who were ultimately found on Robert Pickton's farm. She knew what to do. Bernie led Gladys out the door and took her around the Downtown Eastside, asking everyone she knew—and Bernie knew everyone—if they'd seen Tamara. She introduced Gladys to organizations that worked in women's rights, Indigenous rights, violence and addiction. Bernie walked miles with Gladys around the neighbourhood looking for Tamara; in the coming years, they would walk thousands of miles more together.

BREAKING A SPIRIT

THERE IS A HILL on the south side of Edmonton, on an otherwise flat plain. It has since been swallowed up by large suburban homes on curving streets and cul-de-sacs, but in the early 2000s, it was still a wild place. Looking north, the city stretched all the way downtown, a cluster of modest high-rises jumbled against the North Saskatchewan River. Nearby, power transmission lines zapped and cracked, and cars whistled by on the highway. But if you listened long enough, you'd start to hear other sounds, those that had been here far longer, sounds of the wind rushing through the grass, and the whispers of animals in the distance.

The hill was one of Tim Auger's favourite places. Aielah, his youngest sister, would sometimes come upon him there, while he looked out over the city. She would ask what he was thinking. He always told her, "I'm thinking about you." "Why?" she'd ask. "Because I care about you, that's why," he always replied. Tim worried about her. She trusted people and made new friends with ease. "She wouldn't suspect the worst of anyone," said her sister Kyla. That scared Tim. He was afraid that people out in the world would hurt her, break her spirit. "There's nobody in the world that you look up to more than Mom," he would say to Aielah, "and her life, the hard times in her life, have been given to her by other people . . . They'll do the same to you if you don't try to protect yourself." Aielah would tell Tim: "I wish that the world was filled with a lot more people like you, because then I'd never have to worry."

Aielah Katerina Saric-Auger was born in Edmonton on December 30, 1991. Her mom, Audrey, had five children before her: Sarah, followed by Samson, Tim, Kyla, as well as a son she'd had very young

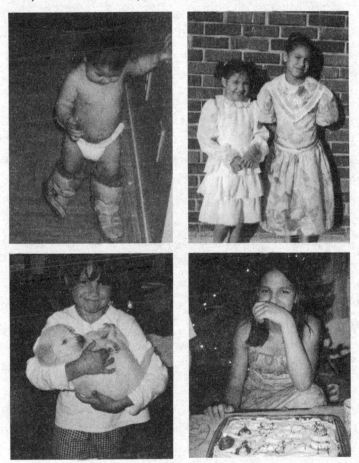

Aielah Saric-Auger adored animals, constantly
bringing home strays until the house was like a zoo.

who was raised by another family in her home community. Audrey jokingly called Aielah her Heinz 57, because she had a little of everyone in her.

The younger four kids—Aielah, Kyla, Tim and Sam—were a team. The family moved around Edmonton a lot, and each new neighbourhood was a place to explore—the kids discovered the hill Tim so loved when trying to locate the sound of frogs. When they arrived home, Audrey was always excited to hear about their travels and discoveries.

Audrey had to fight hard not only to raise her children, but to keep social services at bay. She didn't always succeed. Child welfare authorities were always on their backs; the kids learned to lie in order to not be split up. "She did her best," said Tim. "She tried really, really hard. She'd fight for us all the time. It was like they didn't want us to be a family." They lived in poverty; there were times when there wasn't enough money for bills, let alone food. Audrey struggled with addiction and the scars of abuse and mistreatment she'd survived as a girl. "She'd go through these points where she was strong," said Sarah, her oldest daughter, "and then she'd get weak again. I think it was just wanting to have a family so bad, and people that cared for her." Audrey used to tell Sarah that she wished she could be more like her. At the time, Sarah didn't know what she meant. "But I was standing up for myself, and she couldn't. She couldn't. She figured she deserved to be treated like shit. She needed to be treated like shit in order to feel normal because she was so used to it growing up.

"But my mom was beautiful."

Darrell Auger, Audrey's older brother, has a memory from when he was very young of the blankets their mother used to make, huge quilts stuffed with down. The family slept together, the children burrowed into the middle of the bed under the blanket, everyone together, safe. They'd wake in the morning knowing life was coming and that it might be hard, but also knowing that at the day's end, they'd come back to this warm place. "I think that's what Audrey was always looking for," said Darrell. "That warmth."

Audrey was one of nine children born to Jane Rachel Auger. In Audrey's early years, the family lived in the Gift Lake Metis Settlement. The community is a four-and-a-half-hour drive north of Edmonton, along roads where fields and prairie give way to rolling hills blanketed in scrubby pine trees, the edge of the boreal forest that stretches across the Canadian Shield all the way to the Arctic tundra. The occasional pumpjack dots the landscape. The vehicles that roar past on Highway 43 are mostly pickup trucks and semis, and on the few radio stations it's all country music, with lyrics along the lines of "God is great, beer is good and people are crazy." Gift Lake lies six kilometres from Highway 750. It's a pretty community, homes separated by huge yards with patches of forest and fields in between. Signs point the way to the pizza joint and a general store. Near the shore of Gift Lake sits the band office, the community centre and the school; the police detachment is housed in a trailer.

Audrey's early years were tough. Jane was a residential school survivor. She struggled with the trauma of those years and turned to alcohol to numb the pain. "She always wanted us to be different," Darrell said. "She tried for us to be different." Audrey was a toddler when Jane gave her up to be raised by another family on the reserve, under pressure from an abusive partner and struggling to care for her children. As a child, Audrey was beaten and abused. "If you hear all the time in your life that you're dumb and you're useless, after a while you start to believe it," said Darrell. "A lot of my family was told that and they believed that. They all hurt. We all hurt."

When Darrell was about seven, Jane moved with her remaining kids to Prince George. They lived on Gillett Street near the Nechako River where a cluster of cabins, long since torn down, once stood. Life was good, or at least better, there. Jane married a man with whom she'd spend the next thirty-five years and who took in the kids as his own. He was a good man. For Darrell's tenth birthday, his stepfather gave him a fishing rod and reel; all he'd had before was a handline that he'd take down to the river near the old wooden bridge. But Darrell always thought about the little sister they'd had to leave behind, worrying about her being alone in Gift Lake without him to protect her. Sometimes he went down to Highway 97 as it rolls into Prince George and watched the cars go by, looking for her. One day, he was sure he caught sight of her and chased the vehicle, calling her name, until he was too exhausted to go any farther. He spent days waiting for her by that highway, but she never came.

When he was in his early teens, he started to run wild, getting into trouble and hanging out with a gang. Jane decided to put him on a bus back home to Gift Lake, where he was taken in by a family headed by a warm, strong matriarch who became like a second mother to him. It was a safe haven, a place he didn't have to worry, a kind of security he hadn't much experience of, despite his mother's efforts. In those days, before anyone talked about residential school and what happened to the children sent there, he didn't understand what haunted his mother. "I didn't understand what those things would do to a person until later."

Not long after arriving in Gift Lake, he went to see his little sister. He knocked on the door and opened it. There she was, a little girl washing the floor. He told her to put the mop down. She just looked at him, then asked who he was. When he told her he was her big brother coming to check on her, her eyes lit up in recognition and she ran into his arms. He told her he was back now, that he'd never leave her, that she didn't have to be afraid anymore.

But Darrell couldn't protect his sister from the world. Years later, when he was about twenty-one, a time in his life when he was angry and violent, she made him swear to keep a secret. She told him that she had been raped by people in the home she grew up in. It broke his heart. "Those fucking bastards, they're dead," he said. He stormed to his truck, Audrey's arms around him as she tried to keep him away from the hunting rifles stored inside. He loaded a gun and started for the house as she tried to hold him back. It was her voice that stopped him. Sobbing, Audrey said, "Bro, please, I don't want you in jail, it's not worth it. They're not worth it." Not long after, Audrey left Gift Lake for Edmonton, and there, in the Alberta capital, built her life and her family.

Audrey worked hard. Darrell, who had a contracting company at the time, hired his sister as a labourer; she could do twice the work of the guys. She was a talented artist as well, beading and making coats and moccasins. She could walk into Value Village with ten or twenty bucks and come out fit for a fashion runway. Despite living in poverty, Audrey literally gave the clothes off her back to homeless people she encountered during Edmonton's frigid winters, when the wind screams across the prairies and temperatures can drop to minus thirty degrees Celsius and lower. She volunteered at a support centre for homeless people, and kept her door open to friends and family in need. Things weren't perfect, and sometimes they were really hard. But Audrey always

Audrey Auger worked hard to keep her family together.
"She did her best. She tried really, really hard," said her son.

bounced back. She had her family, and together, they always found a way through.

Audrey and her children moved to Mill Woods in about 2000, and this quiet expanse was one of the best places they ever lived. It was the sort of neighbourhood where families walked their dogs down the wide tree-lined sidewalks, kids played in the well-equipped parks, and everyone looked out for the children always roaming about. Development on the south side was booming, with kilometre after kilometre of what had been grassland getting chewed up by heavy machinery to put in roads, power lines and pipes for suburban communities. It was, for Audrey's kids, a wonderful playground.

Up to that time in his life, Tim had not known hatred. He remembers the feeling still: "I would always wake up and think, 'There's nobody on the planet that I hate.' God, that's an awesome feeling." Then a relative came to stay with them; Audrey would not turn away anyone in need. They later came to suspect that he had been abused as a child, and, while living with them, he mirrored what had been done to him: he abused Aielah. "It wasn't something that we thought could happen," said Tim, "and when it did, it blew me away—it blew us away. Families are not supposed to hurt each other." That was when Tim felt hatred for the first time, and he felt it for a long time afterward. But he tried to focus on a positive: he would never let it happen again. They would get through it together, and it would never happen again. "It broke my mom's heart," said Tim.

Soon after, the family left Mill Woods, moving into a series of motels before authorities apprehended the kids again. Aielah was sent to live with her paternal grandparents nearby, while Tim and Kyla were moved to a foster home in Leduc, south of the city. They were separated for about a year while Audrey scrambled to rebuild her life to appease the authorities and regain custody of her kids.

One of the best days of their lives was when the news came that they could go home to their mother. Audrey had a place in Beacon Heights by then, with her boyfriend Sheldon. The basement of their house was equipped as a suite, with a kitchenette and living area, where Audrey had offered an acquaintance a couch to stay on. Tim's room was down there, too. One night, he woke to the sound of his sisters arguing outside, not far from the kitchenette's window. Tim couldn't hear what they were saying, just a rush of fierce whispering and shuffling. He climbed up on a chair and carefully opened the window, poking his head out. He could hear them clearly now. And he knew what, and who, they were talking about. He shut the window and headed for the stairs. As he passed the man sleeping on the couch, he said, "Wake up."

Tim went outside. Aielah and Kyla were standing by the garage under the glow of the street light. Trying to be nonchalant, he asked what they were doing. Aielah tried to change the subject. But Tim wouldn't let her—he wanted to confirm his suspicions. "You're not supposed to know," Aielah said. Tim told them, "I'm going to fix this." His sisters grabbed him by the arms, pleading with him not to ruin his life on account of that asshole. But Tim shrugged them off and went into the upstairs kitchen. He took a knife and went downstairs to confront the man on the couch. "You messed around with my sister," he said, holding the knife to the man's throat. "I'm going to tell my mom and Sheldon what you did. I'm not going to ruin things for myself . . . because you're just not worth it. But they will destroy you when they find you." He stabbed the knife into the pillow beside the man's head and said, "Well, good night, then." He went back into his bedroom, sat down on the bed and tried not to cry.

Audrey could always read her kids. It didn't take her long to figure out what had happened. They went looking for a new start.

Tim doesn't remember what they did with their stuff. He thinks they left it behind, packing just a few bags and setting out on foot across the northern stretch of the city, leaving it all behind. Kyla thinks maybe they took the bus, but Tim remembers that walk vividly, how the city looked different—felt different—after what had happened. Trudging westward along the road, all they wanted was to get away. It was the end of the summer of 2004, and Sarah was living in Enoch, a Cree Nation reserve about thirty-five kilometres west of Edmonton. Audrey could leave the kids there with their oldest sister while she went farther west to Prince George to find a new home for her family. Her oldest brother lived in Prince George, and, Audrey would later write, she believed that in a smaller city, far away from what had happened, "things would be at ease for my daughter and she [would] no longer have to look over her shoulder or feel afraid."

Tim wanted to go with her, but he couldn't leave his sisters. He didn't trust some of the people who hung around the house where Sarah was living; there was a lot of drug use going on there. "Drugs and alcohol back in those times was just something that really haunted and destroyed my family, in so many ways," said Tim. He hated staying there, but at least he could protect Aielah and Kyla. The girls shared a room in the basement. Every night, Tim was the last one to go to sleep, waiting until they were both safely in bed. Then he dragged a couch in front of their door and lay down. If anyone came downstairs looking for his sisters' room, they'd have to get past him. He was fourteen years old.

It was getting cold when Audrey came back for them, October or maybe early November. Audrey's oldest brother drove down with her in his van to pick up the kids. They loaded up and set out for their new home, following Highway 16 through the mountains and western foothills, eventually arriving at the edge of Prince George, where the highway dips down past the prison, over the Fraser River and into the bowl. It was foggy and dark when they arrived, the humid air heavy with the stench of the pulp mill. Looking out the van window, Tim suddenly missed Alberta.

Audrey had found a trailer to rent just off the highway on the western edge of the city. It was surrounded by woods, nestled between a field, a motel and a small strip mall. Tim quickly dropped his earlier impressions. "It was awesome," he said. "It just felt different. It's so beautiful down there." The kids started school and explored the area. They had never had nature so close by.

But by late spring, things were getting tough again. Sheldon was deported to his native Barbados, and the owner of the trailer wanted them out. Money was tight, and for a time they moved into an emergency shelter. They finally found a place in a duplex on McIntyre Crescent, a short, rundown street just south of the Nechako River, lined with small apartments and duplexes.

Not far from the river, a trail leads up to a place called Blue Rock, a boulder with a slightly bluish hue. It's a spot where teens go to drink or do drugs, a gathering place for the young and unruly. Aielah had started hanging out there. She was getting into drinking and smoking weed, running with a crowd that made Tim uneasy. She always invited him to come out with them, but he rarely went. He didn't like her new friends, especially her boyfriend.

Over the summer, Tim spent less and less time with his sisters. Sarah had moved from Enoch into a place on the other side of the duplex. Audrey was falling back into addiction and would leave her bank card with Sarah to get groceries and pay the bills because she didn't trust herself. Sarah didn't know what exactly Aielah and her younger siblings were getting up to. As the eldest, she'd long been a "second mother" figure, whom they'd nicknamed "the sergeant." They kept things from her.

One day that summer, Tim was on the front stoop when a slew of police cars drove by, so many that he jotted down the car numbers on a scrap of paper to figure out if the same cars were circling the area. Then the thought came to him—and once it did, he couldn't shake it—that what if today was the day his sister never came back. He looked across the street to a gap between two apartment buildings that Kyla and Aielah walked through on their way home, and he wondered what he would do. He sat down, and the feeling, the loss, coursed through him. Tears came to his eyes. At last, Aielah and Kyla emerged from between the buildings, chatting and laughing. Tears were still on his face when they got to the porch and offered him some pop they'd picked up at the convenience store. They teased him, asking whether he'd been staring at the sun all day, if that was why he was all teary. He told them it was dust. And the rest of the day, he was just really happy.

On Thursday, February 2, 2006, Tim and the girls headed to the mall. Audrey would later write:

Tragedy once again hit my family hard and changed everything forever. A parent's most feared nightmare came to reality and still haunts my family to this day. I will never forget as I watched my children heading out to the Mall feeling happy waving and blowing kisses at me with big bright smiles on their faces. 'I love you mom don't worry, we'll be back, see you.' I always taught my children not [to] say 'goodbye' because they're not crossing over. I stood outside when my Sweetie Pie Aielah ran to me gave me a big buffalo hug and a kiss. As she walked away she says 'Good Bye,' then reassures me. 'Oops sorry mommy, I love you mommy, don't worry' as she blew me kisses again.

The Pine Centre Mall, about four kilometres from their home, is the largest in Prince George—and thus northern B.C.—with nearly a hundred stores. It was, to the kids raised in Edmonton, home to what was once the largest mall in the world, a tiny place. But it was a hangout nonetheless. It didn't take Kyla long to spend all her money from a job she had as a janitor. She's not sure what she bought in all, but she definitely sprung for a Ciara album Aielah wanted. They ran into some friends and decided to go out drinking.

Kyla and Aielah invited Tim to come along, but he didn't want to. He told his sisters to keep an eye out for each other and warned them not to accept open drinks or drugs from anyone. Aielah tried one last time to persuade Tim to join them, but he declined. When her friends teased her, asking why she wanted her brother to come so badly, she replied, "Because he cares, that's why." Tim headed home, looking back over his shoulder as he crossed the parking lot and calling out, "I'll see you all tomorrow." He tried to ignore his unease, telling himself that he was needlessly worrying.

At some point that night, the kids got split up. Kyla remembered heading home when it was nearly dawn, expecting to find her little sister there. Aielah wasn't, but Kyla figured she had probably decided to stay the night with a friend and would be home soon. "We waited, and we didn't see her." It didn't take long for the worry, and soon panic, to set in. Audrey quizzed the kids: where had Aielah been headed, who was she with? Audrey would later write that she tried to track down Aielah that day, and when her efforts failed, she went to the police the following morning. Kyla remembered the police telling her mom to wait and see if Aielah turned up; if she didn't, Audrey could come back later to file a report. "No Amber Alert was sounded and they told me to come back in 78 [hours]," Audrey wrote. Police later said that the family filed an official missing person report early on February 6, four days after Aielah had gone to the mall with Kyla and Tim.

For Aielah's family, the days that followed passed in a blur. Audrey trawled the city for her daughter, carrying a bag of food and extra clothes in case she found her hungry and cold. Kyla and Aielah's best friend called around and visited places where they hung out, hoping to catch sight of her or find someone who'd seen her. Sarah stayed by the phone in case she called, and Tim drove around with Audrey, imagining that if they found her, he would jump out of the car and wrap her up in a huge hug, and tell her, "See? See? We care about you. Let's go back home where we can be safe. Let's go back home where we can take care of you." As the days passed, Audrey hardly ate or slept. Tim found her on the couch in the living room one day, screaming, the way someone might if they were locked in a dark, tiny room with no way out and no one to help them. Other times, she searched the streets late at night, in the rough part of town known as the Hood, led by rumours of sightings of Aielah. She shone a flashlight into yards and down alleys, handed out posters and called Aielah's name, hoping her daughter was out there somewhere and that her voice would lead Aielah home.

On February 7, the *Prince George Citizen* ran a short story in which Audrey asked for the public's help to find her daughter. "I was told that she slept at a friend's place on Thursday and at a different friend's place on Friday," Audrey said. "She was last seen getting into a black van." It's not clear where Audrey got that information. Three days later—a week after Aielah vanished—the paper published another article, quoting the police saying the last confirmed sighting was February 3 and there was nothing new to report.

That same day, a driver who police would later describe as "a very alert motorist" noticed something in the ditch beside Highway 16, about twenty-three kilometres east of downtown Prince George, past the gas stations and homesteads that dot the outskirts of the city.

There was a body.

It was a young female. Reporters who went to the spot, just past the turnoff to the Tabor Mountain Ski Resort, noted the shallow depression in the snow beside a small creek, between the highway's shoulder and the treeline.

It was days before the police confirmed who it was. It might have been the next Monday or Tuesday that officers arrived at Audrey's front door. One officer had a piece of jewellery that had been found;

they wondered if Audrey would recognize it. She did: it was a necklace she had given her daughter. It was all that was found with her—her clothes and her bag were gone. Audrey didn't want to believe that it was Aielah they had found. She couldn't believe it. The officers showed her a photo in which half of Aielah's face was visible. When Audrey asked why it didn't show her whole face, the police told her Aielah had been out there so long, animals had got to her. Kyla saw the photo, and so did Tim. Police told them that there was no struggle, that Aielah did not suffer. She was hit on the head with something heavy and died from the blow.

Late on Wednesday, February 15, Aielah was identified publicly as the victim found in the ditch. A newspaper story described Aielah as a caring, well-liked teen. Anjula Corbin, the vice-principal at Vanway Elementary School, which Aielah had attended when the family lived in the trailer at the edge of the forest, remembered her volunteering in the office and being kind to a "little kindergarten buddy."

"I remember one incident when a boxed science project arrived and a science-related jigsaw puzzle spilled out on the floor," said Corbin. "I couldn't make the pieces fit but Aielah spent the day putting it back together."

The next day, *The Province* picked up the story in Vancouver. RCMP media spokesperson Const. Gary Godwin told the paper that police had interviewed Aielah's family and friends during the days she was missing. "We were working on the assumption that she was staying with friends," he said. But by then—February 17—it was a murder investigation, and in the media and the communities along the Highway of Tears, the story was raising the names and faces of all the girls and young women vanished or killed before. Godwin said, "I understand they're all individual investigations. Until we get something that ties them together, and we haven't got that yet, they will continue to be investigated individually . . . They've all been extensively investigated, and this one is being extensively investigated."

It was one of these stories that Darrell came across as he sat down in an A&W in Kelowna to have breakfast. "And just, what the fuck is this?" He phoned Audrey. But he didn't go to her. He'd spent all his money relocating to Kelowna for work a couple of weeks before, and he hadn't accrued any time off. He would have lost his job if he left. He wishes he had gone.

A teacher at D.P. Todd Secondary School wrote a letter to the editor of the *Prince George Free Press*, begging for help for the family. Gail Morong wrote that since Tim, Kyla and Aielah had enrolled in September 2005, the school had been aware of the family's financial hardship. "This is a family that was struggling financially even before this tragedy with Aielah occurred and they are reeling from the many unfortunate events which keep coming their way," she wrote, noting that local agencies were doing what they could to help with donations of groceries, but food was running out and there was a funeral to pay for. Audrey wanted to take Aielah back to Gift Lake for a traditional burial. The teacher signed off with, "We are counting on PG residents to show the Auger family that we are caring people with big hearts."

Audrey couldn't believe that Aielah was really inside the box as it was lowered into the frost-hardened earth in the cemetery behind the fire hall and band offices on the shores of Gift Lake. She couldn't quite believe that Aielah wasn't out there somewhere, waiting for her mother to find her, to bring her home. Kyla had the photo the police had shown the family etched in her memory; it was enough for her to know Aielah was gone. Tim tried not to let the image into his mind. Instead, he tried to remember how fun it had been with his little sister, the endless joking and laughter that bound their family, the warm cocoon of love that Audrey wrapped around them. "When they were together, they were strong. They were very strong," said Darrell.

But Audrey and her family and everything she had built and worked so hard to hold together now fell apart. Tim and Kyla went northeast, to stay with relatives in Gift Lake. Tim felt close to Aielah up there. Sarah and Samson moved back to Edmonton. Audrey packed their belongings in Prince George and left them for safekeeping before returning to Edmonton, where she gave up. There, she lived on the streets, refusing offers of help, of a place to stay, from Sarah and others. She drank heavily and used a lot of drugs. She felt numb, she would later write, with no will to live. She felt that she had failed. "It broke her spirit," said Darrell of his little sister who had gone through so much, been knocked down so many times, but always, always got up again.

Not this time. "It broke her," he said.

THIS WE HAVE TO LIVE WITH EVERY DAY

IN FEBRUARY 2006, as news swirled around Prince George about Aielah Saric-Auger's disappearance and murder, Rena Zatorski was a new mother and a new band councillor. She had been elected to the Lheidli T'enneh council less than a year earlier and had recently given birth to a baby girl. Aielah's death hit home for Rena in a major way, she said more than a decade later during a panel discussion hosted by CBC's *The Current*. She knew about the history and systemic issues underlying the violence against First Nations girls. And she believed that being a leader meant being an activist.

Less than two weeks after Aielah was found, the Lheidli T'enneh band council fired off a press release calling upon First Nations, police, government and the public to put a stop to the violence battering so many young lives, particularly those of First Nations women and girls. "It is clear that the recent murder of 14-year-old Aielah Saric-Auger has not only stunned aboriginal communities and the city of Prince George, but it has also brought to the forefront the critical issues of race, poverty, women's rights, the isolation of our youth and our justice system," read the statement. "Let us put an end to these disappearances and murders by empowering our youth, by being involved in their lives and by treasuring who they are." The band offered $1,500 to get a symposium off the ground to find a way "to put an end to these horrific murders." The matter, Rena stressed, was urgent. "There are nine women listed as victims of the Highway of Tears," she told the *Prince George Citizen*. "If something isn't done you will see a number 10 and I don't think anybody wants that to happen. This has gotten way out of hand, way beyond what it should have."

The response was overwhelming. Rena and other leaders at Lheidli T'enneh were inundated with calls. Pledges of support—financial, logistical, moral—came from all over: the B.C. government, First Nations, Indigenous organizations, health agencies, domestic violence and sexual assault centres, the public, the police. The attention and support weren't limited to the symposium, either. By the end of the month, B.C. solicitor general John Les announced a slew of police officers had been assigned to the Highway of Tears cases: twenty-two working to find Aielah's killer and another fifteen to review the previous deaths and disappearances. News stories went up on the Canadian Press newswire and were picked up by newspapers across the country, from Victoria to Halifax.

"This has been a long time coming—too long," Rena told the *Globe and Mail*. "But at least it's happening now. At least we don't have to wait like they did in the Downtown Eastside [of Vancouver] where dozens and dozens of women disappeared before anything was done." Rena estimated the cost for the symposium to be about $100,000. Carrier Sekani Family Services anted up $10,000 in early March, and its then executive director Warner Adam issued a challenge to the provincial government to provide some real funding, over the $1,500 John Les had agreed to contribute to match the Lheidli T'enneh pledge. "I hope the government and all its agencies will seriously participate to make this happen. Most bands don't have sufficient funds to participate in these ventures on their own.

[Government's] responsibility is the safety and security of all humanity, especially to ensure the most vulnerable are looked after. I am sure they will come through."

Rena's anguish at the news of another victim had driven her to push the issue, which had now snowballed into a nationwide concern. At long, long last, something was being done. The date for the symposium was set for March 30 and 31, mere weeks away.

Four hundred kilometres away in Witset, Florence Naziel also felt she had to do something. She just didn't know what. She'd been thinking about it since the previous fall, when her daughter, Priscilla, called and told her to turn on the news. That was how Florence found out that Tamara Chipman, the only daughter of her cousin Tom, the girl she considered her niece, was missing. That was when it hit her family.

But Florence knew there had been so many girls before. She had worked alongside Alberta Williams's family in Prince Rupert's canneries, and knew the families of Cecilia and Delphine Nikal and Ramona Wilson. She had followed the stories for years, clipping out articles in papers, watching the short documentaries that occasionally appeared on the news.

The idea came to her gradually, although in retrospect, it seemed she had been laying the foundations before she came up with a plan. She had begun working out a lot—walking ten kilometres a day, doing aerobics, going to the gym—and just couldn't get enough exercise. "I guess I was conditioning my body, but I didn't know at that time," she said. Spring was approaching, and Florence's two foster daughters would soon be off school for March break, when it would be easier for Florence to get away. She decided she would drive to Prince Rupert and then walk the highway to raise awareness about the missing and murdered women and girls.

Florence Naziel came up with the idea of walking the highway after she learned that Tamara, her cousin's daughter, had vanished.

Florence told the staff at the Friendship Centre in Smithers about her plans. She went to the radio station and the newspaper. "When?" they all asked her. "Two weeks," she replied with a laugh. Word quickly got around and her phone was ringing off the hook. Reporters from Prince George and Prince Rupert called her up for interviews, and offers of support came in from across the province. Not one for the spotlight, she kept thinking, "What's happening?" When the day came to drive to Prince Rupert, she put on her running shoes and tried to coax Kena, her German shepherd, along for company and protection, but the dog refused to get in the car. Betty Joseph, Florence's sister, responded decisively: "My sister is not going to walk alone." Betty appeared in Florence's driveway with an overnight bag and climbed in the vehicle. The two sisters set out for the coast.

In Smithers, Matilda Wilson was considering a 370-kilometre walk to the symposium in Prince George. She had continued to hold her march every year on the anniversary of her daughter's disappearance. She had watched as girls continued to vanish from the highway. Each time, Matilda cried. "It brings back how much it hurts," she said. A walk all the way to Prince George for the symposium might be a big enough statement to ensure that something would get done.

Down in Vancouver, Gladys Radek, Tamara's aunt, got a message on Facebook from Florence, advising her of the walk. Gladys wrote back right away—she was in. She invited Bernie Williams, who immediately agreed; they convinced the Union of British Columbia Indian Chiefs to cover their bus fare. A few days later, Gladys, Bernie and a handful of supporters climbed on a Greyhound bus for the twenty-two-hour trip to Terrace, then got straight into Gladys's sister's car to meet the other walkers in Prince Rupert.

When Florence arrived at the Friendship House in Prince Rupert the morning of March 11, 2006, she was stunned. There were so many people there. She trembled as she approached the video cameras and outstretched microphones and the crowd of supporters that included the city's mayor Herb Pond and the local MLA Gary Coons. She hadn't expected this. When a journalist tried to interview her, she just shook, unable to speak until he took her hand and told her, "Florence, I'm a human being just like you. You talk to the camera like you're talking to me." She appreciated that, yet when it was her turn at the mic, all she managed to say to the crowd was: "Thank you."

As the walkers prepared to depart, the officials addressed the crowd. Gary Coons vowed to push the issue in the provincial legislature, where his party, the NDP, sat as the official opposition. "I think this is an issue that has been haunting not only communities along the highway but throughout the province," he said. "We need to find out the real issues, it's not just solving the atrocities and the murders and disappearances, it's looking at the real issue: women's rights, poverty and all the social issues and challenges we encounter in the North." The mayor told Florence, standing beside Tom Chipman, that the entire city of Prince Rupert was with them, every step of the way.

Gladys arrived and greeted her cousin. She asked if Florence had heard of the symposium in Prince George happening later in the month. Florence had not. She didn't even know what a symposium was. Gladys asked her, "Instead of just walking to Terrace, how would you feel about walking to Prince George?" Florence quickly conferred with Betty, then said, "Yep, we're in." As they set off through downtown, dozens of people Florence had never met walked alongside her. Social media and cell phones were at work spreading the word. Panic tugged at her, but she breathed deeply and told herself, "It's not about me. I better get my grip now." She threw her shoulders back and continued marching through the city and out onto the Highway of Tears.

As the walkers left Prince Rupert, they stopped to lay flowers in the industrial park where Tamara was last seen. They marched on and crossed the causeway connecting Kaien Island to the mainland. Trudging behind a pilot car driven by Florence's daughter, they continued through the moss-covered, cathedral-like forests under the snow-covered peaks of the rugged coastal mountains. They passed Diana Lake and Prudhomme Lake as low-hanging clouds threatened snow and freezing air whipped their faces, before cresting, on the second day, the Rainbow Summit that overlooks the Skeena River and, not far beyond, the Tyee overpass where Alberta Williams was found. Florence Naziel stopped there for a few moments, as snow began to fall, and laid flowers for Alberta.

The crowd of about a dozen that marched out of Prince Rupert had dwindled after the first day, as the winds rose and snow pelted the north coast, and people returned to jobs and families. A core group that included Florence, Betty, Tom and Christine Chipman, Gladys and Bernie continued, walking about thirty kilometres each day before marking their spot at dark and returning the next morning to go on. The distance between Prince Rupert and Terrace is nearly 150 kilometres, the longest stretch on the Highway of Tears with no communities, and in those days, no cell service. (Even in 2019, there are only a few spots with marginal cell coverage.) In many places, the highway is wedged between the Skeena River and the railway tracks, the forest-blanketed mountains rising just a few feet beyond the rail ties. Aside from the odd pullout, there is nowhere to go beyond the roadway. Mountains tower in every direction, mist shifting here and there. It is a place of profound beauty, but it is also remote, and minutes would pass with nothing but the sound of rain falling and trees rustling before a vehicle would roar by, occasionally splashing slush and water.

Some walkers later said they felt the spirits of the girls and women walking with them; some felt peace, others anger and sadness. Some found themselves thinking about what had happened to the girls: Were they in the wrong place at the wrong time? Who had picked them up? What had been done to them? How much had it hurt? When they were tired, or cold, or hungry, the walkers only had to think of what the missing had gone through to know that their own pain and discomfort were not important. Their mission was what mattered.

A woman drove by to hand Florence money she'd collected to help them cover their costs. The Kasiks Wilderness Resort, about sixty kilometres west of Terrace, gave the walkers a place to stay for the night and offered them a huge steak dinner complete with all the trimmings. Florence asked for soup instead. No one had the appetite for a heavy meal—they had eaten so little, and walked so much. Florence lost ten pounds between Prince Rupert and Terrace. Florence had brought along her hiking boots, plus two pairs of running shoes and extra socks donated by the

Moricetown Band Office. She'd heard that changing her socks every few hours would help prevent blisters. Gladys, who lost a leg after a motorcycle accident decades earlier, could do nothing about the sores that formed on her stump, but fellow walkers helped clean and dress her wounds each evening, while she massaged their aching muscles.

And they walked on.

They made their way into Terrace in a chilly fog. A crowd had gathered to welcome them and usher them to the Kermode Friendship Centre, where lunch was waiting. Members of Tamara's family led the way behind a banner that read: "Highway of Tears, Remember our Lost." Florence remembered Tamara's two-year-old son, Jaden, seeing the crowd and yelping with excitement, "Did they find my mommy?"

"This, we have to live with every day," said Florence.

She would have loved to stay behind the scenes, but the other walkers once again brought her before the cameras, journalists and supporters. She remembered most a little girl, perhaps four, approaching to give her flowers. Florence knelt down and gave her a big hug, trying not to cry because the gesture so touched her heart. The attention the march was receiving was overwhelming; it was all Florence had ever hoped for.

By then, a new plan had fallen into place. Florence would lead the walk past Terrace to Kitwanga, another hundred kilometres inland at the junction of Highway 16 and the Alaska Highway, not far from Gitanyow, where both Alberta Williams and Lana Derrick had grown up. From there, the Gitxsan Spirit Walkers would lead the walk 150 kilometres farther to Smithers, where Matilda Wilson would take over to lead the walk to Prince George.

The next morning, Florence laid flowers outside the Terrace Inn and the Petro-Canada station beside the highway, the last places Lana Derrick was seen. Another eighteen supporters joined the group as they left the city.

In Kitwanga, the diner at the community gas bar fed all the walkers for free—they were told they could order anything they wanted from the menu—and then Florence passed over the banner to the Gitxsan Spirit Walkers. Her daughter was waiting in the pilot car to drive Florence home to Moricetown to rest. But at the last moment, she decided she couldn't leave. She would walk on. Tom and Christine, too, had planned to turn back, but felt it wasn't time yet. They walked on, too.

More supporters joined them in Gitsegukla, a Gitxsan reserve of about five hundred people twenty kilometres east. Just east of the village, a long road led to a train station from which children had been taken away to residential schools. Jean Virginia Sampare had been headed toward that road when she disappeared. The eighteen-year-old, known as Virginia, was one of the first young women to vanish, at least as far as the present record goes. Virginia was a quiet person, raised under the watchful eyes of her parents and older siblings. The Sampare kids were brought up to work hard. Theirs was a strict household where the kids weren't allowed to run wild or stay out late at night. Virginia had celebrated her birthday the previous month. On October 14, 1971, she seemingly got into an argument with her mom and left the house around 11 P.M. "I tried to ask her what was wrong, and she just went straight to the door, opened the door and walked out," Violet Sampare, Virginia's sister-in-law, said forty-six years later. Virginia's mother told Violet not to worry about going after the girl, certain that she'd be back soon after she'd cooled off. But she didn't come back. The family would later hear that she and her cousin had set out for the store by the train station, just a few kilometres away. The cousin left her for a moment to collect his bicycle. When he returned, she was gone. He'd later tell them he heard the sound of a car door slam. They are still looking for her.

The walkers reached Hazelton, where still more supporters joined them, and carried on to Witset, where Florence finally veered home for a break. By the time the walkers came into view of

Search
called off

Hazelton RCMP have called
off the search for 18 year old
Virginia Sampare, who went
missing from her home at 11
p.m. October 14.
No conclusive signs were
found in the two week search,
although a police dog had been
brought in from the Peace
River area. RCMP said that no
doubt the villagers will continue

Virginia Sampare was a quiet girl who grew up in Gitsegukla
under the watchful eyes of her parents. She vanished in 1971.

Hudson Bay Mountain, towering over Smithers, and passed Yelich
Road, where Ramona Wilson was found eleven years earlier, there
was a core group of about twenty. In Smithers, Matilda Wilson,
along with her family and supporters, met the walkers for a pan-
cake breakfast in the muddy parking lot of the museum that sits
at the intersection of Highway 16 and Main Street. Dozens of people arrived to show their support. Many donated money to help the
Gitxsan Spirit Walkers continue on to Prince George. A woman
arrived asking for the organizer of the walk, the person who started
it all. People pointed her to Florence, who she approached and gave
an angel pin, saying, "You're like an angel—you opened the doors
for all the missing women."

On March 23, as a light snow fell and the ground crunched with frost underfoot, Matilda Wilson led the procession east of Smithers, over the Bulkley River. Dozens of people were walking behind the families by now, including a group of nurses from the Smithers hospital, where Ramona and Delphine were born. Each time the walkers arrived in a community, people waited along the highway, joining them for some of the distance. In between towns, on the empty expanse of the highway, numbers fell again. Matilda walked and walked, as her feet blistered and her knees throbbed. They passed the place just east of Burns Lake where Roxanne Thiara was found dead shortly after Ramona went missing, and as they neared Prince George, the elementary school where kids had come across Alishia Germaine. A little farther on, they passed the gas station where Nicole Hoar was last seen.

As she neared the end of the journey, Matilda told a reporter that she was astounded by all the support they'd had. "I feel over-whelmed by the whole thing, because it all just fell into place. Knowing I will be opening the symposium, it brings it all to light: the missing women and all the messages we have to give the public and those in authority. We need to say so much to them about what needs to be done for all the loved ones that are missing right now."

As the walkers made the 725-kilometre journey along the highway to Prince George, the Lheidli T'enneh council led by Rena Zatorski pulled off an incredible feat by getting the symposium off the ground in just weeks. Organizers had ensured the attendance of high-powered politicians and authorities, including B.C. solicitor general John Les and federal MP Nathan Cullen, whose riding encompassed much of the highway. Various provincial government ministries provided funding to pay for the event. High-ranking RCMP brass would be there, along with First Nations leaders and the majority of the victims' families.

After so many years of speaking to a world that would not hear, families were inundated with attention. The symposium, and the girls and women missing and murdered along the highway, were national and even international news. Newspapers in communities along the highway ran near daily updates on the walkers' progress and the upcoming symposium. It was, it seemed, the turning point that families had sought for so long. Finally something was going to be done.

Prince George in March is a dreary place. The city is built upon and around a traditional settlement of Lheidli T'enneh at the place where the Nechako River flows into the Fraser. The name means "where the two rivers meet," though Lheidli T'enneh territory stretches from the central plateau all the way to the Rocky Mountains. Spring temperatures hover a few degrees on either side of zero. It takes a long time for snow to melt and even longer for things to start growing. Dirty snow piles drip in the corners of parking lots and in patches through forests that in spring are a dull, monotonous shade of brownish grey. The CN Centre, named after the Canadian National Railway, sits in the middle of Exhibition Park on the western side of the city, near the University of Northern British Columbia campus, just up the hill from downtown. The six-thousand-seat arena is home to the city's Western Hockey League team, the Prince George Cougars, and is the only major concert venue in the province north of Kamloops. It was there that the symposium would take place.

The walkers had arrived a couple of days before the start of the symposium and were met by drummers on the city's outskirts who escorted them into Prince George. Under overcast skies on the morning of March 30, a crowd gathered at the corner of Massey Drive and Ospika Boulevard to begin the last steps of the journey. The families led the way as the crowd behind them swelled past the sidewalk and into a lane of traffic, the walkers holding banners and posters showing the faces of the victims. They moved down

Ospika Boulevard in the early morning fog as cars honked in support, past the horse-riding rings and the rodeo chutes and the stables until they finally arrived at the Highway of Tears Symposium. Matilda Wilson, wearing a yellow reflective vest with her daughter's name written across the back, entered the arena to the sound of drumming and singing. She had been upbeat during the walk, cracking jokes, offering kind words and thanks to all around her. But as she took the stage to begin her speech, Matilda collapsed into choking sobs.

Marchers made their way into Prince George in 2006
for the Highway of Tears Symposium.

The first day of the two-day symposium was dedicated to families and loved ones to tell their stories, while the second day would focus on devising recommendations. The arena floor was filled with hundreds of family members, along with police, community workers, First Nations leaders, politicians and members of the public. Representatives of more than ninety organizations were there, surrounded by easels displaying photos of the girls and women lost along the Highway of Tears. A large map was marked with a pair of moccasins showing the place where each girl or woman had disappeared. When Florence stepped into the arena and saw it full, brimming with people, she felt relief. "Now we're going to talk about the missing women," she thought. "Now, what are we going to do? How can we prevent it? It was my desire to have all this out in the open, right across Canada." It was, for Brenda Wilson, Ramona's sister, like a large funeral. One by one, families climbed the stairs onto the stage and, in front of a wall of cameras and five hundred people, honoured the lives and relived the loss of daughters, sisters, mothers, grandmothers, aunties. There were just so many cases. Family after family, flanked by friends and supporters, took their places on the podium to tell their stories. Each story was different, but there were so many similarities.

Brenda, standing shoulder to shoulder with Matilda, told the crowd that for First Nations people, there is no help when someone goes missing. "First, you have to make people believe your child is lost," she said. Lucy Glaim, Delphine's sister, said police initially refused to look for her. "It was brushed off," she told the crowd. "The officer wouldn't even get out of his car to make a report. We had to start the search by ourselves." Communities, she stressed, had to stop blaming victims. Audrey Auger held up a photo of Aielah and sobbed as she recited a prayer in Cree and recounted the last time she saw her daughter, just two months earlier. "Justice is what I want," she said. "What should come out of this is for people's cries to be heard." Sally Gibson spoke of how the negative stereotypes harboured by mainstream society resulted in apathy and indifference when First Nations girls and young women met with tragedy and violence. When Lana went missing, said Sally, the public and police did little more than go through the motions. "She is not just a name on a list of missing people," Sally said. "She was a daughter, a niece, a granddaughter, much loved by many people. She wasn't doing anything wrong when she disappeared." All these families, said Sally, are walking wounded. They always will be.

Partway through the first day, Nicole's family took the stage. Unlike the other families there, they were not from the area; they were not First Nations. Unlike other families there, they did not have extended family or friends present for support. It was just Barb, Jack, Michelle and John. So the Gitxsan Spirit Walkers, who had been on stage to support previous speakers, stayed there. One woman kept her arm firmly around Michelle, who was struggling to remain composed. Another took her hand. At least six others stood behind them. "That was really powerful. I remember how hard it was to stand up on that stage again, I remember crying and shaking at the podium," said Michelle. "I was just so touched by that act, and so blown away that a community that's gone through so much pain, not just the loss of women on the highway but so much loss and trauma period, that they could show so much kindness to us." Michelle later wrote, "I know that one of the biggest memories my mom, dad, brother and I will keep of the symposium was of the overwhelming warmth, support, and friendliness showed to us by other families going through the same thing, and members of all the Aboriginal communities along Highway 16, the Gitxsan Spirit Walkers included."

Jack spoke first. "I never thought I'd be standing up here saying I was one of the lucky ones," he said. But after hearing all the other stories, he knew he was. Police had responded immediately and overwhelmingly to Nicole's disappearance; hundreds of people had turned out to search for her. "I felt so sad hearing of the families that were ignored," he said. "That is unacceptable."

The *Prince George Citizen* summarized the first day: "Many of the grieving families said they had been victimized on top of their loss by a society that doesn't show an emotional attachment to aboriginal people. Some of the dead were involved in drugs, prostitution, reckless behaviour, and that has spawned minimization in casual comments and in the media that add insult to their injury." Beverley Jacobs, then the president of the Native Women's Association of

Canada, said she had proposed, in September of the year before, that violence against Indigenous women be on the agenda of the national first ministers meeting. It was rejected. The next day, Tamara went missing. "This is a daily issue. This is a crisis. All across Canada we can see a trend where women are treated like garbage. Who killed [these women]? We are all responsible."

The Highway of Tears Symposium left families exhausted but, for the first time in years, hopeful that there would be answers and action. If nothing else, things would be put in place so that no more girls and women were lost but, if they were, there would be help, support, maybe even intervention in time to save them. This way, all the pain over so many years would not be in vain. "We had such high hopes," said Sally Gibson. "Now it's out there, now people know about it. Now maybe we'll get something done."

The front page of the *Prince George Citizen* the day after the symposium called it "a huge step forward towards the prevention of deaths along Highway 16 West." Minister of Children and Family Development Stan Hagen called the symposium "without question the most powerful gathering that I have ever been at." Solicitor General John Les promised to give concerns "serious consideration," adding that "people feel a sense of abandonment [by authorities] that needs to be addressed." Federal MP Nathan Cullen, highly critical of the Canadian government's failure to address the Highway of Tears situation and of the province's and RCMP's "lacklustre" efforts to date, said he would take "the messages from this conference to Ottawa" and do all he could to "get the support that families deserve in bringing these crimes to closure."

Top RCMP officers, including Supt. Leon Van De Walle, in charge of major crime in B.C., had been present for the two days, meeting with families. "We hear you," he told the symposium. "We aren't just sitting here taking notes. We know we need to improve. You are our clients, we work for you." No one, aside from a victim's loved ones, wanted to solve the cases more than the police, he said.

"I can't tell you about all the ones I've solved, but I can tell you a lot about the ones I didn't solve. That stays with you for a long, long time." The RCMP said it would send the Highway of Tears files to Vancouver to be reviewed by a team of specialists looking for connections between cases in the northwest and across Canada. The Mounties also promised to improve communication with families. A couple of months later, senior RCMP officers sat down with families as a group for the first time, meetings that they said would continue, to update them on the investigations and to tell them they were entering all the evidence from Highway of Tears cases into a central database.

In June, the symposium's organizers, led by the Lheidli T'enneh First Nation, released a report on the gathering, including thirty-three recommendations. The launch was held at Lheidli T'enneh Park on National Aboriginal Awareness Day, which happened to also be the fourth anniversary of Nicole's disappearance. The report is subtitled: "A collective voice for the victims who have been silenced." Described as "a community response to a deadly serious situation," it recognized the enormous efforts of families to raise public awareness and implored action to stop the killings: "It is the sincere wish of the First Nation and non-First Nation communities that all levels of government, both the opposition parties and the sitting government, work collectively and collaboratively to support the recommendations contained in this report." And it directly addressed communities, municipalities, cities and organizations along the highway to work together to see the recommendations through to reality. "On behalf of all past Highway of Tears victims, and in the interest of preventing further victims, this multi-community initiative must not fail." The recommendations hashed out by grieving families, social workers, cops and politicians over those two days were broken down into four categories and further divided into short- and long-term goals; only those that were "realistic" and "achievable" were included, each a direct call to action. The report was a concise roadmap to what needed to be done. "It's not just up to the RCMP," said author Don Sabo as he released the document publicly. "There's a lot communities can do."

About half the recommendations focused on preventing more disappearances. It noted a "hunting pattern," whereby victims tended to go missing off the highway during warm summer months when hitchhiking was most prevalent. During the cold winter months, when fewer people were out on the highway, the disappearances happened in Prince George, where young people, many of them vulnerable, congregated. The crimes, it stressed, were crimes of opportunity. Getting girls and young women off the highway would make it harder for predators to target them. But that meant addressing the poverty that put many of them there in the first place. "Young aboriginal women are placing themselves at risk by hitchhiking because they simply have no other transportation options. They have very little money, and vehicles are considered a luxury item that many families cannot afford," the report noted. Not only did poverty leave people with no choice but to hitchhike, it also made them vulnerable to being lured by promises of money or work. In 1989, an entire family—Ronald and Doreen Jack and their sons, Russell and Ryan—disappeared after telling relatives they were going to work at a logging camp or ranch.

Short-term recommendations focused on reducing the number of girls and women hitchhiking. The report called for a shuttle bus to link each community along the entire highway, for increased RCMP patrols, and for a new policy whereby officers had to stop to check in with any girl or young woman they passed hitchhiking and encourage her to find a safer way to travel.

Greyhound buses, the only public transportation between Prince Rupert and Prince George, should stop for female hitchhikers, the report said. Public sector employees who travelled the highway frequently should be used as a "female hitchhiker detection network," reporting where girls and women were hitchhiking. It called for safe houses along the corridor that would double as check-in points, a highway watch program modelled on Crime Watch, emergency phone booths in places with no cell service—most of the highway in those days—and billboards and posters. It called for awareness and prevention programs in schools and universities and at tree-planting companies, along with similar education in First Nations communities and a far-reaching media campaign.

The report noted that better recreational and social programs for First Nations youth were needed, in both rural areas and urban centres. Similarly, First Nations communities needed to be better equipped with health and social services, so people did not have to hitchhike to obtain basic services like medical care. Other recommendations focused on planning an overwhelming response in the event of another girl or woman going missing, and developing an emergency readiness plan that articulated procedures and roles. Such a plan would detail timelines for the RCMP and community emergency response teams to act upon a missing person report and create an alert system in every community. Overseen by local coordinators, the emergency response teams would incorporate existing responders, among them search and rescue and fire departments.

The final recommendations revolved around providing support for families. "For these families there has been no closure for their missing or murdered women whose cases remain unsolved. The Highway of Tears Symposium listened to these grieving family members and it was apparent that their needs for healing and support would be long-term." Permanent crisis response plans for families and communities experiencing a traumatic event, such as murder, suicide or disappearance, needed to be developed, including a roster of Indigenous mental health specialists ready to deploy at a moment's notice, followed by long-term counselling and support. "Readers of this report must understand that First Nation communities are closely knit, and when a tragic event occurs to a First Nation community member . . . the event's impact goes beyond the immediate family. Its effects are felt throughout that entire community." It recommended that the RCMP "re-establish and maintain communication" with families, a major concern brought up by almost every family at the symposium. And lastly, it called for a First Nations advocate to help bridge the gap between the police and victims' families.

To see all these recommendations through to fruition, the report detailed a structure: a board of directors that would manage funding and establish working committees in each community, with two full-time coordinators—one at each end of the highway— to support the committees. The committees would meet each year at an annual symposium to update each other on their work. The report also called for families "to meet and comfort each other in expression of common loss and mutually support each other in their journey toward healing and closure." The report didn't address how much implementing the recommendations would cost. But, as its author said, "cost is secondary when it comes to nine lives."

The last recommendation spoke to the widespread belief that the police had simply never looked for some of the missing and too easily given up on others. It called for the RCMP to continue its investigation into how many women and girls were missing, noting that no one knew the exact number. "This ongoing official RCMP investigation should determine the number of missing women and verify their identities. More importantly, this investigation needs to acknowledge the fact that each individual number from nine to possibly thirty-two missing victims is in fact a valued family member's life that deserves the same respect and attention presented at the Highway of Tears symposium. Whatever the eventual number of missing victims, all remain unsolved, and all of these victims' families have yet to receive full closure."

The RCMP publicly endorsed the report, as did the provincial solicitor general, calling it "practical" and the recommendations "bite-sized and in some cases . . . doable without too much effort," and praising it for resisting the urge to lash out at anyone. By the time the report was released, the Mounties had already started to make changes. North District Supt. Barry Clark said police had increased highway patrols and advised officers to stop and check in with hitchhikers, along with planning meetings with families. "None of these recommendations come across as being problematic, in my opinion," he said.

Diane Thorne, the provincial opposition critic for women and families, called the report "fantastic," noting that it laid out things that could be done immediately while longer-term solutions were found. "God knows we need to do something," she said. John Rustad, the MLA for Prince George–Omineca, promised it would happen. Government officials were impressed with the recommendations on transportation and emergency planning. "I can tell you it will be given heavy consideration," Rustad said. "We all agree this is a very serious issue, as serious as it gets when you talk about people dying and it needs to be addressed." He was not, he said, intimidated by the costs and challenges of tackling poverty in the north. "I want to do everything possible to make sure the Highway of Tears becomes a memory by finding solutions." An editorial in the *Prince George Citizen* stressed the importance of the moment. It read, "The momentum and public awareness generated by this week's report shouldn't be allowed to slip away . . . The challenge ahead is daunting, but there may be no better way of honouring the memory of those who have died."

A groundswell of support rippled across the northwest. Musician Ray Bessette released a two-song CD as a tribute, with proceeds going to pay for billboards warning of the dangers of hitchhiking. The College of New Caledonia, in Prince George, unveiled a memorial bench as a tribute to the victims. An association sewed a memorial quilt. Town and city councils passed motions to work together to prevent further violence, to erect billboards and to get going on transportation issues.

Carrier Sekani Family Services had assumed the helm of seeing the recommendations through. With $50,000 from the province, the agency announced plans to hire a coordinator who would oversee the process from Prince George. But the agency's director, Mary Teegee, stressed that the coordinator's first task would be finding more money. "At the end of the day, the workload coming out of the recommendations . . . is quite a massive amount," she said, adding that at least one more position was likely necessary to "ensure the coordination is done properly." By September, the agency was wrapping up the hiring process for the one position for which it had funding. "I am really happy," Mary said. "I am really excited."

Back in March, on the last day of the symposium, fog blanketed Prince George. It had been overcast for days, still chilly enough to need a warm coat. By afternoon, while the symposium's attendees hashed out recommendations, Gladys and Christine left the arena and crossed the parking lot to Tom's car. They needed a break, a chance to unwind and talk. Gladys had fought hard, and had had to face down long-held fears to do so, planting herself in front of RCMP officers to grill them and "give 'em what-for." She had lived her life in terror of the police. She'd been beaten and raped by cops, and incarcerated, but in March 2006, after all that had happened, she was no longer afraid. She wanted recognition, and she wanted accountability. By the end of it, she was exhausted. The two women sat in the Mustang and talked. "This isn't going to go away, I hope you know that," Gladys said. "We're not gonna leave any stones unturned. I'm going to keep searching for Tamara until we find her."

Christine looked over at her. "I know you will," she said.

They went back into the building in time to catch the news, expecting the symposium to be front and centre. It wasn't. A few days earlier, police in Victoria had posted a $100,000 reward for information about Michael Dunahee, a four-year-old boy who had been abducted from a playground in 1991. Police were getting a fresh wave of tips. That was the top story. Later in the broadcast, there was a quick piece about the Highway of Tears.

It pissed off Gladys. All those people calling in with information on Michael now that there was a six-figure reward—where the hell were they when he vanished fifteen years earlier? What the hell was wrong with people? Did they really care that little? And why would police announce it at the same time as the symposium? She feared that even with the walk and the symposium, the Highway of Tears wasn't going to be a high priority.

WHERE WERE YOU TWENTY YEARS AGO?

STEVE PRANZL JOINED the Vancouver Police Department in 1976. By the late 1980s, he had worked his way up to the Sex Crimes Unit and joined Homicide in 1991. He investigated murders in Vancouver for eleven years before moving to the provincial Unsolved Homicide Unit in 2002. That unit was formed in the mid-1990s to probe long-unsolved cases around the province. Under the leadership of the Mounties, it was a joint effort that included detectives from municipal police forces, mainly Vancouver.

Staff Sgt. Bruce Hulan, who was then in charge of the unit, approached Steve in late 2005 with an assignment: take another look at some of the Highway of Tears cases. "There was a lot of pressure at that time from a number of different quarters," said Steve. The prolific media attention when Nicole Hoar disappeared in 2002, Amnesty International's *Stolen Sisters* report in 2004, First Nations organizations' ever-louder advocacy and the disappearance of Tamara Chipman that fall had contributed to a mounting sense that something had to be done.

The big question, Steve said, was whether there was a serial killer. That spectre had been raised a decade before, when the team of profilers met in Prince George to review the cases and concluded that three of them—Ramona Wilson, Roxanne Thiara and Alishia Germaine—were possibly linked. The prospect of a serial killer had come up repeatedly ever since, said Steve, as different investigators and profilers examined the cases. Reviews "happened many times." In 2004, the RCMP's Behavioural Sciences Branch had once again determined that the deaths of Ramona, Roxanne and Alishia could be linked.

Steve read up. Estimates of the number of victims diverged wildly and with increasingly high numbers—some sources cited a hundred or more. He went back to Hulan and said, "This has just become silly. We keep doing this and we just keep accepting what to me are these arbitrary numbers and names. Let's start this by having a good, hard look at who we think are related. It's going to require a project." Hulan gave the go-ahead.

Steve and RCMP investigator Peter Tewfik began looking through old unsolved files and devising a proposal for determining which cases, if any, might be related. The resulting list of murders and disappearances shared common criteria. First, according to an RCMP report, each involved a female. Second, the victims were "engaged in one or more 'high risk' behaviours," defined as "behaviours which would tend to place them in the control of strangers in isolated environments without witnesses, easy avenues of escape or sources of assistance—the primary examples of this would be hitch-hiking alone or sexual exploitation through prostitution" (though some of the cases don't seem to fit this criterion). Third, they went missing from or their bodies were found on certain sections of Highways 16, 5, 97 and 24. And fourth, the "evidence indicated a stranger attack," which the RCMP defined as occurring when "no suspect was seen or identifiable and there was no grounds to believe that death was the result of suicide, misadventure or domestic violence" (though, again, in at least one of the cases, investigators had a suspect who was known to the victim).

Initially, the RCMP said publicly that it was reviewing three cases, and then another six, almost all Indigenous girls and young women gone from the northwestern stretch of Highway 16. Soon after, nine more cases were added, bringing the total to eighteen. Most of the additional nine cases had occurred elsewhere in B.C. in the 1970s and '80s. And in most of those cases, the victim was white. "We started doing the review," Hulan said, "but very early into it, we recognized that, if we are looking for this serial killer, we'll have to broaden our scope and have a look at other files."

The decision to expand the probe beyond the geographic boundaries of the Highway of Tears was controversial, and highly criticized in some circles. David Dennis, then the vice president of the United Native Nations, called it "one of the most disgusting and despicable displays on the part of the RCMP . . . It seems they don't take the disappearance of any of these women seriously," and Gladys Radek accused the force of trying "to get rid of the whole Highway of Tears concept." Kim Rossmo, the geographic profiler formerly with the Vancouver Police Department, said, "There's absolutely no reason in the world to connect [cases from the early 1970s] to the ones that originated the concern over the Highway of Tears." In his assessment, the Highway 16 cases in the mid-1990s had a "reasonably high" probability of being connected; those in 1989 and 1990, along with those in the early 2000s, were possible. "The police should be dealing with anything where there's a reasonable chance that it's linked," he said. "That's why I questioned why were they going back so many years for stuff that's not likely to be related, given that they have limited resources. The focus should be on the ones that are most likely connected."

Expanding the investigation beyond Highway 16 made sense, said Steve, because if there was a serial killer, nothing was to say the predator would be confined to the strip of road between Prince

Rupert and Prince George. "If somebody's a trucker or something that's moving, he's going to be moving to some of these other areas, too," he said. And it made sense to narrow down the cases to a list of eighteen, on certain highways, otherwise the investigation would simply be too large to handle. "It would be impossible. It would be decades. It would require a new police force to be able to do it," he said. The rationale behind the final list was that if a serial killer could be identified, investigators could probe what else he might have done in the area and time period. "Justification for being smaller was, if we have a serial killer operating, he's going to have touched on some of our girls. And then if we find him, we focus on him and see who else he could have done."

Ten of the cases occurred along the Highway of Tears: Ramona, Roxanne, Alishia, Tamara, Nicole, Alberta, Delphine, Lana and Aielah, as well as Monica Ignas, a fourteen-year-old who had vanished along the highway just outside Terrace in 1974. Her body was found four months later near a logging road. Seven other cases occurred elsewhere in B.C., along with one in Hinton, in western Alberta. The project was given the moniker E-Pana, the "E" denoting the RCMP's B.C. division, and "Pana" for an Inuit goddess who cares for the souls of the dead. Its mandate was to determine whether a serial killer was involved and, regardless of whether investigators found evidence of one, to develop investigational plans for each case.

Word of the task force was kept fairly quiet during the first two years, when the work was largely administrative. Investigators collected files, most of which consisted of notes, reports and exhibits stored in bankers boxes in whatever detachment had performed the original investigation. "It sounds easy," said Steve. "It's not." They flew around the province gathering everything related to the cases, then recruited data experts to enter all the information into a computer database.

As data was entered, the team cast around for investigators with major crimes experience to start reviewing the cases. That wasn't easy, either. "You can't just push Play and there they are," said Steve. "It was tough, because there's a lot of competition for those people." The project hired retired investigators, from the Mounties as well as those, like Steve, from municipal forces, to help out.

The investigators pored over the files, noting gaps, people of interest to interview and leads to follow up, creating what amounted to a gigantic to-do list. Exhibits were re-examined, particularly for the possibility of DNA evidence, given the tremendous advances in the years since many of the cases occurred. Review teams then presented their findings to the entire project staff for feedback and suggestions. By 2008, E-Pana was kicking into high gear. There had been file reviews of the cases in the past, but this was different. "We don't care if a file review's been done," Steve said. "We're going to investigate this again from scratch. That hadn't been done."

Around this time, in late 2007 or early 2008, Dave Aitken sat down for a beer with Steve. The two had been partners in the Homicide Unit at the Vancouver Police Department for eight years. Dave had retired from the VPD in 2001 and then worked on the Pickton investigation for a few years under a contract with the RCMP. He'd had enough of Pickton, and when Steve mentioned that E-Pana was looking for investigators, Dave decided to talk to Hulan. Dave said Hulan asked him what kind of role he was interested in. "I said, 'Well, I'm an old murder guy. Put me on an investigative team.'"

The cases were always going to be difficult to solve. In most, police believed, the perpetrator was a stranger. That runs contrary to the norm: most homicides are committed by someone known to the victim, so catching the assailant is a matter of following the trail from victim to perpetrator. But when it's a stranger, there's no trail. "They're the tough ones," said RCMP Staff Sgt. Wayne Clary, who later led the task force. The vastness of the landscape in the northwest and its sparse population worked against investigators. So much can happen without anyone seeing it, and there are so many places where the wilderness can swallow a person. It's easy to hide a body there, and nature doesn't take long to dispose of it.

In five of the cases, there was no body, nowhere to even start. Don Adam, who headed the Project Evenhanded investigation that ultimately led to Robert Pickton being convicted of six counts of second-degree murder, described the difficulty of investigating the Vancouver missing women cases in an article he wrote for the *Vancouver Sun* in 2010. "In a homicide investigation, there is normally a logical, chronological progression. The crime scene is almost always the starting point of the investigation as it tells us the forensic facts and of course supplies us with concrete evidence. It also gives insight into the killer, and the whys: Why kill this way, why in this place, why now and of course why this victim," Adam wrote. "If you pictured a rock dropped into a pond, the investigation flows out from that epicentre much like the waves would. The crime scene is processed, neighbourhood inquiries start and move out. In a more figurative way, the investigation will move back in time tracking the movements of the victim and later the suspect. It will move forward in time looking at actions which occurred after the murder. Witness[es] will be discovered, statements taken, persons of interest will be surfaced. They will be investigated and eliminated or elevated to suspect status and the investigation evolves." In missing person cases, he wrote, police were "operating blind."

Other factors were working against the investigators. "It lost the advantage of being a timely response," said Rossmo. Michael Arntfield called it "an uphill battle." The creation of a task force, he said, is itself an acknowledgement of a certain degree of failure, leaving investigators to "stop-gap" previous oversights. "Their job is that much harder because they not only have to pursue people who have few, if any, rules, but also mitigate the deficiencies of earlier investigative missteps by their own people." To be a homicide investigator, he said, "you need to assume that you are smarter, faster, more resourceful, more diligent and craftier than the psychopath you are pursuing. To be on a cold-case task force, you need to believe all those things. But you also need to believe about your own people that they fucked up."

Dave, who reviewed several of the files, said his impression of the earlier investigations was that officers did their best. "You got to realize that techniques change over the years," he said. "A lot of the original interviewing and stuff was done by street cops, people with limited investigative skills. So a lot of the initial interviews were sad, you know, really not what you'd expect in a city like Vancouver. But they did their best with the limited resources they had. In the ones I looked at, we didn't notice any real fuck-ups."

Steve retired from the Vancouver Police Department in 2007 but remained with E-Pana for another decade before finally leaving in the spring of 2017. He knew the cases well. The quality of earlier investigations varied, he said. Cases where a major crime unit was called in tended to be handled better, investigated more thoroughly. "A lot of them, there wasn't a lot [left] to do," he said. "Some of them, there was a lot to do."

Steve won't criticize officers working in small detachments where they are responsible not just for a major investigation—a missing or murdered person—but everything else, too. "They do the best they can," he said. But they lack specialized training and experience, staff and time. "Small communities are often slow to get off the mark because they don't have the same amount of resources that they can spend on a murder investigation," he explained. "So they're more easily dissuaded from thinking, 'This is a murder, or could be a murder, or could be something we need to be alarmed about,' as opposed to, 'It's a troubled young woman who in all likelihood has run away.'"

Statistically, the latter is usually true. In small communities, where the police may have encountered the potential victims, witnesses, friends or family, officers can be too quick to write off their concerns or information. "You need someone who can look at it with an unjaundiced eye. [They'll] probably come to the same conclusion, and others might look from the outside and say, 'That was a waste of time, money and resources.' But if anything, some of these have shown that some cases were wrong to not be hitting the ground running. It might have made a difference."

He confirmed that some of the girls, including Monica Ignas and Delphine Nikal, were assumed to be runaways. "Some of them, because of things the family said, because of things witnesses said, were not taken as seriously for a long time." In those cases, the files had a "huge gap where almost nothing was done, and now you're trying to play catch-up."

More than once while reviewing files, he commented, "They didn't do a very good job here." Some earlier investigations, Steve said, suffered from misdirection and a lot of delay. "We're going years later, talking to people, and they're saying, 'Where were you twenty years ago?'" There were cases where he read a one-page interview of a "pretty good suspect" and felt the investigators should have probed more. Even though the RCMP is generally strong in its reporting requirements—"the RCMP is an anal organization," said Steve—there were cases where more note taking and report writing should have happened. Many earlier investigators, among them Garry Kerr and Rick Ross, who investigated the murder of Alberta Williams, took their notebooks with them when they retired. Some just threw them out. "There's more information in those notebooks than there is half the time going to be in the police file," said Garry. "Bits and pieces of [an] investigation are in ten basements across the country."

Steve said investigators found exhibits were missing—investigators went looking for items only to find they were gone, "because it was a pain in the ass sitting in the corner of the property office and people kept tripping over it," he said. "I recognize it's a storage nightmare, it's a cost, but we shouldn't be throwing out exhibits. If it's related to a missing, unsolved person, homicide, major sex offence, you do not destroy it. And if that means the Mounties are going to pay, VPD, whoever, for a warehouse forever, then you do it, because we had cases where we could not find reports and we could not find exhibits." One such exhibit was a shirt thought to have blood on it, found in a rural area near Smithers after Delphine went missing. A police officer apparently retrieved the clothing, but there was no record of it being collected and investigators never could find it. "I think it was turfed, myself," said Steve. "I think [the officers] were sent out, they were not happy about it: 'Yeah, yeah.'"

But, after working twelve years on the files, he said he's certain E-Pana cleared up those loose ends. "I'm confident that no murderer went free because the investigation wasn't done properly."

E-Pana wasn't without its problems. Dave Aitken, Steve's former partner, was impressed with the initial review process. But when, in 2008, the group split into investigative teams and got to work, "in my estimation, things started to go off the rails." Dave's concerns about the task force are myriad. The cumulative result, in his opinion, was that "a lot of people got shortchanged during these investigations."

Dave said the task force had been advised that once the investigative phase was underway, no one would be transferred. "We wanted a dedicated group of people who had file knowledge to do the investigations," he said. "Well, that lasted about two months, and people started jumping in and out, going to greener pastures or whatever . . . We're left in a void, and they'll parachute in some character who knows nothing." Many of the RCMP officers assigned to E-Pana had little or no investigative experience. "We were getting people in who had essentially no reason or right to be there," Dave said. One of them "was a small-town cop one day and the next day she was in Vancouver being a murder investigator. That's just inappropriate." Dave said he asked one of the officers in charge of the task force why unseasoned investigators were being assigned, and he was told it was a training exercise. "I said, 'You know, if my daughter was killed or missing, I would want the A-team. Not some kid whose most important arrest has been an impaired driver and who has never investigated shit.'" Steve agreed that the lack of experienced RCMP investigators was a "big issue." Had it not been for E-Pana's ability to also hire retired detectives with extensive experience, the task force would have been "in dire straits," he said.

Wayne Clary, who moved from the Pickton investigation to lead E-Pana in 2011, said it's always difficult to find large numbers of good people and competition for them is fierce. "When you go from, let's say, ten unsolved homicide members and then you want to gear up to sixty investigators, you're not going to get the cream of the crop," he said. "It's hard to get good people in that volume because everybody wants them." As a manager, he said, "you find the weak ones and you get rid of them, you find the diamonds in the rough and you develop them, and you get average folks and you put them in work that they can handle."

A further complication arose when it became clear that the retired investigators hired as civilian contractors, like Dave and Steve, were not allowed to actively investigate or conduct interviews. Dave had signed up with the understanding that, as "an old murder guy," he would be out pounding the pavement looking for murderers. "There was no job description attached, it just kind of evolved, what we were doing," he said. "I assumed we'd be actively participating in interviews and things of that nature." That wasn't the case. During Project Evenhanded, retired officers working under contract such as Dave did perform policing duties, like conducting interviews, until higher-ups and the public service caught wind of what was going on. "We may have got our wrist slapped," said Wayne.

So the practice was scrapped, and at E-Pana veteran detectives were left in the office, while inexperienced investigators went out to conduct interviews, which they'd bring back for review by the team. "I'm not saying they weren't people with talent—they were," said Steve. "But some of them had never been to court, they had never had training in interrogations and in-depth interviewing, and some of the work they brought—well-intentioned, doing the best they could—but it showed. We had to train them in house and then send them out, and then review what they'd done and say, 'Well, this is something, this is an interview that could have gone a little differently, you really should go and do it again.'" That response didn't always go over well and it was frustrating for everyone involved.

Despite the difficulties, though, Steve said the RCMP impressed him over the course of E-Pana. With the exception of not providing all the crack investigators they wanted, the Mounties anted up the resources the task force needed. The project's expenditures ballooned from $20,000 in the 2005/06 fiscal year when it got underway to more than $5 million a year from 2009/10 to 2011/12. "We spent millions of dollars . . . Anything we wanted to do—surveillance, wiretaps, undercover operations, travel, live on the road for weeks," Steve said. "I was in charge of the thing for quite a while. No one ever said no." Nevertheless, Dave is critical of RCMP culture, which he said prioritized appearance over substance—to the detriment of investigations. "Their prime motivation was, don't do anything to embarrass the buffalo," he said.

Dave left in disgust in early 2011, insisting on an exit interview to voice his concerns. "It was a terrible, frustrating experience and it still irks me to this day," he said. "The ball was dropped in just about every fashion I could think of. It was a useless investigation. They didn't follow best practices. They didn't use people who were adequately trained to be doing it. The whole thing was just a huge disappointment."

Wayne Clary maintains that the cases were investigated thoroughly from the start and that the failure to solve them was not the result of either police indifference or incompetence. "The opposite is true—they were incredibly thorough investigations," he said. The widespread sentiment among families that the RCMP did not respond quickly is false, he said. "It didn't happen in any of the E-Pana files. I've seen what the response was." The RCMP, he noted, is a "very military type organization," with a lot of reporting up the chain of command. Cases like missing people or homicides required reports to be sent to headquarters, where "readers" went through the paperwork to make sure everything was done correctly. The process is "pretty thorough," he said. But detachments are busy and officers struggle to keep up with the day-to-day workload. "So when you get an unsolved major case, you need a dedicated resource, in my opinion, to work it properly. Not to say it wasn't worked properly initially, but to keep it going."

Where the RCMP failed on these cases, he said, was in communication—or lack thereof—with families. "That's where we deserve criticism, quite frankly, because we didn't do it, not in all cases. It's different today and so it should be." In its early years, E-Pana held regular gatherings to update the families on the task force's progress. Investigators also made themselves available to the families. Wayne, when he joined the task force in 2011, began visiting families in their homes, travelling to wherever they lived to get to know them and explain the investigation to them. "I think that's the way to go. They deserve it," he said. "They want to know that somebody's working, somebody cares. They know these are tough, and I tell them it may never get solved, but at least they know that you've given the effort." He and other investigators also made a point to show up at memorial vigils and took part in walks such as the one organized annually by the Wilson family.

Their efforts did not go unnoticed. "It was good because we got to see other people, other families," said Sally Gibson, Lana and

Alberta's aunt. "We came up with ideas." It was the first time she felt someone from the RCMP genuinely cared. Matilda Wilson said communication with the police improved "80 per cent" when E-Pana launched. The police brought families to the RCMP headquarters in Surrey and showed them the room containing all the files from all the cases. Matilda saw the boxes with her daughter's name written on them. "It was very hard, difficult, to grasp everything," she said. "It just felt like a graveyard." But she understood then how much work there was to do, and she trusted they were doing it. "I've been close to them, and I understand where they're coming from. I really appreciate their work."

Around the time that E-Pana began its work, private investigator Ray Michalko was watching the news at his home in Surrey. There was a story on about the disappearance of Tamara Chipman, and he was complaining to his wife. "Look at this, I could solve this," he said. Ray had been in the RCMP many years before, two stints that added up to nine years, and he, like many former police officers, was "a great armchair cop." To shut him up, his wife said, "You're a [private investigator], why don't you see what you can do?"

He began looking into a few of the cases, browsing the web and visiting the library to review old newspaper articles. Not long afterward, he took a job in Prince George. There, Ray found himself driving past places he recognized from the articles he had read—the spot along the highway where Nicole was last seen, the schoolyard where Alishia was found. He thought about what could have happened to them and what it must be like for their families. "The more I learned, the more I wanted to learn, and the more I felt sorry for the victims' families," he said. "It was just a snowball effect."

In February 2006, he placed an ad in the *Terrace Standard* with a phone number to call with tips, a move that brought on teasing from a friend who told him, "You might as well give me your money—nobody's going to call you." But people did call. And Ray's ads sparked newspaper stories in local and provincial papers. He told the *Calgary Herald*, "I've been watching this over time, came up with a few theories and set out to prove or disprove them. I'm going to spend a little time and a little money and a little effort to explore this hunch. If the worst thing that happens is that a few people think I'm a fool, so be it. I just want to help."

In June that year, Ray accused the police of failing to follow up on tips about Nicole's disappearance. One man he'd spoken to had seen a car matching the description of a vehicle possibly associated with Nicole. The man had called the Terrace RCMP to report the vehicle, only to be told to call Prince George, where he left a message but was never called back. And a woman who'd found a broken tree planter's shovel near Terrace told Ray she'd been "dismissed outright" when she contacted the police. (Ray photographed the shovel and showed it to Jack and Barb, who confirmed it was not Nicole's.)

But the police insisted they had followed up on every tip. "We're taking this very seriously, and no, race is not a factor," Staff Sgt. Eric Stubbs said. "We deal with a lot of calls and a lot of tips, and some of them we investigate ourselves and some we pass on. Some fall through the cracks, but the overwhelming percentage are looked at." By the fall, Ray said he'd identified five persons of interest and received funding from an anonymous Vancouver-based women's group to help cover his costs. In October, he said he believed a number of people were present when Ramona Wilson was killed, and took out another ad that implored: "If you were one of the people that was present during this horrific crime, or know who was, for the sake of Ramona Wilson's family, do the right thing and call Smithers RCMP immediately." He was, he said, trying to "rattle some people up. I'm hoping that somebody's got a guilty conscience and says, 'I should have come forward long ago.'"

The next spring, in May 2007, Ray organized a volunteer search of a swath of wilderness west of Prince George, near Cluculz Lake. Tips had led him to believe they might find Nicole there. The RCMP was less optimistic. Staff Sgt. John Ward said, "The RCMP are not convinced that Michalko's tips are bona fide clues." More than a hundred people showed up to scour the wooded area, and they turned up dozens and dozens of bone fragments. But none were human. Nicole's family had travelled north to help search. They were devastated. "We hoped that we would come across something that would help somebody—whether it was our daughter or anybody else," Barb Hoar said. "But it's part of working through this. I didn't know I would be able to do this, it just seemed too hard. But I am glad I did. We all needed this."

Ray became something of a media darling, doing dozens of interviews with reporters about his work and, increasingly, using his pulpit to needle the RCMP. In the first year or so of his probe on the Highway of Tears, he'd largely avoided criticizing his former employer. For its part, the RCMP said they had a positive relationship with him. But when the force announced it was adding another nine names to its list of unsolved missing and murdered women cases along the Highway of Tears and elsewhere, Ray said he was "disgusted and embarrassed" and that, if the officers who'd thus far failed to solve any cases worked in the private sector, "they'd be fired." Ray, in turn, was publicly chastised by the RCMP in March 2008 after he told a radio talk show that he was optimistic that at least one case would be solved that year. "Where did that come from?" said RCMP spokesperson Pierre Lemaitre. "That is the kind of information that should only come from the official investigators and we would not ever go to our partners in the media saying there is a break imminent, because there are parents and loved ones involved who don't need to be upset or [given] false expectation in case it doesn't pan out."

Ray later wrote in his 2016 memoir, *Obstruction of Justice*, that he had interviewed a man in March of 2008 who claimed to be a witness to Ramona's death and provided the names of other witnesses and a suspect. The man took Ray "to the alleged crime scene and to the location of the now-wrecked suspected vehicle thought to have been used in the crime." Ray recounted that the man agreed to accompany the private investigator to the Smithers RCMP detachment to share the information. At the station, the officers did not know who Ramona was; when Ray explained, they told him it was Vancouver's case. Ray wrote that he had to push the officers to interview the man. A couple of months later, Ray followed up with the potential witness and learned "that no one else, including E-PANA investigators, had spoken to or re-interviewed him."

So Ray wrote to Bruce Hulan, advising the staff sergeant that unless the RCMP had objections, he planned to interview the alleged suspect during an upcoming trip to the Smithers area. Hulan thanked Ray for the information and said: "I have no doubt you are aware the investigation of a homicide is a complex matter. The investigation is ongoing, the focus of homicide investigations constantly changes and an independent investigator, unaware of all the facts, may in spite of best intentions adversely impact the investigation, or profoundly jeopardize the safety of potential witnesses." Hulan requested that Ray not contact potential witnesses or "take any action that in any way might characterize an investigation into the death of Ramona Wilson." Ray agreed to refrain from interviewing the alleged suspect but stated he was "unable to comply with [Hulan's] request not to take action in regard to Ramona's death or any of the other Highway 16 cases" because of the tips regularly coming in to him. Hulan wrote back: "Your reluctance to comply with my request that you do not take any action that might in any way be characterized as an investigation into the death of Ramona Wilson continues to cause me concern, and to that end I must advise you that your conduct with respect to this investigation could adversely affect and obstruct the investigation to the extent that it could defeat the course of justice. I would ask that you carefully reconsider my concern, and in doing so review Section 139 of the Criminal Code of Canada." That's the section that deals with obstruction of justice.

Not long after news of that exchange got around, families sent a letter to media outlets praising Ray's work. "Families of four girls missing from the Bulkley Valley and Prince Rupert areas are questioning the heavy-handed and hair-trigger response of the RCMP, who have never made an arrest on this 30-year-old case," it read, signed "Families of the Disappeared." It's not clear which families were involved, though the Wilson family was outspoken in their support.

Soon after, the RCMP issued a statement praising Ray's contributions. "There are now those with the false impression the RCMP may harbour ill feelings against Mr. Michalko for his personal involvement in attempting to gather witnesses or evidence that may be of assistance to our investigation," Supt. Russ Nash said. "The truth is that I applaud Mr. Michalko's commitment and resolve and am certain the families of those victims, both missing and murdered, are equally appreciative. It must be stressed however that his role as a private citizen is much different than the role of a police officer." Later that year, Ray set up a toll-free hotline for tips and blanketed the northwest with flyers advertising it.

What was hoped would be the task force's first success came in the summer of 2009. "It is the break investigators, family members and the public have been waiting for—a reason to believe police have zeroed in on the location of the remains of at least one of the missing victims of the Highway of Tears tragedies," read an editorial in

the *Prince George Citizen*. The RCMP descended on a property outside Prince George with dogs and backhoes in a search related to
the disappearance of Nicole Hoar. According to news reports,
"investigators excavated dozens of sites in densely wooded sections
of the two-hectare property, climbed down an old well and scoured
a nearby dump, while dogs trained in detecting human remains
were led through the area for two days." The RCMP seized various
material for forensic testing, including a vehicle from a nearby
informal garbage dump.

The property had, at the time Nicole disappeared, belonged to
Leland Switzer. Two days after Nicole went missing, in 2002,
Switzer shot and killed his brother. He was charged with second-
degree murder and sentenced to life in prison without possibility of
parole for ten years. Switzer had a lengthy criminal history, including such offences as aggravated assault, extortion, possession of
prohibited weapons and assault with a weapon. "Your violence has
included other family members, neighbours and dogs. You have
used physical violence, weapons, and threats to intimidate and
harm your victims," noted a 2016 parole board decision.

Long before he went to prison for murder, Switzer was infa-
mous in the rural logging area of Isle Pierre where he lived.
Neighbours shared a litany of rumours and suspicions with reporters during the 2009 search. One woman said she had called police to
tell them to check his well, reporting that she had seen him pour
diesel into it and light it on fire. A man showed a reporter to a junk
heap where he said he'd found a bag of bones. A couple that lived on
a property backing Switzer's said he "terrorized and threatened
everyone in Isle Pierre, even scaring off a young couple on the next
door lot with a shotgun." Parole board records detail a long history
of substance abuse and mental illness, contributing to repeated
delusional episodes and erratic behaviour. The *Prince George Citizen*
described Switzer as "highly thought of by the people who knew

him unless he was drunk or on drugs. Then he was to be avoided. They also described him as being 'a little bit haywire' even at the best of times."

Switzer gave a statement to police in 2004, in which he told officers that he and a friend had stopped to urinate on the side of the highway near the place Nicole was last seen. "Switzer told police about this because he said he didn't know if police used a 'fine tooth comb' to search the scene," reported the *Vancouver Sun*. "During his police statement . . . Switzer provided the name of a friend and neighbour whom Switzer claimed had broken down crying when Switzer asked if he was responsible for all the 'girls' going missing along Highway 16" and claimed his daughter had heard a gunshot that night.

But nothing ever came of the investigation at the property in Isle Pierre. Switzer later claimed, in parole hearings, that he passed a polygraph test, absolving him of any involvement in Nicole's disappearance, though the RCMP did not publicly verify his assertion at the time. Wayne Clary later confirmed that police are "no longer interested in him."

The cases included in E-Pana received many hours of police attention. The media devoted a great deal of space to the girls and women's stories, and their names and faces were splashed across newspapers, websites and TV broadcasts for years. They got recognition, if not answers.

But there are more women and girls lost along the Highway of Tears who did not.

Vicki Hill was on her knees, digging.

It was early May in 2017, and the earth in the Prince Rupert cemetery was damp and covered in moss. In between two old grave markers, Vicki was searching for another one, sinking her long nails into the sod and pulling it up in clumps that she stacked neatly to the side. She studied the dark brown soil underneath. "It should be here," she said. "She should be here."

A few moments before, in the cemetery office, a worker had pulled out an old map and pointed out the spot where Vicki was now working. A few hundred metres away, cemetery workers were excavating a new grave. They kept glancing over, until finally one of them cut away from the crew and walked toward her. She figured he'd be mad at her for digging up the sod. But when she explained what she was doing, he didn't get mad. He said he'd be right back. He went to get a shovel.

Vicki was looking for her mother.

Vicki never knew her mom. For many years, she didn't know what had happened to her. The absence is etched deeply on every aspect of her life. She spent her early years in foster care in Gitsegukla. Her dad, Oscar Hill, struggled with addiction, particularly to alcohol, and visits to his children were not frequent. In Gitsegukla, Vicki was abused throughout her childhood. As she was approaching her teen years, social services placed her in a foster home in Prince Rupert. There, she was happier, safer, but those early years had done so much damage. She sought solace in alcohol. She was missing something—someone—she had never had. But she thought for so many years that she would, someday, somehow, find her mom and they would be together.

She was well into her twenties when she learned that her mother was dead. An aunt told her that Mary Jane had passed when Vicki was a baby, but didn't give any details about how, or when, or where, or why. It felt like losing her again. "I was really kind of heartbroken," Vicki said. "It just seems like everything was just taken away."

In about 2004, a support worker helped Vicki dig up some old newspaper clippings about her mother's death. Mary Jane was thirty-one years old when she died; her body was found along

Highway 16 east of Prince Rupert in March 1978. A coroner's inquest found that she had died of pneumonia and manslaughter but offered no explanation of the finding, nor of how a young mother could have ended up out there, naked, to die in the cold. Vicki was devastated—and determined. She wanted to find answers, to know what happened, to get justice. If she didn't do that for her mother, she said, no one would.

In 2006, Vicki spoke to several reporters for the first time. As news swirled about the Highway of Tears, the Prince George symposium and the RCMP file review, she hoped that the police would take another look into her mother's death. "The police never found anything that I know," she said. "I've been trying to find out myself, it's been too long not knowing." Over the next few years, she continued to collect bits and pieces of information, along with a grainy black-and-white photo. Like Vicki, Mary Jane was born with a cleft palate; relatives said they looked just alike. Mary Jane was from Gingolx, or Kincolith, a Nisga'a community in the Nass River valley north of Terrace. She was one of seven children. She was a mother of four. Vicki wanted her included in the E-Pana investigation. But the RCMP explained to her that Mary Jane did not meet the criteria.

Vicki did not understand how a finding of manslaughter as a cause of death did not warrant further police investigation. She wanted to know how her mom ended up out on the highway, alone, dying. "How much evidence do I need for them to actually understand that my mom was part of this?" she said. "She should have been on there."

That day at the cemetery, the worker came back with a shovel and dug down into the ground. Headstones can sink quite a bit over time, he said, in this wet ground. He dug down farther than Vicki's nails had been able to. He dug and he dug, and then he apologized. A couple of tears rolled down Vicki's cheeks. There was nothing there.

Like Vicki Hill, the family of Virginia Sampare wanted her included in the E-Pana investigation, believing it might lead to answers after decades of not knowing what had become of her. Virginia's disappearance seemed to fit the criteria: she was a young woman who went missing along a highway. But, police said, foul play had to be confirmed, and in her case it was not.

In other instances, families either did not know what authorities had determined to be the cause of death of their loved one, or felt that the determination was wrong. Pauline Morris was fourteen years old in 1978 when a teacher drove her to a doctor in town and then dropped her off at a ferry across the lake from her home. The ferry connects communities on the south side of François Lake, where Pauline lived, to the highway that runs into Burns Lake, along Highway 16. Pauline vanished. Four months later, ferry workers moving a barge discovered her body underneath.

As far as Laura and Ted Morris, Pauline's older sister and brother, know, the police didn't investigate what the family believes was a murder. But Ted was given the names of men who had apparently been bragging about raping and killing a young Indigenous girl. "My sister got murdered and there was no investigation at all, it was just another dead Indian," Ted said. Women in the community told Ted and Laura, separately, that the men, who are white, had raped them when they were young. Laura remembered being bullied and called a squaw by the same men when they were boys in school, and beaten to such an extent that she dropped out. Many years later, a man told her at a party that he was a witness to Pauline's death and apologized. He said she had been gang raped. When they were finished, she tried to run away with nothing but her bright red runners on. There was ice on the lake—it was March—and she fell in.

Almost forty years later, the RCMP would tell the family that Pauline had been drunk and her death ruled an accidental drowning.

The family doesn't buy it. They want a thorough investigation. "If there was further investigation, it could put our family's mind at ease and our heart at ease, and we don't have to think that the case was just dropped," said Laura. Ted agreed. "If they're found guilty there should be a penalty, otherwise other people will take native women and girls and continue abusing them and killing them. If it were any other race they would continue investigating that and not stop."

CANADA'S DIRTIEST SECRET

GLADYS RADEK RETURNED to Vancouver after the 2006 symposium. She kept working on social justice issues in the Downtown Eastside. She kept hoping for information about Tamara. But by fall, it seemed the investigation was stalling. Gladys was determined that all these missing and murdered women and girls not be forgotten, that the issue not fall to the wayside again. She started to walk.

The idea had been simmering since she marched to the symposium. As the months following the symposium dragged into years and the final recommendations foundered, Gladys felt compelled to do something to keep the issues and the victims' stories in the public mind. She knew there were far more women missing and murdered on the Highway of Tears than those on the E-Pana list, and she knew that was probably the case across Canada. So along with Bernie Williams, she launched Walk4Justice. The organization would build a comprehensive list of victims to show the public and the government just how bad the situation was. The plan was to walk across the country collecting the names of those who'd disappeared or been murdered and gather signatures on a petition calling for a national inquiry. The group would then visit Parliament Hill—which Gladys calls "the house of ill repute"—and meet with then prime minister Stephen Harper to give him the list of names and the petition. Maybe, finally, something would be done.

On National Aboriginal Day, June 21, 2008, a group of about a dozen people, including a toddler and a seventy-four-year-old, gathered at Trout Lake in Vancouver's John Hendry Park, just east of downtown. It was a warm morning as they ate breakfast at picnic tables. Gladys had brought her old minivan, which she had plastered bumper to bumper with photos of missing and murdered women. She called it her war pony. They finished eating and set off on a 4,500-kilometre walk across the country.

The first stop was the Pickton farm. It's an eerie place, surrounded by upscale developments built upon land the Picktons sold off over the years, places now of quiet cul-de-sacs and manicured lawns and BMWs parked in driveways. The walkers gathered in front of the chain-link fence encircling what remains of the farm and said a prayer. They laid flowers. They set off again.

Lorna Brown, Tamara's auntie, and Christine Chipman, her stepmom, had left Prince Rupert on foot the previous week, retracing the steps they had taken to the symposium in 2006. In Kamloops they met the group coming from Vancouver, and together they all continued north from the city through the high, dry hills of scrub brush and cactus and into the tiny town of Barriere, on the banks of the South Thompson River. Along the way, a woman rushed over to them, sobbing. She recognized one of the photos on Gladys's van. It was a friend from high school.

By the time the walkers neared Edmonton in early July, they were about twenty strong. A handful of people had joined the group along the way, including Carole Fletcher, a fifty-nine-year-old white woman from Ottawa, who flew out to take part. Carole had never met any of the members of Walk4Justice and had never participated in such a cause. But when she read about it in the newspaper,

she knew she had to support it. "Their cause is our cause. It's humanity's cause," she said.

When the walkers arrived in Edmonton, they were met by family members of dozens of missing or murdered women from that
city. Edmonton, like northwestern B.C., has been the location of
clusters of missing and murdered women for decades. According to
a *Globe and Mail* analysis, nearly fifty women had been murdered
since 1986 in similar circumstances, including that their bodies
were found outside. Many of them were street-level sex workers; a
grossly disproportionate number were Indigenous. Despite an
RCMP-led task force, dubbed Project KARE, that investigated
many of the murders, charges had been laid in just eleven of forty-
nine cases as of 2016.

The walkers met for a feast that night at a Friendship Centre,
drumming and praying and singing. And then they carried on—
through Regina, Saskatoon, Winnipeg, Thunder Bay. It was gruel-
ling. Outside Edmonton a truck T-boned the lead vehicle, injuring
two elders. There were thunderstorms and blazing hot days. There
were racial slurs hurled from the windows of passing cars. But
there was also a groundswell of support as communities welcomed
them, provided them with names and pictures of more victims,
signed the petition and contributed food, shelter and money.
"Since I started organizing this in January I have learned that we
do have a very caring society," Gladys told a reporter. By the time
they reached Ottawa that fall, after eighty-three days of walking,
they had nearly three thousand names of missing and murdered
women. "I kind of knew how big Canada was, but it really opened
my eyes even more about the plight of the missing and murdered
women right across the nation," Gladys said. "I think it's Canada's
dirtiest secret."

On September 15, 2008, the walkers held a rally on Parliament
Hill calling for a public inquiry. About five hundred people turned
out to support them. They had hoped to meet with the prime

minister but were told he wasn't available. Gladys vowed that "one way or the other" he would get the petition and list of names. Momentum was building. Canadian media had covered the walk, and so had international journalists. Gladys was fielding calls from the United States, Australia, Germany and France. Families were forcing the issue into the spotlight.

The Native Women's Association of Canada (NWAC) had launched a campaign in 2004 to document missing and murdered Indigenous women and spur authorities to action. "This is Canada's shame. Native women are being marginalized from life to death," said Terri Brown, then the group's president. "The only thing Canadians know about us is that we're drug addicts, drunks, prostitutes and people who live on welfare. They don't know us for our kindness, our generosity . . . and our love for one another." The Canadian government granted the initiative, dubbed Sisters in Spirit, half of the $10 million it had requested, disbursed over five years. Sisters in Spirit held vigils and gatherings where families came together to share stories and support, and it created toolkits on topics such as dealing with the media, the process of reporting a loved one missing and safety measures for Indigenous women. It conducted research on missing and murdered Indigenous women and girls, building a database of cases from across the country. As of March 2009, the initiative had documented 520 cases—126 involving missing women and girls, the remainder women and girls who'd been killed. "We were starting to get a lot of international attention, people were starting to talk about it," said Dawn Lavell-Harvard, who was president of NWAC in 2015 and 2016, after decades spent advocating for Indigenous women and girls. Sisters in Spirit was viewed by many as a success.

But when its funding ran out after the five-year term, the Canadian government refused to renew it. The Conservatives had been elected in 2006, under the leadership of Stephen Harper, with policies many Indigenous organizations viewed as openly hostile. The government claimed the initiative had achieved its aims and it was "time to move to action, by taking the research and implementing it on the streets," referencing funding it would provide to another NWAC project and the recent announcement of a $10-million strategy to reduce violence against women. NWAC had previously criticized that strategy as too broad, having little to do with violence against Indigenous women specifically. Much of the funding was slated for the RCMP.

Dawn said the federal government made it clear that NWAC had to drop the Sisters in Spirit name. "We weren't even supposed to be using the [words] Sisters in Spirit, using the logo, we weren't supposed to be talking, that if we even called it anything close to Sisters in Spirit, that we would get zero funding at all, for anything," she said. The federal government denied this at the time. The ministers of justice and status of women wrote that "the ability of NWAC to continue to use the Sisters in Spirit name or to conduct further research using other funding sources is not in doubt."

The organization tried to keep research going with volunteers, but the threat against other programs created a chill. "You get caught between a rock and a hard place, because there are other things we're doing as an organization to help support women," said Dawn. "It's potentially putting other things in jeopardy. With the Harper government, it was very obvious that it was a total backlash to end the attention Sisters in Spirit was getting."

But although the government succeeded in putting an end to Sisters in Spirit, it couldn't shut down the conversation. "It almost had the opposite effect," said Dawn. "Once people saw how hard they tried to silence it and shut it down, people were appalled."

———

In July 2007, just over a year after the symposium, Audrey Auger also began to walk. She told reporters that she wanted to memorialize Aielah, show support for other parents who'd lost a child to the highway and raise awareness of its dangers. But it was more than that, too. "You know," said her brother Darrell, "I think she was looking for her daughter. She was still looking, looking for closure, looking for something, something to make the pain go away."

Audrey, her daughter Kyla and one of Aielah's friends travelled to Prince Rupert, where they planned to set off walking on July 1. They weren't entirely sure how far they'd go. They'd talked about walking as far as Prince George, but Audrey mulled carrying on to Edmonton or to Gift Lake in northern Alberta, where Aielah was buried, if they received enough support. They made it most of the way to Terrace, five days of walking the highway in pouring rain and camping in the bush at night, when they had to turn back. Things hadn't worked out with the driver, who was supposed to trail them to ensure their safety; they had run out of food because promised donations didn't materialize; and they'd been spooked by numerous signs of bears. The trio returned to Prince Rupert, where they stayed at the Salvation Army shelter to plan their next move. After some discussion, they decided on a new route, and in mid-August, Audrey and Kyla set out once again, this time from where Aielah's body had been found, twenty-three kilometres east of Prince George, to Gift Lake.

Each day, they walked as far as they could, taking only short breaks to eat. Each night, they placed a marker where they stopped and pitched their tent. They walked for hundreds of kilometres along townless stretches of highway, traversing the continental divide through Pine Pass, then crossing the northern prairies, a flat, windswept expanse where the earth blends into the sky. Audrey called Darrell wherever there was cell service: Mackenzie Junction, Chetwynd, Dawson Creek, Spirit River. On one of the last days of the walk, just before she reached her daughter's grave, she told him people had seen hundreds of others walking with her. At first she was confused—it was only her and Kyla. Then she realized. "Those are spirits," she said. "Those are the grandfathers and grandmothers walking with me."

She would do two more walks, one in 2008 and one in 2011, looking for the healing, the peace, the daughter she could not find anywhere else. It helped her, her brother thought. But when she wasn't walking, the peace would evaporate and grief and pain would return. She was plagued by guilt, by a voice in the back of her head that said, "Why did you let her go out that day? Why did you let her go?" "It would come back and it would haunt her," said Darrell. On March 5, 2013, at about 1:20 A.M., Audrey was driving west from Edmonton along Highway 16. She had been drinking, and she veered into the path of a tractor trailer. She died at the scene.

In 2009, a year after the walk to Ottawa, Walk4Justice organized a 1,500-kilometre march from Vancouver to Prince Rupert. Their message the previous year had fallen on deaf ears, so they'd decided to try again. Bernie Williams said, "And we will keep walking [until it is heard]. We will not go away. We will keep rolling. We will keep raising our voices up." This walk was meant to draw attention to the recommendations hashed out at the Highway of Tears symposium three years earlier. Although the Carrier Sekani Family Services in Prince George had launched the Highway of Tears Initiative, a project meant to shepherd the calls to action into existence, there was virtually no money to implement the recommendations. The roadmap drawn at the symposium to address the tragedies was fading, and that was crushing for families. "It just seems like we complain," Sally Gibson said. "We do everything that ordinary people would do and they'd get some action, but it seems like we're just talking to space . . . It just seems to be their

answer was to do this great big report. The thing I know about all
the reports that are ever done . . . they must have a warehouse
somewhere where they stick those after they're done because nothing, absolutely nothing, happens."

That fall, NWAC organized vigils across the country in what
was the largest, most coordinated event to date. In seventy-two
communities, from Victoria to Halifax, people gathered to com-
memorate missing and murdered Indigenous women and girls and
to demand action. And in July 2010, Walk4Justice continued its
campaign, this time walking the length of Highway 16, from
Kamloops to Winnipeg, where the highway ends. "Throughout each
and every journey we gained momentum by getting support from
all our First Nations leaderships, employee unions, politicians and
thousands of family members across the nation who fully support
our walks," Gladys and Bernie later wrote. "They gathered in soli-
darity to have their voices heard to the top levels of government."

In the late summer of 2010, British Columbia announced an
inquiry to examine problems with the investigation into missing
and murdered women from Vancouver's Downtown Eastside.
Although families had long called for such an inquiry, it was
panned in many circles when its terms of reference were announced.
Its scope was seen as too narrow, looking at criminal investigations
but not the larger systemic issues that left the women vulnerable in
the first place. It included only investigations from a five-year span,
ending when Robert Pickton was arrested, and would not delve
into any of the Highway of Tears cases because those investigations
remained open. And it was to be chaired by Wally Oppal, who had
served as B.C.'s attorney general from 2005 to 2009; there was
skepticism that he could serve as an impartial leader.

In response to criticism, Oppal did broaden the probe, and he
agreed to meet with families of Highway of Tears victims. But that,
in turn, angered families who saw an expanded probe as misguided,
for it would treat girls and women missing and murdered from the

north like those of the Downtown Eastside, when in fact each group encountered a very different set of challenges. Sally Gibson was among those outraged with the "lumping together" of women, as if the problems faced by sex workers in downtown Vancouver were equally applicable to Lana, a college student in a small town 1,500 kilometres away. Increasingly, families were calling for a national public inquiry that would tackle the deep-seated causes behind the staggeringly high rates of violence against Indigenous women and girls—and put a stop to it. "It's going to be up to the people," Gladys told a reporter. "It's going to be us, the grassroots women that are going to make that public inquiry happen."

She would keep walking and pushing for a national inquiry for years to come.

Meanwhile, Indigenous women in B.C.'s northwest continued to disappear.

Fort St. James, a forestry, mining and tourism town founded in 1806 by explorer Simon Fraser, lies about fifty kilometres north of Highway 16, along Highway 27. The region is the territory of the Tl'azt'en, which means "people by the edge of the bay," part of the Dakelh people, known to Europeans as "Carriers." The Tl'azt'en traditional territory is vast, stretching about 100 kilometres from Stuart Lake to just south of Takla Lake. For thousands of years, the Tl'azt'en people hunted and fished the land, but in the late nineteenth century, during the inpouring of settlers, the Tl'azt'en began getting pushed into central communities and, later, reserves.

The road from Fort St. James to Tachie, the largest Tl'azt'en community and the hub for services like daycare, elementary school and the Tl'azt'en administration, is long and winding, crossing pine-blanketed hills that offer the odd glimpse of Stuart Lake. Trucks loaded with logs roar past, along with pickups pulling boats and campers, a sign of the region's recreational fishing industry.

Tachie sits on the lake's shore near the Tachie River and is home to a couple hundred people who live in houses sprinkled along a scenic rise.

In the space of less than five years, two women from this community, both mothers, disappeared.

Bonnie Joseph spent her childhood in foster homes, some in Tachie, others in Yekooche, a Dakelh community on the other side of Stuart Lake. At times, she lived with a foster family in Vanderhoof, more than a hundred kilometres away. She was a happy, kind girl who was always laughing—even in adulthood, she was always laughing. Bonnie's children were her world; she would do anything for them. "She was always a stay-at-home mother, she was always happy, loving, caring," said Indyeyah Tylee, a long-time friend. "She was just a really good person."

Child welfare authorities apprehended her children in about 2000. A diary kept by Bonnie and her husband tracked in painstaking detail their efforts to stay connected with their kids and regain custody. They noted the dates and times of conversations with a foster parent and officials, along with Bonnie's visits to breastfeed her baby and their concerns about the children's well-being. They struggled to survive in Fort St. James, far from their homes but close to

Bonnie Joseph loved her children more than anything and was devastated when authorities took them away.

where their kids were placed. They noted the long winter walks, often late at night, that Bonnie took to feed her baby, and her difficulty finding transportation to attend appointments with authorities and support workers. The entry on March 22, 2000, read: "But things could be better if the kids come home so we both can start living the way we want to without people stressing us out we are not criminals so thing we do and talk about is how to [cope] with life and how to deal with it." There followed a list of strategies, including parenting classes, anger management and drug and alcohol counselling. There is a floor plan sketched out of the home they wanted to build for their family. A 2001 entry by Bonnie is simply messages to her children, telling each of them, "I love you a lot."

The majority of Indigenous children, who are vastly over-represented in the care system across Canada, are there because of "neglect," not abuse. What constitutes neglect is, in some cases, dubious—in some provinces, too few windows in a home is grounds enough to remove children—and largely stems from pov-erty. "Children from low income families are many times more likely than other children to experience neglect," noted a 2015 report. "Given that First Nations people on average have higher unemployment rates, lower incomes, and more pervasive poverty compared to non-Aboriginal people, First Nations children also have a much higher likelihood of being placed in care as a result of a substantiated neglect investigation."

The Canadian government has long failed to provide basic necessities such as clean drinking water and adequate housing to Indigenous communities; in 2016, the Canadian Human Rights Tribunal found the government racially discriminates against 165,000 First Nations children through its failure to provide them with equitable services—basics like schools and health care—that most Canadians take for granted. In 2018, then federal minister of Indigenous services Jane Philpott described the country's child wel-fare system as riddled with "perverse incentives," whereby child welfare agencies receive funding based on how many children are in care. "So the more children in care, the more money comes out of government coffers," said Philpott, who called the situation a "humanitarian crisis." "It's really a matter of changing the headspace, the policy space to say let's not have a system that's prioritizing and funding apprehension, let's have a system that's prioritizing and funding prevention." There are now more Indigenous children in the child welfare system than at the height of residential schools; in fact, the system has been called "a second generation of residential schools."

Not only are children involved in the child welfare system at high risk; their parents and extended families are, too. Mothers of children placed in care are more likely to die young. A study published in the *Canadian Journal of Psychiatry* in 2017 showed they have a suicide rate four times higher than mothers who maintained custody of their children. The study attributed this partly to "feelings of guilt, responsibility, shame, stigmatization, and loss of self-worth [that] are often associated with this type of custody loss." Another study found these mothers were three and a half times more likely to die of avoidable causes, such as unintentional injury and suicide, and nearly three times more likely to die of unavoidable causes, such as heart disease and vehicle accidents.

Bonnie tried, but she did not get her kids back and, according to her family and friends, she sank deeper into addiction as a result. "She was hurt because her kids were everything to her. Everything," said Indyeyah. Bonnie never missed visits with her kids, or the meetings and court dates about custody. Because she didn't drive, she usually had to hitchhike. For appointments in Vanderhoof or Prince George, she left a few days in advance to make sure she got there in time—there was no way of knowing how long it would take to get a lift—and stayed in shelters. "She made every appointment no matter what," Sharon Joseph, her sister, said.

That's why Bonnie's friends and family began to worry that something was wrong as soon as she missed appointments concerning her kids. A family member saw her in the fall of 2007 along Highway 16 in Vanderhoof. They chatted for a little while, and then Bonnie set off up a hill that leads out of the small town and toward Prince George. She was reported missing that December. A search of an online news archive brings up only one story, published in the *Prince George Citizen* just over a year after she was last seen. "She's been fighting for her kids since day one; she never misses her court days or her visitations, but now it's been more than a year. It's not like her at all," it quoted Dean Joseph, her cousin. Another cousin, Jo-Anne Bertram, said Bonnie had fallen through "some significant cracks" and had little in the way of community or family support, which was "partially why she was not considered missing for quite some time." "Most of her family members are drinking or on the streets. It is a sad, sad story . . . All the people who really cared about her are gone and most of the ones left behind aren't really here, either."

Indyeyah has the same dream over and over, where she sees a small blue house that sits on a reserve 150 kilometres away and, terrified, walks into it. Bonnie is sitting in an armchair in the corner. She says, "How long I waited for you." Bonnie tells her that she's stuck, she can't leave. Indyeyah goes to her to give her a hug, and then wakes up in tears. "I don't know why this happened, but it shouldn't have," said Indyeyah. "She was so loving. I miss her every day."

There have been stories and suspicions: word went around the community that someone found a phone that might have belonged to her; others wondered about a man Bonnie was seeing who she had told friends was abusive and controlling. Years after her disappearance, local papers ran a couple of short stories when police reissued a call for information. But despite disappearing from the Highway of Tears the year after Aielah Saric-Auger was murdered, Bonnie's case has received hardly any attention. "She's native and so nobody cares that much," said Indyeyah. "I think that's so unfair. It's just so unfair that they keep on ignoring stuff like this."

———

Late in 2010, along Highway 27 south of Fort St. James, a police officer noticed a pickup pull out of a logging road and speed off. It seemed suspicious, so the officer pulled the vehicle over. After speaking with the twenty-year-old driver, the police called a conservation officer to come and trace the vehicle's tracks back through the snow, suspecting that perhaps he'd been poaching. The conservation officer found the body of Loren Leslie, a legally blind fifteen-year-old girl who had gone missing earlier that evening after leaving her home in Vanderhoof to meet a friend.

That night, a police officer called Doug Leslie, Loren's father, and asked him if anyone might have been using Loren's ID, which was found in the truck. "They wouldn't say why they wanted to know, but I knew it wasn't good," Doug later said. "They told me they had found something . . . but they never called back and so I just drove out to the scene. I had to know." Police cars were everywhere, and someone told him it was a homicide scene. They wouldn't let him go any closer and sent him home to wait. It was three thirty the next afternoon when police confirmed that it was his daughter out there. At the funeral the next week, an empty coffin sat at the front. Loren's body had been sent to Pennsylvania for examination by highly specialized forensic experts.

Cody Legebokoff, the man driving the truck, was charged with murder. Ten months later, the RCMP announced another three homicide charges against him for the killing of three young mothers: Jill Stuchenko and Cynthia Maas, both thirty-five years old, and twenty-three-year-old Natasha Montgomery.

Jill Stuchenko had five children when she went missing from Prince George on October 22, 2009. Four days later, her body was found in a gravel pit on the outskirts of the city. Cynthia Maas was reported missing the next fall, on September 23, 2010. Her body was found a couple of weeks later in a park beside the Fraser River.

When the RCMP announced the charges, Cynthia's family released a public letter that read, in part: "Cindy had a right to live, to overcome her struggles, to become strong, and to be the mother she wanted to be . . . Cindy was a social victim of disability, ethnicity, class, gender as well as suffering the greatest indignity as a victim of murder, she is a poster child for vulnerability in our society. We are concerned about all the other unsolved missing and murdered women. Murders do not just harm families but our society is harmed as we forget and are numbed by senseless violence perpetrated against women portrayed as deserving of death." Natasha Montgomery was reported missing September 23, 2010, too. Her body has never been found, though police recovered sufficient evidence to charge Legebokoff in her murder.

Legebokoff was found guilty of the four murders in 2014, earning him the ignominious title of Canada's youngest serial killer. He is serving life in prison with no chance of parole for twenty-five years. Police ruled out his involvement in the E-Pana cases based on forensic evidence and his young age, an investigator told *Maclean's*. When it comes to Bonnie's disappearance, the RCMP said they are aware Legebokoff is from the area where Bonnie disappeared, that he was the subject of an extensive investigation and that they continue to actively investigate the file.

Not long after Legebokoff's 2010 arrest, a twenty-year-old white woman, Madison Scott, vanished from a lake near her hometown, Vanderhoof. She'd driven out to a party on Friday, May 27, 2011, with plans to camp for the night with a friend. The friend left in the early hours of Saturday morning; when Madison's parents went to look for her on Sunday, they found her truck and her tent, but not her. She is still missing.

The Leo Creek Forest Service Road veers north from the main road to Tachie a few kilometres before it reaches the community. It is a wide, washboarded gravel road, along which large trucks head out empty and come back loaded with logs. It had been a dry spring in June 2017, and the trucks kicked up great billowing clouds of dust, so much that drivers of smaller vehicles were momentarily blinded.

A few dozen kilometres away, just over a bridge that spans a creek, a crowd began to gather on the morning of June 13. Peter Basil had been there the previous evening until after ten, cutting back the brush and tall grass in a clearing beside the road. Off to the side, a couple of old outhouses tilted next to a rusted-out fuel drum, and facing the creek a few rows of chairs had been set up. Mosquitoes swarmed, and the early summer sun beat down amid the haze of dust that drifted across the clearing each time a logging truck roared by. People arrived in pickups and vans and cars; some came from Tachie, others from Yekooche, Fort St. James and surrounding communities. The Tl'azt'en band's bus arrived, dropping off more people, many wearing bright red hoodies printed with a photo of a pretty young woman who had been gone four years that day.

A priest in a blinding white robe read from the Gospel of John and offered what words of comfort he could muster. It would be easier, he acknowledged, if there was a way to say goodbye, a gravesite to visit. But this, he added, gesturing to the deep forest surrounding the place, is her grave. All of this is where she is.

Immaculate Basil, called Mackie, was one of eight children born to parents who had survived residential school in Lejac. Their mother was expecting compensation for the abuse she had suffered when she was hit and killed by a semi in Prince George. Their dad has never spoken of his own residential school experience; he didn't file for compensation because that would have required him to talk about it. Child welfare authorities apprehended most of the kids, who were split up into foster homes throughout the region. Three of the sisters were sent to Vanderhoof, where two, Crystal and Ida, lived together. Mackie was put in another home by herself. It was a bad experience, said Ida. Mackie was bounced around and abused in some of the homes. They were all cut off from their family, their culture, their community.

Mackie went into independent living when she was sixteen, following in Ida's footsteps, and managed to finish high school while taking care of herself. After graduating, she lived in the Vanderhoof area for a couple of years, and then went home to Tachie. "Even as kids, she said she wanted to come back and get to know family," said Ida, "and that's what she did." Mackie lived with Peter, the older brother she hardly knew growing up, and his wife, Vivian, when she first returned. It was a good time, a happy time, said Peter, as they got to know each other, "laughing around and having fun and teasing." Mackie was shy and hesitant to open up—it took her a while to trust people. "But other than that, she was happy and tried to forget about the past," said Ida. She was fiercely loyal to her family, and her son, Jameson, was the light of her life. She tried to give him everything she hadn't had growing

Mackie Basil graduated from high school in Vanderhoof.

up—love, security, family—and each year started saving money months before his birthday so she could throw him a big party. "She really loved her boy, she'd do anything and everything for him," said Rita Pierre, a friend who spent many hours sitting on the deck of her father's house overlooking the lake, smoking cigarettes and chatting with Mackie. "She'd do anything for anybody."

Mackie volunteered at community events, donating food and helping out at potlatches and funerals. She worked for a time at the elementary school and began fostering children part-time. She knew how abuse gets passed down generation to generation, as it had from her parents in residential school to her in foster care. And she was determined to stop the cycle and prevent other children living in Tachie from being separated from their families and enduring the pain she'd experienced. "She was a good person," said Maureen Felix, her sister-in-law, words echoed by many in Tachie.

On June 13, 2013, the Thursday before Father's Day, Mackie went to Vanderhoof with Peter and Vivian. They had planned to invite their fathers over that Sunday and were driving to Vanderhoof to get a cake for the celebration. When they arrived home that evening, Mackie got ready to go out. Earlier that day she had called Crystal, who was living in Burns Lake, excited about a party that night at a home not far away, down in the old part of the reserve. Mackie left Peter and Vivian's and went to William and Elsie Pierre's house. She was a frequent visitor to their home, and William and Elsie had enjoyed getting to know her. Mackie rarely drank, but that night she had a bottle of Smirnoff Red Label vodka in the pocket of her vest. She hung out on the porch with them for a time and mentioned she planned to stop by a wake nearby on her way to the party. "That was the last we seen of her," said William.

At some point that night, Mackie returned to Peter and Vivian's to pick up a second bottle of vodka. A couple of people, including Rita Pierre, saw her heading to the party sometime between nine and ten.

On Friday morning, Crystal had a bad feeling. She tried to call Mackie but couldn't reach her. Then she called a few places where she thought Mackie might be, but no one had heard from her. Peter and Vivian didn't think anything of it at first. They figured she was still partying—parties often lasted the duration of the weekend. But the weekend rolled into Sunday and everyone resurfaced except for Mackie. Their brother stopped by Peter and Vivian's to ask if they'd seen her. "We said, 'No, why?'" Vivian remembered. "He said, 'Because nobody's seen her all weekend.' And that's when it all started."

Crystal was still calling around. On Sunday, she finally reached one of Mackie's friends, who promised to look into it. Half an hour later, that friend called Crystal back and said, "You're right. Mackie's missing." Crystal called Peter and their father.

Peter and Vivian drove to the house where the party had been. They were told that Mackie had jumped in a truck with a couple of guys and headed up the Leo Creek Forest Service Road. Peter and

"It's kind of tiring, chasing dreams," said Peter Basil,
who, with his wife, Vivian, has been searching for Mackie since 2013.

Vivian went to see the two men she'd apparently left with, who denied having gone anywhere that night. Others who had been at the party said she had left with two other men. Peter and Vivian drove the forestry road but saw no trace of anything. They went home and called the police.

On Monday, Mackie's family began searching. People came from Tachie to help; over the next days, as word got around, people arrived from all the surrounding communities and as far away as Burns Lake. By Tuesday morning, it was a full-blown effort, with the RCMP and search and rescue taking part. The RCMP "jumped into action on the first part of the search right away," said Peter, who praised the RCMP investigator with the Prince George–based Major Crime Unit who had been the police contact for the family. "[He's] been good dealing with me." The police brought in a helicopter, dogs and scuba divers. Officers interviewed logging truck drivers, forestry workers and tree planters.

According to the RCMP, a forestry worker saw Mackie walking on the road in the mid-morning hours. In a media release asking for public assistance, the RCMP said, "Mackie was at a house party in Tachie when she and two other individuals decided to head out to a local cabin. While on route to the cabin, the pickup truck the trio was travelling in became stuck in the mud and efforts to free it were unsuccessful. The three walked to the cabin where they spent some time, then made more attempts to free the truck from the mud. Mackie became frustrated with the unsuccessful efforts and advised the others she was walking back to Tachie and left them with the truck."

Mackie's family erected a camp at the clearing by the bridge, close to where the forestry worker reported seeing her walking, to house and feed volunteer searchers; within days, upward of three hundred people had joined them. They combed an enormous area, including the vast web of roads that sprawls dozens and dozens of kilometres in every direction. They traipsed through soggy cutblocks under a low cover of brush and, in those areas that have been replanted, young pine trees. They picked through the stones along the banks of rivers and creeks. After four days, the RCMP and SAR wrapped up their ground search efforts. But the family and hundreds of volunteers continued, including Rita Pierre, who spent days searching. One day, she was stepping carefully through a cut-block near two swamps and somehow got turned around. It was raining and she was lost, with no idea which direction the road lay. She panicked. "I just ran and ran and ran," she said. She thought of how Mackie must have felt out there, alone. "It was a pretty scary time searching for her, just desperately trying to find her," said Rita. For months, they searched. But slowly, their numbers dwindled. They found nothing. There were suspicions in the community about a man who was "kind of obsessed" with Mackie, who people say exhibited strange behaviour after she disappeared before packing up and leaving. When a group of people gathered on a porch was asked how, in such a small community, no one knows what became of Mackie, they answered in unison: "They know."

Ida Basil says her sister Mackie was fiercely loyal to her family
and to her son, who was the light of her life.

The RCMP said it has conducted "a large investigation" that included scrutinizing those who were last in contact with her. "We have investigated many theories, including is she a victim of foul play, a motor vehicle incident or an animal attack as she became lost in the area, or did she leave the area of her own accord," said Cpl. Madonna Saunderson. Investigators don't know, but believe she would have contacted her family by now if she were still alive.

At the vigil for Mackie in 2017, her son, then nine years old, milled about. He had begun asking his family where his mother was, trying to understand how she could have disappeared. He asked them if the reward money—the band council put up $20,000— was still there for her. He spent a lot of time looking at a photo of her. "He's getting lonely, really bad," said Maureen Felix, his aunt. He asked Ida when his mother was coming back. "I tell him she's missing, we're doing everything to try and find her," Ida said.

The family kept the camp at Leo Creek going for three years, returning each summer to continue the search. They've taken it down now, but they still go out and search whenever they can. When people have dreams—many people have dreamed of Mackie—they try to figure out what they mean, to follow them in hopes of finding her. "That's hard, too," said Peter. "It's kind of tiring, chasing dreams." People have told him that it's time to forget and move on with his life. "I tell them, 'You think it's that easy? It's not. It's just that memory that's sitting in the back of your mind, and that hurt that's still sitting in your heart. How are we supposed to get on with our life?'"

Not long after Mackie disappeared, one of her sisters died of an apparent fentanyl overdose in Prince George that the family believed involved foul play. And not long after that, their youngest brother was shot to death in a homicide that remains unsolved. "It's been ripping us apart, this thing," said Peter.

They want to have a proper burial for Mackie; they want her son to have a place to visit, to be near her. "The only thing we care about is just finding her," said Crystal.

WINDING DOWN

IT WAS RAINING HARD when the group assembled outside Prince Rupert's civic centre, a sprawling, mural-coated building that sits behind a pavilion from which three totem poles rise. A man held an umbrella over Brenda Wilson as she spoke to the crowd about the walk she was about to embark on: a 725-kilometre journey from one end of the Highway of Tears to the other to mark the tenth anniversary of the first highway walk, which had culminated with the symposium. The Cleansing the Highway Walk of 2016, said Brenda, was a way to honour lost loved ones and to find power in the pain. Brenda had always been a shy person, most comfortable as far from the spotlight as she could be. But the murder of Ramona Wilson and the many other women and girls had galvanized her. In the twenty-two years since Ramona had walked out the door on a Saturday night, never to return, Brenda had become one of the most outspoken, persistent advocates for victims and their families along the Highway of Tears. "I had to lose my sister to be who I am today," she said. "She's given me strength . . . and hopefully I'll be able to pass it on."

In the summer of 2014, Brenda took on the job of Highway of
Tears coordinator at Carrier Sekani Family Services, where she
tried to implement the symposium's recommendations. The
organization scrabbled to maintain funding for the position—for
most of her time there, Brenda was guaranteed a job for only the
next few months. That had been the case with the position since
its inception a decade earlier, and whenever funding ran out, they
did what they could. "There needs to be somebody there to advocate for the families, to keep this whole initiative alive," Brenda
said. "I don't care if you pay me. I'm going to do it."

However, without resources, there wasn't much they could do,
so most of the recommendations languished. There was still no
transportation system along the highway corridor—the first recommendation in the report. Safe homes, check-in points, a hitchhiker
detection network, a highway crime watch program, emergency
phones—none of it had been established. A few billboards had
been erected, but with messages like "Hitchhiking: Is it worth the
risk?" and "Girls don't hitchhike on the Highway of Tears: Killer on
the loose!," some criticized them for blaming victims rather than
focusing on perpetrators. While various coordinators for the
Highway of Tears Initiative had presented community workshops
and published information about what to do when someone goes
missing, the project was never able to develop emergency readiness
plans in each community or hire more than one person. Some recommendations were implemented, in a fashion, by communities
themselves or through other initiatives, including those focused on
improving services and opportunities on reserves. But the holistic,
coordinated, well-funded approach called for at the 2006 symposium never came to pass.

The idea for the anniversary walk had emerged a few weeks
before, when Brenda sat down with Angeline Chalifoux, the aunt of
Aielah Saric-Auger, for a coffee at a downtown Tim Hortons in
Prince George. Since Audrey died in 2013, no one had been publicly

advocating Aielah's case. In 2015, Angeline called the family for
permission to take on that role, and later that year organized a
twenty-three-kilometre walk from where Aielah was found to
Prince George. She was thinking of doing it again when she met
Brenda that day, but Brenda had another idea, a bigger one. She
said to Angeline, "Will you go for a walk with me?" "Where are we
walking?" Angeline asked. "From Prince Rupert to Prince George."
"Oh!" Angeline laughed. But she agreed—she'd been quietly hoping to walk the length of the highway. A few weeks later, the two
were in Brenda's pickup headed west, Angeline behind the wheel so
Brenda could field calls from reporters. The walk was to take three
weeks, with stops in communities along the route to hold forums
where families could share their stories and suggestions.

Angeline and Brenda set out, side by side, from Prince Rupert's
civic centre in the pouring rain. "It's cleansing the highway,"
Angeline said of the weather. "These are the tears everyone has

Brenda Wilson and Angeline Chalifoux set out to walk the Highway of Tears in 2016.

cried." Walkers were to travel in pairs, one person walking and the other driving closely behind with hazard lights flashing. Much of the highway, particularly the western section, still didn't have cell service, so there was no way to call for help in the event of a run-in with a bear, a hostile driver or a medical problem. They would "leapfrog" the route, each team covering ten kilometres at a time, the stretches divided with markers Angeline assembled the night before in their hotel room: foam cut in the shape of a dress and attached to a metal pole. The number of walkers would ebb and flow, based on the day and location; the distance covered each day would be determined by who showed up.

This is how I ended up walking the Highway of Tears: I'd called Brenda earlier that week, when I heard of the forum in Prince Rupert that would kick off the walk, and asked if I could attend. When I arrived at the Friendship House, the crowd was sparse. Later that morning, when I asked Brenda how many people were

Brenda and Matilda Wilson at the annual memorial walk for Ramona in 2016, which took place during the Cleansing the Highway Walk.

participating in the walk, she laughed and motioned to herself and Angeline. I was surprised. "Just you two?" I asked. "You want to walk?" she said. I said yes. Brenda loaned me a reflective vest; pinned to the front was a purple ribbon from the annual Ramona Lisa Wilson memorial walk, the one Matilda, Brenda and their family led each year in Smithers, emblazoned with the words "Let her spirit soar."

In 2012, Wally Oppal released a damning report on the police's "blatant failures" to investigate missing women from Vancouver's Downtown Eastside. He had endorsed the recommendations stemming from the Highway of Tears Symposium and stressed the urgent need to improve transportation along the highway. The following year—seven years after the symposium—the provincial government released its report tracking the progress of the Oppal inquiry's sixty-five recommendations. The report stated that the transportation ministry was preparing for consultations with communities along Highway 16 to improve transit options.Those meetings took place the next summer, in June and July of 2014, and revealed local concerns about the lack of transportation options along the highway. Nonetheless, despite the significant amount of attention drawn to the Highway of Tears and its lack of transportation, nearly three years after the Oppal report there was still no transit plan in place.

Halfway through the 2016 Cleansing the Highway Walk, the B.C. government finally provided a transit start date for the region. Buses connecting the many small communities along the corridor would be operating by the end of the year. Not long afterward, Greyhound announced that, as a result, it was ending its service, meaning there would no longer be a bus that travelled straight through over long distances.

At a national level, in 2014 the RCMP released a policy on dealing with missing people. It included risk-assessment forms and a ten-page "intake report" to be filled out in all missing person cases to ensure standardized information was collected, and a requirement that high-risk cases be reviewed by a supervisor. It spelled out how officers must develop an investigative strategy and create a communication schedule with families to keep them apprised of investigations. The changes came the year after a Human Rights Watch report on policing in northern B.C. had documented a litany of allegations against RCMP officers, including rape, assault and failing to protect Indigenous people. (British Columbia enacted the Missing Persons Act in 2015, giving police wider access to information that could help locate a missing person, and in 2016, provincial policing standards for missing persons investigations came into effect, establishing "the overall approach to missing person investigations for all B.C. police agencies.")

The Human Rights Watch report, along with other complaints, triggered an investigation by the arm's-length Civilian Review and Complaints Commission into the conduct of North District detachment officers on a number of issues, including the handling of missing person reports. The CRCC's final report contained a number of troubling findings regarding missing person cases, including that the RCMP lacked mandatory training on how to handle the files. As the report documents, the RCMP agreed with all the CRCC's findings except four regarding missing persons: namely, that nearly half the occurrence reports it reviewed failed to show the RCMP investigated missing person cases promptly and thoroughly; nearly half the missing person cases involving someone identified as high risk failed to show a prompt and thorough investigation; missing youth identified as "habitual, repeat or chronic" were more likely to have "deficiencies in the documented investigative actions, including unexplained gaps in the investigative timelines and failures to document risk assessments or missing persons debriefs on file"; and in over half the files reviewed, "North District supervisors failed to comply with the policy requirements to document observations and directions on file, and showed no indications of follow-up on member compliance with directions." On those points, the RCMP simply responded that new provincial standards addressed the majority of concerns regarding missing person investigations. "This response," noted the CRCC, "directly ignores any acknowledgement of the deficiencies that were identified as a result of the Commission's review of RCMP occurrence reports—deficiencies that are apparent on the face of the police files."

The RCMP also compiled national statistics on missing and murdered Indigenous women that, for the first time, put a number to the ongoing tragedy, albeit one that many advocacy groups believed was far too low. The 2014 "operational overview" reported 1,017 Indigenous female homicide victims between 1980 and 2012, and 164 missing, with some of those cases dating as far back as 1951. Just over a hundred of the missing cases were categorized as "unknown" or "foul play suspected," and 120 of the homicide cases were unsolved. The national homicide "solve rate" of nearly 90 per cent was similar for Indigenous and non-Indigenous women. B.C.'s solve rate was lower, at 82 and 84 per cent, respectively.

While the RCMP did not release a list of victims' names, missing women and girls from along the Highway of Tears during that time period would account for more than 6 per cent of the national total, while unsolved murders would account for 4 per cent, a vastly disproportionate number given the population of the region. Nationwide, Indigenous women accounted for more than 11 per cent of the total number of missing females, despite making up just 4 per cent of Canada's female population. Similarly, 16 per cent of female homicide victims were Indigenous women. And, while rates of homicide of non-Indigenous women had been steadily declining since 1980, that of Indigenous women remained constant, leading to their representing an ever-higher proportion of women murdered in Canada.

Further, Indigenous women were significantly less likely to be killed by a spouse or former partner—the rate was 29 per cent for Indigenous women versus 41 per cent for non-Indigenous women— and more likely to be murdered by a "casual acquaintance." Almost none of the Indigenous victims—fewer than 2 per cent—had links to the drug trade or organized crime.

In September 2012, the RCMP E-Pana task force announced a breakthrough. Colleen MacMillen was sixteen years old in August 1974 when she disappeared near her home in Lac La Hache, a small town three hundred kilometres south of Prince George along Highway 97. Her body was found a month later, dumped beside a logging road fifty kilometres away.

Investigators had submitted exhibits from the scene during the E-Pana investigation. DNA was identified, but there was an insufficient amount to be useful. It was only later, after DNA technology had advanced, that the lab could develop a profile from the sample. It was male, but didn't match anyone in Canadian databases. But when they ran it through Interpol, they had a hit: Bobby Jack Fowler, an American drifter with a long rap sheet of violence, including kidnapping, sexual assault and attempted murder. His was the sort of background that would have automatically made him a person of interest in Colleen's murder—if police had known he was in the area. Yet there was no record of his ever being in B.C. or elsewhere in Canada—not with other police agencies, the motor vehicle branch, employment insurance agencies or border patrol. It was only after the DNA hit that investigators uncovered a presentence report in the U.S. in which Fowler said he had worked as a roofer in Prince George in 1974. Based on that information, police were able to learn about his movements in the region, which led investigators to "strongly suspect" he was also responsible for the deaths of Pamela Darlington and Gale Weys, two other young women whose murders E-Pana investigated, though they lacked conclusive DNA evidence in those cases. "Talk about a needle in a haystack," said Wayne Clary. "I suspect there's others that are like this."

But by the time this discovery was made, Bobby Jack Fowler had been dead for years; he had passed away from lung cancer in 2006 in an Oregon prison where he was serving sixteen years for kidnapping, assault and attempted rape. "It was kind of a shallow victory," said Wayne. "It was a victory because we cleared that up, but you don't get to put the handcuffs on anybody."

Two years later, in 2014, Shari Greer stood on an RCMP podium in Surrey. She'd been there many times over the past four decades, pleading for information about her daughter, Kathryn-Mary Herbert, who was only eleven when she was murdered. "This is a moment I've waited for for thirty-nine years," Shari said. "Finally, it's here." That December, police charged Garry Taylor Handlen with two counts of first-degree murder in the deaths of Kathryn-Mary and Monica Jack, a twelve-year-old who disappeared riding her bike near Merritt in 1978. Her body wasn't found until the mid-1990s. Monica's case had been included in the E-Pana investigation, while Kathryn-Mary's was not. Handlen, a twice-convicted rapist, had been a suspect in both cases from the start, but it took nearly forty years for police to gather evidence to lay charges.

Evidence supporting both charges included confessions Handlen made to undercover RCMP officers posing as members of a criminal organization in a so-called Mr. Big operation; such confessions are "presumptively inadmissible," requiring a judge to decide "whether the circumstances in which the confessions were made, and the markers of their reliability, render their probative value greater than their prejudicial effect, on a balance of probabilities," notes the ruling that allowed the confession in the Jack case but found the Herbert confession inadmissible. After his arrest, Handlen denied committing the murder. The ruling noted that some of the details Handlen shared with the undercover officers did not match evidence and that other information could have been gleaned from media reports and documentaries. In January 2019, Handlen was convicted of the first-degree murder of Monica Jack and sentenced to life in prison with no possibility of parole for fifteen years. The charges against him for killing Kathryn-Mary were dropped.

Kathryn-Mary's mom, Shari Greer, who spent four decades fighting for justice, passed away in 2016. The task force made headway on other investigations. In two cases, the police identified persons who they believe were responsible, but the suspects, and the key witnesses, are dead.

At its height, from 2009 to 2012, the E-Pana task force had about seventy investigators, along with support staff and an annual budget of more than $5 million. But its budget dropped in the 2012/13 fiscal year to $1.8 million; the following year, it was allotted just $800,000, with an additional $1.55 million for personnel costs. B.C.'s justice minister at the time, Suzanne Anton, said that the task force had the resources it needed for its current investigations. But a draft memo penned by the RCMP's commanding officer for the province, Dep. Comm. Craig Callens, warned that the budget cuts would impede the force's ability to continue its investigations into missing and murdered women and girls on the Highway of Tears. "The termination of funding for project E-PANA would impair the ability to effectively conduct historical homicide investigations" in the province, Callens wrote. "At present, the loss of resources in project E-PANA would result in no other Highway of Tears historical homicide investigations being undertaken for the foreseeable future."

Many families learned of the budget cuts through the news. In 2015, Sally Gibson, Lana and Alberta's aunt, said it had been two years since she'd heard any updates from E-Pana, though Wayne Clary and other investigators still came to the candlelight vigil for Lana each fall. "I miss E-Pana," said Sally. "We learned a lot from them. It seems to be the end result of everything that government or anybody has to do with it is, 'Oh well.'" By then, the dozen or so staff members remaining on the task force were largely working on preparing disclosure for the upcoming Handlen trial. The project's expenditures from 2015 onward have been a mere $30,000, along with $1.55 million a year to cover staffing.

By 2015, E-Pana had identified more than 1,500 persons of interest and eliminated over 90 per cent of them. Its investigators had made more than 18,000 inquiries and conducted 2,500 interviews, polygraph tests and DNA tests. Wayne said they had sufficient resources for what they were doing; if a promising tip was to arise or there was some sort of breakthrough, resources could be shifted around within the RCMP to make sure E-Pana had what it needed to pursue it. But the investigation was "naturally winding down."

"There's not as much to do," he said.

The RCMP has released little information publicly about what investigators did in the course of E-Pana, beyond general details such as how many inquiries were made and how many persons of interest were eliminated. Steve Pranzl, who spent twelve years on the task force, takes a different tack. If you've got nothing else, it's time to be bold. The E-Pana cases, he said, "have been worked as hard as we can." Investigators ran every lead they had into the ground. "My interest is to solve these, if at all possible, and my philosophy is a little bit different than the RCMP philosophy. I believe in putting information out there," Steve said. "Sometimes this elicits information we can use . . . You get to a point where you've got nothing else. Poke. Tell people." So Steve spent more than four hours in a Langley coffee shop in January of 2019 describing the work E-Pana did, what they had found and how much they still don't know.

In the investigation of the disappearance of Delphine Nikal, the fifteen-year-old who went missing in 1990 while trying to hitch a ride home to Telkwa from Smithers, detectives put numerous earlier theories to rest. There was suspicion about her uncle, long since dead, who lived across the yard from her Telkwa home. "He was gone at hard before he died," said Steve. "There's lingering suspicion because he's dead and you can't keep going at him, but there was nothing there that said she made it home. In fact, there was evidence to suggest that she didn't make it home." There were stories she had ended up at a property in Driftwood, a rural area near Smithers, where a rough group of older men partied, one of whom apparently "had the hots for her." (Driftwood is the same rural area where someone reportedly found an article of clothing with what looked like bloodstains and called the police to collect it; the detachment had no record of the item and it was never found during the file review.) "She was not there, based on my investigation and my review and what we sent people and [they] came back with. No. She never made it," said Steve. Investigators also pursued the tip about her getting into a red sports car on the highway, the same lead that Rhonda Morgan, of the Missing Children Society of Canada, still wondered about more than twenty-five years later. "Nothing came of that either. I'm not saying it's not possible, but our evidence was not likely."

Wayne confirmed that investigators looked closely at her friends and associates, along with rumours circulating at the time, and "we're left with what we have." (Still a manager with E-Pana as

of April 2019, Wayne also answered some specific questions about
the cases and confirmed portions of what Steve had said, though he
was far more circumspect in his comments.) He said, in March
2019, that someone came forward to investigators within the previous six months who had never before spoken to police. "She gave us
some information about Delphine . . . it just confirms that she was
probably picked up by a stranger heading out of town," he said.

Steve said he came up with one possible suspect who, to his
knowledge, has not been ruled out: a man who lived in the area at the
time and had a criminal history of violence and sexual assault against
a teenaged girl. Steve said the man refused to take a polygraph test
on the advice of a lawyer, which is standard. "It's not someone I can
tell you I'm even fifty per cent sure," said Steve. "This guy was never
really hammered . . . And I want him to be hammered."

In the murder of Ramona Wilson, investigators ruled out a
suspect over whom a question mark had hung since shortly after
her body was found near the Smithers airport in 1995. They
believed she had made it to the apartments at Lake Kathlyn, just
west of town, before walking back toward the highway to head for
the dance in Hazelton. They followed up on a story that after leaving the apartment, she was walking in the direction of Smithers
when some locals left the party in their truck, "snorting off down
the road in the direction she's gone . . . and then there's a big wham,
and a screech, and our witness goes running down the road and
she's under the truck," said Steve. "No. Didn't happen." They followed up on a story that she had been at the rugby fields, a popular
party spot just north of the runway close to where her body was
found. "There's no evidence to suggest that she made it to that
party," he said. They took a hard look at some local "thugs" who
were rumoured to be involved. "They were our best suspects," said
Steve. But there was no evidence to suggest they had anything to do
with it. As far as he knows, the case is still a complete "whodunit,"
said Steve.

What happened to Roxanne Thiara, the fifteen-year-old who vanished from Prince George shortly after Ramona Wilson and was found dead near Burns Lake in August of 1994, is another mystery. For a time, investigators thought they had something, even a possible murder weapon. "We thought, this has gotta take us somewhere." It didn't.

In the murder later that year of Alishia Germaine, who was found stabbed in a schoolyard in Prince George, investigators have DNA and a suspect. They wrote up a report and took it to the Crown, but there wasn't enough to lay a charge, said Steve. "I think we got a guy who knows, but he's not dumb and he's saying what he has to say and clamming up on all the rest, so we don't have enough," he said. "One of many frustrations." They are also still looking for a female whose DNA was found at the scene. So far they haven't been able to match it to anyone.

The case of Lana Derrick, the nineteen-year-old college student who went missing from Terrace in 1995, is "an absolute mystery." Investigators took a hard look at the two men a witness described her getting into a car with—the same men police had released sketches of and then ruled out. E-Pana looked into them again. They also looked into her boyfriend, the fellow from Kitwanga who committed suicide the same night she vanished. They don't believe it was him, either.

When it comes to the investigation into Nicole Hoar's disappearance, Steve is aware of criticism that more was done in that investigation than some of the others because she was white. "It wasn't that," he said. "There was a lot more coming in about her." Unlike the earlier cases, Nicole's was widely covered in national media, and the entire region pulled together in the search effort for her. There were hundreds upon hundreds of tips, including a couple of vehicle descriptions that were promising. They had tips that pointed to Switzer and the farm at Isle Pierre, which resulted in the excavation of numerous sites on and around the property in 2009.

They found nothing. It was a case "where you thought you knew," said Steve, and "our work has said, no, you don't." They spent years trying to get Switzer to undergo a polygraph test before he finally relented. Police are no longer interested in him.

Tamara Chipman, the young mother who disappeared hitchhiking to Terrace from Prince Rupert in 2005, is one of the cases where the RCMP is fairly sure they know what happened. She had made some enemies in Prince Rupert and was trying to get home to Terrace. She made her way out of the city to where she was last seen hitchhiking east. A trio of people, two men and a woman, heard she was there and picked her up. The woman would later recount to police that one of the men began arguing with Tamara as they drove toward Terrace. He grabbed her, hit her and then strangled her to death in the car. They pulled over in a remote spot and left her there; not long afterward, the man who purportedly killed her went back to better hide the body, burying her in the forest. The police searched the woods with the witness a couple of times, bringing cadaver dogs and digging up some areas, but they never found her. The witness and the two men are now dead. "That's the best information we have now," said Wayne. "Everyone's dead, so that makes it difficult." Steve said the investigators are not certain—it's possible the witness made up the story, though it checks out as far as they could discern. "That's another that is, in my view, pretty much concluded but not with the same degree of certainty as some of the others, only because the witness, the only one alive at that time—not anymore—is iffy." Her family wants to know where she is—Gladys believes others have information about what happened. They want to bring her home.

The investigation into the 2006 murder of Aielah Saric-Auger, who was separated from her friends in Prince George and found dead in a ditch about a week later, suggested she had turned up at a friend's house late at night asking for a ride home. The friend's mother couldn't take her, and Aielah didn't want to call her mom.

She was seen heading toward what Steve called a "crack shack" across the street. "Well my God, did we spend time on that," he said. They looked into dozens of people who hung out at the house. They questioned and polygraphed a police officer who had run Aielah's name that night. "He was questioned as a possible suspect—he was a scared boy," said Steve. He was ruled out. For a long time, the drug house was the focus of the investigation, until an investigator reviewing security footage—they'd gathered up every bit of video they could from gas stations—came across her later that night. There were two sightings of her at gas stations, heading in the direction of home "considerably" later than all other information police received about her that night.

Steve has a favourite line from the TV show M*A*S*H, when Major Freedman, a psychiatrist, is questioning a soldier who arrived at the army field hospital claiming to be Jesus Christ. "Tell me, is it true that God answers all prayers?" Freedman asks the man lying in a hospital bed with a bandaged head. "Yes," the soldier replies. "Sometimes the answer is no." That sums up the cases that are still open, Steve said. "It's not that we don't care, we're not working. Sometimes, it just isn't there." If new information arises, if someone comes forward, investigators will jump on it, he said. "The ones that we don't know, they're not concluded." Investigators have worked through many persons of interest, some specific to particular cases, others who were "bad guys" in the area at the time, said Wayne. "I only hope that when some of these are solved that their names aren't in our database," he said. "It would bother me to think that we missed something."

The Canadian government under Prime Minister Stephen Harper long refused calls for a national inquiry into missing and murdered Indigenous women, repeatedly describing the violence they face as a criminal issue rather than a social and systemic one. The Conservative government refused further funding to the Native Women's Association of Canada to continue its Sisters in Spirit initiative, which had been counting the missing and murdered Indigenous women and girls across Canada. Although the government did fund Evidence to Action, a subsequent initiative, to the tune of $1.89 million over three years, the funding was provided on the condition that it not be used to conduct research into missing and murdered Indigenous women. Infamously, Harper said that the issue of missing and murdered Indigenous women "isn't really high on our radar, to be honest."

That particularly galling comment came just months after the murder of a First Nations teenager rocked the country. Tina Fontaine was fifteen years old when she left her home at Sagkeeng First Nation, Manitoba, where she'd been raised by her great-aunt, to visit her mother in Winnipeg. In Winnipeg she landed in the care of Child and Family Services. Tina went missing for brief periods several times that summer, but despite her numerous interactions with authorities, none intervened to help her beyond the CFS workers who drove her to the hotel where she was housed, unsupervised. Her body was found in the Red River on August 17, 2014, wrapped in a duvet and plastic and weighted down by rocks. The man later charged with her death was acquitted in 2018.

Indigenous issues were getting more notice among the general public, owing in part to the Idle No More movement and the ongoing hearings into residential schools conducted by the Truth and Reconciliation Commission. Tina's death galvanized public sentiment across Canada. Her family spoke out about the failures of the system that left a troubled girl grieving her father—who had recently been beaten to death—vulnerable, and how authorities charged with her protection failed her repeatedly. Social media campaigns and online petitions garnered widespread support. The Canadian Human Rights Commission requested an inquiry into how many Indigenous women were missing and murdered in Canada; street marches took place across the country. And, crucially, media covered the events, thrusting them to the front and centre of the national discourse.

A 2013 monitoring study by Journalists for Human Rights had examined coverage of Indigenous affairs in Ontario over the previous three years. *Buried Voices* found that "Indigenous people were vastly underrepresented in the media compared to other stories. Seven times less, in fact, than what should proportionally reflect the population." Although a follow-up study three years later showed little improvement in the representation of Indigenous people in Ontario media, "there [was] a major shift of tone," with far more coverage identified as positive. In an expert analysis included in the report, CBC host Duncan McCue attributed the decrease in negativity about Indigenous issues to the rise of social media and Indigenous people's skilled use of it to broadcast their stories to the world. "Indigenous voices are also responding rapidly to mainstream media coverage, holding newsrooms to account by offering critique when journalism is done poorly and rewarding news outlets that take Indigenous issues seriously by sharing widely stories that matter," wrote McCue.

Indigenous social media was beginning to influence mainstream news agendas, he noted. In 2014–15, the survey found that missing and murdered Indigenous women were the most covered Indigenous issue. "Not because the issue itself was new— Indigenous women and girls have been going missing for decades with little notice by mainstream media outlets. What changed is that Indigenous activists and community members now have the means to broadcast stories that matter to them, and that has the ability to influence political agendas, which in turn forces the mainstream media to listen." Canada's two largest daily newspapers, the *Toronto Star* and the *Globe and Mail*, launched in-depth, expensive and ongoing investigations into missing and murdered Indigenous women, as did the CBC, which also added a department dedicated to Indigenous affairs.

International organizations were also pressuring Canada over its failure to fulfill commitments under international agreements to protect human rights. Human Rights Watch's blistering 2013 report on abusive police practices received attention around the globe. In December of 2014, the Inter-American Commission on Human Rights—tasked with protecting human rights in the American hemisphere—released a report on missing and murdered Indigenous women in British Columbia and issued a call for the Canadian government to launch a full-scale inquiry and national action plan. Echoing past reports, the commission urged B.C. to immediately establish safe transportation along the Highway of Tears. And it insisted that the Harper government address violence against Indigenous women not just as a law-and-order issue but as one that takes into account contributing social and economic factors.

In 2015, the United Nations Committee on the Elimination of Discrimination against Women concluded an investigation into allegations that Indigenous women in Canada faced "grave and systemic" rights violations. The international committee found that indeed "Canada has committed a 'grave violation' of the rights of Aboriginal women by failing to promptly and thoroughly investigate the high levels of violence they suffer, including disappearances and murders." For its part, Canada accepted most of the committee's recommendations, though it denied there had been a grave violation of rights and rejected the call for a national inquiry and plan of action.

In the lead-up to the 2015 federal election, the Liberal Party of Canada, under the leadership of Justin Trudeau, ran on a platform that emphasized a new "nation-to-nation" relationship with First

Nations, Inuit and Metis people, along with reconciliation, and promised to hold a national inquiry into missing and murdered Indigenous women and girls. The Liberals swept the October election to win a majority. Within weeks, the new government had set in motion the wheels for an inquiry.

THE LAST WALK

Walkers gather outside Prince Rupert, near the place Tamara Chipman went missing, to begin the 2017 walk to national inquiry hearings in Smithers.

THE GRAND HALL at the Canadian Museum of History in Gatineau
is a cavernous space, with a six-storey wall of windows that faces
the Ottawa River and Parliament Hill. There, on August 3, 2016, the
Canadian government officially announced the National Inquiry
into Missing and Murdered Indigenous Women. "The fact that so
many Indigenous women and girls have been lost and continue
to be lost is a tragedy and a disgrace and it touches all Canadians,"
then minister for the status of women Patty Hajdu said. "We cannot move forward until we face and recognize and put a stop to this
ongoing tragedy. Until that time, our entire country will live under
its shadow and the consequences of our inaction. The journey of
the inquiry will be difficult and it will be painful. But it will also
be the unflinching gaze needed to create a country where all girls
and women are equally safe."

Marion Buller was named chief commissioner. A Cree member
of the Mistawasis First Nation in Saskatchewan, Buller was the first
Indigenous woman to serve as a provincial court judge in British
Columbia and launched the province's groundbreaking First Nations
Court. Qajaq Robinson, a lawyer raised in Nunavut with a long
resumé of work in Indigenous rights and northern communities,
was appointed as a commissioner, along with Michèle Audette, the
former president of the Native Women's Association of Canada.
Also named as commissioners were Brian Eyolfson and Marilyn
Poitras. Eyolfson, a member of Couchiching First Nation, had spent
nearly a decade working for the Human Rights Tribunal of Ontario
and before that for Aboriginal Legal Services of Toronto. Poitras
was a professor at the University of Saskatchewan's College of Law
who focused on constitutional and Aboriginal law.

For all its promise, the commission was beset with problems
almost from the outset. Its mandate, to examine systemic causes of
violence, did not explicitly include probing policing or how investigations were conducted, nor did the commission have the power
to compel police to testify or reopen cases where families were not

satisfied with an investigation. According to the Native Women's Association of Canada and the Feminist Alliance for International Action, "Since the failure of the police and the justice system to adequately protect Indigenous women and girls and to respond quickly and diligently to the violence is a central concern, and since this failure has been identified as a violation of Canada's obligations under international human rights law, the absence of explicit reference to this critical aspect of the discrimination has caused serious concern." The government responded that the terms of reference were sufficiently broad to include policing and the justice system, and the national inquiry later issued a statement clarifying that it was indeed considering police conduct and the quality of investigations.

Confusion reigned. Communication with families, media and the public was poor to non-existent. The first communications director was fired months after starting work; the second resigned. Many months after the launch of the inquiry, many families did not know how to take part—it was up to them to contact the commission, rather than the commission reaching out—and many didn't know it was happening at all. Some of those who called the commission complained that they reached a voicemail service and never received a call back. Family meetings and hearings were scheduled but cancelled at the last minute. In Prince George, family consultations set for May 2017 were abandoned the week they were to take place. Some families threatened to boycott the process altogether. By summer, the commission had held only one family hearing, in Whitehorse, and postponed others until the fall. Indigenous organizations across the country were protesting: the Assembly of First Nations passed a resolution calling on the government to "reset" the inquiry, and calls for Marion Buller's resignation echoed from numerous groups.

In July 2017, commissioner Marilyn Poitras resigned. In a statement, she wrote that she had accepted the position with the belief "the Commission was gifted with the opportunity to find a new path—one that supports healing and transformation of badly broken relationships in Canada, between Indigenous and non-Indigenous peoples." She had imagined the inquiry would "put Indigenous process first" and "seek out and rely on Indigenous laws and protocols." But after serving ten months with the commission, she wrote, she realized her vision was shared by "very few within the National Inquiry" and the "status quo colonial model of hearings" remained "the path for most."

Staff, too, went in and out through a revolving door. Along with communications directors, just a year after its start the commission had already seen the departure of its lead lawyer, a research director, health coordinator, community relations manager and an executive director whose replacement also resigned after a few months of work. More than twenty staff left in less than fourteen months, either through resignations or firings. One former staff member contended the commission was plagued by a "sick internal culture."

Garry Kerr retired from the RCMP in 2012 after thirty-two years. He moved to Vancouver Island, where he worked part-time for the City of Duncan's bylaw department. It was an easy job, "a social," he called it. On the morning of October 23, 2015, he was drinking coffee and listening to CBC Radio. There was a program on about missing and murdered Indigenous women, and he scrolled through the broadcaster's webpage devoted to the topic. He recognized a lot of the faces in the photos of victims; he'd been connected to many of the cases across British Columbia over the years. There were so many. It made him sick. "And then there was Alberta's picture, and it just really hit home. It's one of the investigations, it always really stuck with me." He read the short synopsis about Alberta on the website. Along the left side of the page, there were the words: "CBC needs you. Do you have information on an unsolved

case involving missing or murdered indigenous women and girls?"
He didn't think about it. He just clicked on the email link and
typed out a few words, telling the broadcaster the name of the man
he suspected of killing Alberta. "I hit Send, went back to my socia-
ble, drinking coffee," Garry said.

He got a reply later that day from Connie Walker, an investigative journalist with CBC in Toronto, asking him to call. "Oh shit,
what did I just do?" Garry thought. But curiosity got the best of him.
They spoke on the phone; Garry hedged for a bit before telling her,
"I was the lead investigator on it." Over the next little while, they
stayed in touch. He was soul-searching, wondering how much—if
anything—he should say. He had to be careful about releasing
information on an active investigation. Particularly sensitive is
what's called "hold-back evidence"—facts that only the killer would
know and that can be used to weed out false confessions and confirm the person responsible. Garry talked to contacts in the RCMP
to find out if anything was being done on the file. "I wouldn't have
done it if the case was five years old. I wouldn't have done it if the
case was twenty years old. But it was almost thirty years old, and
I knew nothing was being done on the file," Garry said. "That's why
I went forward."

Connie Walker and CBC producer Marnie Luke flew out to
meet with Garry a few months later. He walked them through the
case from his perspective. It was "almost like a full-time job" for
months, he recalled. The CBC team travelled to Prince Rupert,
where they visited the spot Alberta had been found and spoke with
some of her family and friends. They met with Claudia Williams,
Alberta's sister, in Vancouver. Almost a year to the day after Garry
sent that first email, CBC launched a podcast, *Missing and
Murdered: Who Killed Alberta Williams?* It garnered an instant following across the country.

Within the police community, some people were very upset
about what Garry did. Some were downright pissed off. Rick Ross,

who remained close friends with Garry, answered questions from CBC, but he didn't share his notebooks. "It can jeopardize an ongoing investigation, that would be my concern. That would be my only concern. It's not that I want to cover up for anybody that ever done it," he said. "I told Garry, I said, 'You'll probably be defence witness number one.'" But Garry said, should the case ever get to trial, he's confident he can explain himself and his actions.

The airing of the podcast reignited Alberta's case; Wayne Clary told CBC the investigation was "very active." The podcast put the pressure on, said Steve Pranzl, and investigators tried to capitalize on it. "We had meetings discussing it and what should we do about this? Like, [Garry] said things that we're not at liberty to say, maybe it will have an effect. So we weren't blind to it, and we weren't inactive. But it didn't produce anything."

After the podcast came out, Garry spoke with Claudia Williams for the first time in twenty-seven years. He was really nervous before the phone call. "I didn't know whether she'd yell and scream at me," he said. Yet it was the complete opposite. Claudia said she was grateful he had emailed the CBC and worked with them on the podcast; she told him that all the family wanted was answers. "It was great to connect with Garry, who wants to see Alberta's murder solved as much as our family," Claudia later said. Garry wasn't too bothered about what some of his former colleagues thought in the first place, but after talking to Claudia, he felt a lot better. It had been the right thing to do. He'd do it again.

The water was like glass, reflecting cedar trees and the pale blue sky, soft with morning mists that had yet to burn off. Vicki Hill, Mary Jane's daugther, was smiling, standing at the rest area beside Oliver Lake, where walkers had gathered after marching from Prince Rupert together. "I'm just really surprised with this," she said. It was the first time Vicki had walked the highway. She wore a T-shirt with a photo of her mother on the front; a government employees' union had paid to have the white shirts printed with pictures and particulars of the women and girls who had died along the highway. When Gladys Radek gave Vicki the shirt that morning, as everyone assembled in the restaurant of the Moby Dick Inn for breakfast, Vicki cried.

It was September 21, 2017, and two commissioners from the national inquiry were to preside over hearings starting in Smithers in five days. There was an electric feeling of history being made that morning at the Moby Dick, as a couple dozen people prepared to set out. At the rest area beside Oliver Lake, so many in attendance had been walking the highways for years—decades, even—fighting for this inquiry, this recognition. Tamara Chipman's family was there. Vicki came with her fifteen-year-old daughter, Zoey. Wanda Good, Lana's cousin, was there. Bernie Williams had arrived from Vancouver with other frontline workers and activists, many of whom had walked to the symposium in 2006. People's phones buzzed with calls from commission staff making hasty arrangements for accommodation, transport and meetings at the upcoming session in Smithers. Michèle Audette, one of the commissioners and a former president of the Native Women's Association of Canada, would be joining the walkers along the way.

It was the beginning of Gladys's last walk. She had done six of them in the twelve years since Tamara went missing. She'd sworn that the previous one would be her last—she was in her sixties, had undergone heart surgery and was tired out. But Elder Mabel Todd, who had walked many of the miles alongside her, told her that there was one more she had to do. This one.

Stephanie Radek, Gladys's daughter, divided the highway into ten-kilometre sections and assigned them to teams of walkers, each with a driver to follow behind for safety. I teamed up with Vicki and Zoey, and we piled into the car and drove east, passing other walking teams, to our stretch. Mother and daughter got out. I turned on the hazard lights, and they began to walk.

They walked a long time that day along the stretch of highway between Prince Rupert and Terrace that sits on a narrow shelf wedged between the mountains and the river. Creeks fed by the last of the glaciers still clinging to the mountaintops flowed down the steep, forested hills that plunge into the water, and out on the Skeena River, the sun shone down on the ripples and swirls formed by currents pushing against the sea. When we stopped to rest and wait for other walkers, Vicki stood for a long time on the highway, her face up to the sky, watching the clouds. "Those look like angel wings up there," she said.

Vicki Hill waits for other walkers along Highway 16 beside the Skeena River.

The first night, the Kasiks Wilderness Resort, roughly halfway between Prince Rupert and Terrace, once again opened its doors to feed and house the walkers, as it had done in 2006. The cook, June, made an enormous dinner—three types of lasagna, salads, desserts—and walkers occupied all the rooms at the resort, with a handful camping out on couches in the lounge.

On the second day, as Vicki and Zoey walked, staff from Terrace's CFNR—Canada's First Nations Radio—drove up and down the highway passing out coffee. Gladys, her car plastered just like her previous van had been with photos of the missing and murdered women and girls, boys and men, zoomed past, honking her horn. Michèle Audette was in the back seat.

That afternoon, the walkers gathered again at a pullout just west of Terrace before marching together for the last few hundred metres of highway to Kitsumkalum Hall, where a feast was waiting for them. Tamara's family led the way, Tom and Christine holding the same banner they'd carried in 2006. As they started walking slowly toward the hall, the sound of the "Women's Warrior Song" and drums filled the misty air that mingled with the tears upon so many faces. That evening in the hall, Gladys told those gathered that her walks had never been easy. "When you're walking on those highways, you feel the spirits of those women," she said. "But we did get our inquiry."

When Vicki and I first met, in May 2017, we had visited the cemetery hoping to locate Mary Jane's grave and found she didn't have a headstone. We had also driven out on Highway 16 from Prince Rupert to see if we could locate the place where her body was found, based on scant descriptions in newspaper clippings. After that first meeting, Vicki and I worked together to find more information. I helped her submit an Access to Information request to the RCMP asking for its documentation related to Mary Jane; Mounties who had previously visited Vicki had told her she could do so, but Vicki, like most people, didn't know how the process worked. The RCMP's Access to Information office in Ottawa replied on May 25, 2017, with a standard response: a search for relevant records was underway and it would respond, as required by law, within thirty days. (If institutions require a longer period of time, they must notify the person making the request.) When, by late July, Vicki had still not received anything, we tried a different route. I wrote to the BC Coroners Service.

All deaths in the province that are "unnatural, unexpected, unexplained or unattended" are reported to the coroner's office for investigation. Sometimes, the coroner opts for an inquest, a formal court proceeding in front of a jury to review the circumstances of a death. This happens whenever the coroner "determines that it would be beneficial in: addressing community concern about a death, assisting in finding information about the deceased or circumstances around a death and/or drawing attention to a cause of death if such awareness can prevent future deaths." At the inquest of Mary Jane Hill, the jury found that she had died of bronchitis and bronchial pneumonia but added, "We further find that the death of Mary Jane Hill [was] a result of manslaughter." Vicki had obtained the one-page finding several years before, but it contained no explanation of how the jury had come to that conclusion, or what it meant by manslaughter, though one could deduce that those six members of the public believed someone had left Mary Jane out there to die.

I explained to Andy Watson, the media contact at the BC Coroners Service, that we were looking for whatever documentation might accompany the finding. The coroner's office was helpful from the start. In little more than a month, it mailed a transcript of the inquest proceedings. Vicki planned to read it that night in Terrace in advance of her testimony at the national inquiry; Gladys asked me to stay with her and Zoey so that she wouldn't be alone. It was going to be difficult; Vicki was apprehensive, and so was I. I had read the document already, and it was heartbreaking.

Thirty-nine years earlier, a man named Peter Hunt went for a drive on a Sunday afternoon. It was March 26, 1978, a cold and rainy day, but Hunt and his fiancée nonetheless headed out of Prince Rupert in his pickup. They were, he would later recall, "enjoying going down the road . . . off the beaten track just enjoying the wilderness." They drove east along Highway 16, over the Rainbow Summit and across the Green River close to where it flows into the Skeena. There was a side road there. "I decided why not turn down it," Hunt later said, "so we did." Not far in, his fiancée spotted the body.

Hunt got out to look, wondering if someone needed help. But he could tell the person was not alive. She lay perhaps a metre off the side road, face down in a stream, a clump of leaves resting against her back. There were no clothes or personal items with her. There were welts on the back of her legs and blisters on the bottom of her feet.

They drove back toward Prince Rupert, to the home of his fiancée's parents—her father was the regional commanding officer of the RCMP. Supt. Howard Golard then called the General Investigation Section, and he and two officers drove to Green River, with Hunt showing them the way.

More RCMP members arrived and began combing the area, taking photographs, looking for evidence. The local pathologist, Dr. Ivor Hopkin, arrived about 8 P.M. and documented a young native woman lying face down in a small gulley. Water ran over her hair, though her nose and mouth were not submerged, suggesting that she had not drowned. There was pus coming from her nose, leading the doctor to surmise that she had had an infection. There were no obvious signs of trauma—no stab wounds, bullet holes, severe cuts or broken bones. But she was a considerable distance from the highway. The medical examiner told the inquest he didn't think it was possible she had fallen down there.

A special orderly at Prince Rupert's hospital, Robert Smith, drove out to pick up the body, which was accompanied by Const.

James Wakely. When they removed the body bag at the hospital, Smith, who had worked at the hospital for twenty years, knew right away that it was Mary Jane Hill. He had seen her at the hospital many times, mainly for incidents involving beatings and alcohol, he later told the inquest. "She'd be in a drunken state and be beat up," he said, "usually [that] was the only reason why she was brought to the hospital."

A doctor did a cursory examination, determining that, at most, Mary Jane had been dead for thirty-nine hours, though due to a number of factors, it was probably much less, about twelve. The next day, Mary Jane's husband, Oscar Hill, identified the body. Dr. Hopkin conducted a more in-depth examination, noting scratches on her lower legs, the same abrasions that Hunt had seen. "It could be that the body had been dragged or moved in the wrong way," he said, "and after talking to the police, I decided that it would be better because I felt the circumstances were very suspicious . . . if the body went to Vancouver." The Prince Rupert hospital did not have access to forensics or a crime lab, and Hopkin wanted to ensure nothing was missed. The lack of obvious trauma, he said, made the cause of death unclear. He made arrangements for Mary Jane to be sent to the Royal Columbian Hospital in New Westminster. Police were treating the death as suspicious, a possible homicide.

That Monday, officers from the General Investigation Section and the detachment's staff sergeant returned to the area where Mary Jane had been found. About eighteen kilometres outside Prince Rupert, they found a red coat and a grey sweater that, they would later learn, belonged to Mary Jane. Nearby, they also found a light-coloured bra. Over the course of that day and the next, officers found a long off-white overcoat. Farther down the highway, there was a brown shoe in the ditch, and five or six kilometres past that, another. They found a plastic bottle holding several anti-seizure pills, with Mary Jane's name on the label—she was epileptic. All the items were found on the right-hand side of the road heading out of the city, as if they had been tossed from the passenger's side window of a vehicle.

In Prince Rupert, at the intersection of Fraser Street and Sixth Street, just behind the Belmont Hotel, the sidewalk crosses the hollow of a vacant lot, creating a secluded area underneath where people frequently gathered to drink. There, police found a pair of blue slacks and a black purse that belonged to Mary Jane, along with a few empty liquor bottles. Police got fingerprints from some of the bottles but weren't able to match them to anyone.

One of the officers later told the coroner's inquest that he spent nine days investigating—nine "24 hour days, you might say." Patrols scoured both sides of the highway and the canine unit was brought in from Terrace. In places, officers searched boulder fields rock by rock. But they found nothing further.

Const. James Wakely took Mary Jane's body to Vancouver and stayed with her through the autopsy. He also took exhibits to the crime laboratory for further examination. Those exhibits included hair samples, fingernail scrapings, swabs and hair pins, among other items.

Dr. Edwin Shiau, a pathologist at the Royal Columbian Hospital who routinely conducted some two hundred autopsies a year, found "a fair number" of small reddish spots on Mary Jane, but they did not form a "specific injury pattern" such as might be left by fighting or the use of a weapon. He thought it "not likely" the abrasions were caused by dragging her, because they did not form the kind of line usually consistent with hauling a body over uneven ground.

In her lungs, he found inflammation indicating she had pneumonia when she died, as well as scars suggesting previous bouts of pneumonia. Pending the results of toxicology tests, the doctor concluded that Mary Jane had died of pneumonia, possibly brought on by a seizure. Epileptic seizures could, he said, be brought on by stimulant drugs or by circumstances that were exciting or upsetting, including fear and exposure. After epileptic attacks, people sometimes go into a drowsy state and, if unattended, might inhale fluids that will cause pneumonia. Pneumonia could also set in if someone was unconscious from drinking, he said, and thus unable to cough up fluid dripping into their lungs. It could kill a person in a matter of hours. The toxicology report showed that Mary Jane had no alcohol in her body, nor any illicit drugs. All that was detected was a trace amount of her epilepsy medication, indicating she hadn't taken it for some time, probably a couple of days, before she died.

Const. Wakely continued to try to determine how Mary Jane had ended up out there in the bush, alone. In the following days, he logged seventy-eight hours of overtime on top of his eight-hour shifts. Then he stopped claiming the extra hours because it was getting too expensive. But he kept working on it, putting in what he estimated to be a hundred hours of his own time. At the time of the coroner's inquest in June, a couple of months later, he was still looking for answers. After the inquest, Wakely told the local newspaper that he was not giving up, that whoever played a part in Mary Jane's death was going to be brought to justice.

But that would not be what came to pass.

The afternoon was warm and sunny when the vehicles turned onto the short road leading to the golf and country club on the edge of Smithers. Drivers parked along the shoulders and people gathered, some in traditional regalia, others holding banners and placards. The families of most of those lost along the Highway of Tears were there. Around them, reporters from all the big news outlets—CBC, APTN, the Canadian Press—milled about. The crowd began to march, about sixty people walking slowly behind Gladys's car as she led the way to the inquiry for which she had fought for more than a decade. She sobbed the whole way.

They passed the golf course, the Harley-Davidson shop and the swimming pool as traffic lined up behind the marchers and the sounds of voices and drums rose in the air. Some walkers cried; others laughed. The procession turned onto Main Street and slowly proceeded past the shops and boutiques and accountants' offices. Some people stopped; others hovered inside doors and windows to watch. Some passersby fell in behind the walkers as the sound of drums echoed off the alpine façades. The march looped in front of the courthouse at the end of Main Street before making its way to the Dze L K'ant Friendship Centre, where everyone gathered in a large circle.

Two of the inquiry's commissioners—Michèle Audette and Marion Buller—stood beside family members, who stood beside hereditary chiefs, town officials, politicians, RCMP officers. Tears streamed down Gladys's cheeks as she spoke about Tamara, about the years of fighting for this inquiry, about the justice everyone still needed to find. As she struggled to speak, Brenda Wilson went to hug her.

"Brenda, we did it," said Gladys. "We did it."

The national inquiry sessions in Smithers were only the second to take place since its launch the previous September. Disorganization was obvious—and painful for families. The inquiry was responsible for arranging accommodations for families, yet Vicki and Zoey didn't know where they were to stay as they walked to Smithers. Vicki didn't know when she was slated to speak until late the night before.

On Tuesday, the hundred or so chairs set out in the Dze L K'ant Friendship Centre were nearly filled by nine in the morning. Vicki was scheduled to be the first person sharing her story with the commission, and she was nervous. But she held herself together, and when she entered the hall, she looked firm and resolute. Vicki and Zoey sat near the front, in the section reserved for family, as reporters and camera operators set up in a line facing the front of the room, where bright blankets with well wishes—"You got this" and "One love"—partly encircled the chairs for family members and commissioners. Gladys and the other walkers sat with Vicki as the inquiry staff explained the process and supports available. Vicki was shuddering, and Lorna Brown, Tamara's aunt, leaned in close, stroking her hair. Then Vicki took a deep breath, stood up and walked to the front of the room, Zoey by her side.

In answer to gentle questions from inquiry lawyer Breen Ouellette, Vicki told the commissioners about her mom—about how she was found naked on the side of the highway outside Prince Rupert, about how she left behind four children, including Vicki, just six months old. She told them about how she was raised in Gitsegukla until she was thirteen. "There was so much abuse and stuff going on, nobody would believe me," said Vicki. "I don't want to talk about it." She told the commission about how she began to search for answers about what had happened to her mom, about support workers helping her comb the archives of the Prince Rupert library to find old newspaper clippings. She spoke about meeting with E-Pana a few years earlier and being told that her mother's case "doesn't fit the criteria." Breen had her read the response to the Access to Information request we had made in May that promised a reply within thirty days. "It's now September 2017. Have you received anything yet?" he asked. "No," Vicki replied. (She got a call from the RCMP shortly afterward, telling her the information was on the way.)

About halfway through her testimony, after she took a break to compose herself, Vicki's voice grew louder, more assured. "I'm not only speaking for my mom; I'm speaking for the rest of the families. I understand what they're going through. I feel the pain, I feel their hurt, I can see it. I'm not afraid. I have my rights, too. I do. And things have got to change no matter what," she said. She pointed

(Top) Mary Jane Hill stands on the bridge in Gingolx. Her daughter, Vicki, was in her twenties before she learned that her mother was dead. (Bottom) Vicki Hill and Zoey Hill-Harris take a rest during the 2017 walk to the national inquiry in Smithers.

out that there was still no cell service along vast stretches of the highway corridor and few options for transportation; if Vicki was to return by bus to Prince Rupert after the hearing, she would have to catch the Greyhound at 3 A.M. She had called for a cab the previous night, she said, only to be told there weren't any running until 6 A.M. She wanted transportation and cell service to be developed and cameras to be placed along the highway similar to those already in place to monitor weather and road conditions. She wanted answers. She wanted justice. "You can't imagine what my mother went through, or the rest of the women, how they ended up the way they were," Vicki said. "We're the voice for them. Are we ever going to find the answers? Are we ever going to get what we want?"

Tamara Chipman's family was supposed to speak after lunch that afternoon, but there was a scheduling conflict and it was pushed to 3 P.M. Then later. It was 4:30 before they took their place before the commissioners. Tom's face was grief stricken as he told the commission about how Tamara's phone calls stopped coming, how he realized that something was wrong.

Gladys talked about the search in Vancouver for Tamara, about the walk in 2006 to the symposium and how few of its recommendations had been implemented, about the other six walks she undertook in the coming years. "We love her, we really, really miss her. And we know that there's not just one Tamara that's missing. We know there's hundreds. We know there's thousands. And I think that losing Tamara has kind of lit a fire in us, in our hearts," said Gladys. "We've heard from so many other families the need for justice."

Stephanie Radek told the commissioners how involvement with the foster care system heightens the vulnerability of children and how few resources are available in northern British Columbia to support those overcoming addiction. Partway through her testimony, the inquiry lawyer pointed out the time. Dinner was at six, and it was 5:45, she noted. "I know that people are sort of assessing and balancing priorities here," she said, "but I don't want to take away from your prime time." After fifteen years of searching for Tamara, of trying to find justice for their family and all the other families, the Chipmans had just over an hour and a half to share their story with the inquiry for which they had fought so long and hard.

Despite not being an official part of the proceedings, the RCMP maintained a presence that was distressing for some families. On the first day of hearings, uniformed officers stood at the back of the room by the doors. They had been invited by the Wet'suwet'en hereditary chiefs, but some families felt intimidated and afraid to voice their concerns about policing. Wayne Clary and Ron Palta, investigators from E-Pana, lingered outside the proceedings. Victim services had asked them to attend to meet with families in the days leading up to and during the inquiry session. Some family members had requested meetings in hopes of learning more about their loved ones' cases. Still others were drawn into meetings without understanding what was going on.

Roddy Sampare, Virginia's brother from Gitsegukla, told the commission of one such instance. The day before the family's testimony, they had been called to a meeting with the RCMP investigators, the first time the family had spoken to the police in years. Their last interaction had been when an officer collected DNA from them during the excavation of the Pickton farm, in case Virginia's remains were found there. During the meeting, police told the family that a former chief counsellor from the village had reported, in the days after Virginia vanished, finding footprints near the river believed to be hers. No one had ever told the family that information. "We didn't even know about it," said Virginia's sister-in-law Violet. "So this is something that really, really shocked us yesterday and was very upsetting to find out . . . To me, that's assuming that our sister went in the river and drowned. And they never, ever told the family that."

At the meeting, the officers read from files that they would not share with the family; Violet and Roddy were allowed to look at a piece of paper containing a synopsis of the investigation, but they were refused a copy. The inquiry lawyer asked Roddy if they felt they'd had enough time to read the paper and get the answers they needed. "No, we didn't," said Roddy. The lawyer asked if they felt they were adequately prepared for the meeting and the information they'd receive. "No, we weren't," said Roddy. The lawyer asked him how he felt, overall, about the meeting. "Well, I find it very surprising that they contact us so close to the hearing, and how they knew that we were going to be part of the hearing."

When Ted and Laura Morris addressed the inquiry about their sister, Pauline, they said they'd been called to a meeting that morning. It was at 8:15 A.M., and they'd only arrived in Smithers at three, but they went, thinking they would be meeting with an inquiry lawyer. It was the RCMP. Just hours before they were to appear at the commission, an officer reading off what they believe was a coroner's report on his phone told them Pauline's death had been ruled an accidental drowning—the first time they'd heard this—and that she had had a blood alcohol level of 0.11. They had never known her to drink; she was only fourteen. "I just found it strange that she [would] even have alcohol in her system, because the only way she'd have it [is] if they forced her to. That's what I figured," said Ted. "They say in every death they have to have a thorough investigation, but if that was the case they would have went after more."

Claudia Williams travelled to Smithers to speak to the commission about the murder of Alberta. She had not seen Garry Kerr in nearly thirty years, but she asked him to come along as her support person. Although they were on the same flight from Vancouver, they didn't get a chance to speak until they arrived at the tiny Smithers airport. A CBC News crew was there to record the moment; so were Claudia's son, daughter-in-law and grandsons, who came to surprise her for her birthday. As luggage began trundling around the conveyor belt in the airport, Garry entered from the runway, followed shortly by Claudia. The two did a few double takes before shaking hands and then hugging. "I'm so glad you're here," Claudia said. "I'm so pleased. You don't even know what this means."

"It means a lot to me, too," Garry said. He wished, he said, that he could turn back the clock. He wished he'd had more of a bond with the family, that he'd nurtured that relationship better. It was a thorough investigation, he believed, but there were so many barriers between the police and the family; if those hadn't been there, and more information had been shared, it might have helped. It might have led to charges. "Hopefully, this is maybe one small step, albeit thirty years later," he said.

The next afternoon, Claudia sat before the commission, her son on one side, Garry on the other. Claudia had prepared a written statement; she wanted to be careful not to say anything that could jeopardize the newly active investigation into her sister's murder. She told the story, and she urged people with information to come forward. "It shouldn't have taken a podcast for people to come forward. It shouldn't have taken a podcast at all," she said.

She asked Garry to speak. There is one thing, he said, that is absolutely crucial in investigations: trust. When Alberta went missing and after she was found, there were many things the police didn't know, he said. People hadn't trusted them enough to talk to them. It may not have solved the case, but it "would have truly made a difference."

On the Monday morning before the inquiry was to start in Smithers, Lucy Smith asked me to come to a meeting with her in Burns Lake. I had met Lucy the previous year, during the 2016 Cleansing the Highway Walk, when she and her brothers shared the story of their sister Beverly Williams. I went back to Burns Lake later to talk to them further, but they knew few details of what had happened to her. She went missing in 1985 and was found murdered in 1986. A man named Thomas Cunningham had subsequently been convicted in relation to her death, but the family wasn't sure what he'd been charged with or whether he was still in prison or the conviction had been overturned. Lucy had long been trying to get the records from the trial to find out what happened; she wasn't successful. "None of those details were given to us," Lucy told the inquiry.

"There was nobody telling us what happened, where she was, what happened before. We didn't know anything like that. The cops didn't tell us nothing." But in advance of the inquiry, a victim services worker had offered the family the chance to sit down with the RCMP to find out the basics of what had happened, and they'd agreed.

RCMP Staff Sgt. Wayne Clary, beside Brenda and Matilda Wilson, addresses supporters at the 2017 memorial walk for Ramona.

Lucy and I met at an A&W. Soon after, Breen Ouellette from the inquiry arrived, along with a support worker who would be observing. Lucy was nervous. It had been more than thirty years. She was afraid of what she would find out, and she was afraid to meet the police, but she needed to know. We drove to the hotel where the meeting was to take place and found our way to a small room on the second floor, with more than a dozen people jammed inside. Her brothers, Herbert and Norman, were there, along with Willie Williams, their father, and Rita, Beverly's daughter.

E-Pana investigators Wayne Clary and Ron Palta walked them through the case, reading from a summary put together from old police files. They handed the double-sided page to Rita when she requested it, and she passed it to Lucy. Lucy read until she got to the part about how her sister's body was found and crumpled into sobs. That was when Ron asked for the paper back, explaining that the police couldn't give the family any documentation. "We're just making sure we're giving you information in a manner that's not too hurtful here," he said. But, as Lucy would later tell the commissioners, she didn't have enough time to read the entire paper. After thirty years of not knowing what happened to her sister, she still had questions.

The next day, Beverly Williams's family gathered in the Elders Room in the entrance hall of the Dze L K'ant Friendship Centre and donned their regalia. They have another family member, Olivia Williams, who is missing. Given where she lived—the Downtown Eastside—and when she disappeared, in 1996, police suspect she was a victim of Robert Pickton, though no evidence has been found.

When the family entered the hall, everyone stood. They sat in front of the commissioners, Beverly's ninety-eight-year-old father, her brothers, her sister and her daughter. Partway through the proceedings, Herbert fetched a chair and placed it between the family and the commissioners, facing the room. "That's my sister," he said. "Now I feel a little better. My sister is sitting with us."

Beverly Williams was born on May 6, 1953, the daughter of Willie and Mary Williams. She was a happy girl. She spent a lot of time with her grandmother, a hereditary chief, and was deeply connected to her Wet'suwet'en culture and traditions. As a woman, she was given a traditional name and became a hereditary chief. Beverly worked hard, "like a man," at the sawmill and farm she ran with her common-law husband. Lucy remembers going to Beverly's place when she was ten or eleven years old, helping her older sister move hay. Beverly could fling the fifty- or sixty-pound bales like they were air. She loved baseball, playing throughout the region, and competed in logger sports at local fairs. She adored her mother and father, and checked in on them often, helping out, driving them around. "She always dreaded the day that they were going to leave us," said Lucy. "She never wanted to be without them." No one thought it would be her to go first. She was the rock of her family, the person everyone relied on and admired. "Everybody loved her," said her daughter, Rita, who was only four years old when Beverly went missing. "Anybody that I meet they just kind of melt down and say, 'Oh, your mum. Oh, she was loved. We loved your mum.'"

On Friday, May 3, 1985, Beverly picked up her two sons from their father's place, near Houston, and drove them to her parents' home on the reserve in Burns Lake. She was living with Willie and Mary at the time and had the boys for a visit; she was due to take them back on Sunday. Early the next morning, she asked her parents to watch the kids. Rita remembered that day, sitting on the couch up against the big front window of her grandmother's house, her mom standing beside her red station wagon in the driveway. The kids wanted to go with her, but their grandmother had locked the door to keep them at home. "That was the last memory I have," said Rita.

Willie Williams reported Beverly missing on Tuesday, May 7. Some family members came across her car in Prince George the next day and waited by it for her to return. Instead, a man did, telling the family she'd headed for Vancouver and left her vehicle with him for safekeeping. Her family and the police were immediately suspicious. The man, Thomas Cunningham, was questioned several times, and the car was searched for evidence. Meanwhile, Beverly's family kept looking for her. Willie and Mary didn't drive, but a community member, Charlie Joseph, took them out, day after

day, week after week, month after month, to search for their daughter. They searched from Burns Lake to Vanderhoof to Prince
George all that summer and into the fall, through the winter and
on to the spring.

One day in April, almost eleven months to the day Beverly
went missing, the RCMP told her family that Beverly had been
found. Her body had been dumped in an old gravel pit about
ninety-five kilometres east of her parents' home. A dog had found
part of her and brought it home, leading police to search the area,
where they found clothing—her beloved baseball jacket—and her
ID. The cause of death, determined by an autopsy, was blunt force
trauma to her head.

It was another two years before Thomas Cunningham was
charged with manslaughter in her death. At the same time, he
was charged with second-degree murder in the killing of a man in
Port Coquitlam. Beverly's parents testified at the trial, but neither
spoke English fluently, and they and the rest of the family didn't
understand everything that was going on. Cunningham was found
guilty in 1989 and sent to prison. He was released on parole in 2000.
He has never admitted to killing Beverly and suggested at parole
hearings that it was someone else. But the investigation is closed,
the matter resolved as far as the police and courts are concerned.
But not for Beverly's family. They are still looking for the truth.

In the months and years after Beverly went missing, her
brother Herbert nearly drank himself to death. But he eventually
turned his life around, going to work for the church and dedicating
himself to helping others. He does it for her, he said. Her daughter,
Rita, was raised outside her culture, cut off from her family. She
was taught that First Nations people are "devil worshippers" and
unworthy. "As a little girl you feel lost. I still do today," she said.
"This is my family, I shouldn't feel that way about them." Her
brothers, Beverly's sons, took her death really hard. They are homeless and struggling with addiction. "They never resolved in their

(From top left) A cross erected on the side of Highway 16 where Aielah Saric-Auger was found; the grave of Ramona Wilson; Wanda Good at a memorial cross placed for Alberta Williams; and Tamara Chipman's family marching into Terrace in 2017.

mind, in their hearts, what happened to their mother, and that hurt is carried on down," said Lucy. "How far is it going to go? How far is it going to go before it stops?"

The family spoke for hours that day at the inquiry, and when it was all over, Lucy went outside for a cigarette. "That hurt so much," she said, sobbing. "That hurt so much." She took a shuddering breath. "Please, please, don't let that hurt be in vain."

A SAFER PLACE

Brenda Wilson and Gladys Radek embrace outside
the national inquiry in Smithers in 2017.

VICKI HILL DID NOT know it at the time, but when she began to speak publicly about her mother, the RCMP took notice. Shortly after the national inquiry sessions in Smithers in September 2017, Vicki received a response to the information request she had submitted the previous spring. The RCMP released hundreds of pages of documents, which included internal correspondence about how to respond to Vicki's public appeals that had started a decade before. According to those documents, E-Pana had tried to find the original file of the investigation into Mary Jane's death. No one could locate it. Investigators then "took another approach to see if [they] could glean enough information to conduct a proper review without the original file" and contacted the officers who had worked on the case in 1978 to request any documentation they still had. Some submitted notes, and others relied on their memories. The notes indicate that investigators felt the circumstances were suspicious, but that they could not find evidence of foul play.

RCMP correspondence in 2008 noted that the inquest's finding of manslaughter together with bronchitis and bronchopneumonia seemed "quite conflicting." However, it posited the verdict likely came from factors such as how Mary Jane was found. "We think the jury was considering these facts in finding that there may have been an offender involved in this matter. Was she possibly left there after a[n] epileptic attack or high fever resulting in exposure and, ultimately, her death? If so, was the offender that left her there negligent to the point of manslaughter? Again we can only speculate on the jury's conclusions. As HILL may have died of causes other than that of an attack by an unknown person(s), her case does not fall into our mandate."

The national inquiry provided modest funding for families to pursue activities that would help them to heal. Vicki used the money to purchase a headstone. When Vicki passes away, she wants to be laid to rest beside her mom. She wants to finally be with her.

On a soft grey day in late August of 2017, four men unloaded a headstone from a red pickup truck and carried it over the grass of the cemetery in Gitanyow. One of the men was Francis Williams. Francis and Claudia had fundraised for many months to cover the cost of headstones for Alberta and her sister Pamela. It had been twenty-eight years since Alberta had vanished from downtown Prince Rupert, and finally her siblings were able to lay her to rest, beside Pamela and close to her parents. Claudia and the family stood beside the graves as Francis and the others brought over the gleaming marble that bore an inset photo of Alberta and an inscription that read:

> There Is No Death, The Stars Go Down,
> To Rise Upon Some Other Shore,
> And Bright in Heavens Crown,
> They Shine Forever More

Earlier that summer, Francis had erected a cross near where Alberta was found, just west of the Tyee overpass. The podcast and the renewed attention it generated had brought a wave of hope to Alberta's family, but as time passed without charges or resolution, disappointment set in all over again. Francis would not attend the national inquiry that fall; he didn't see the point of rehashing Alberta's story and the family's frustration before the commission. He told Claudia that now, with the headstones, their sisters could rest. That's what the headstones were for. But it's hard, he said.

Roddy Sampare told the story of his sister Virginia to Commissioner Marion Buller in a college classroom in Smithers. He told the commission of how, when their mother was diagnosed with cancer and given a week to live, the family flew her home for her final days. She held on for three months. She was waiting for Virginia. Almost fifty years after Virginia vanished, the family is still searching for her, still waiting for her to come home. On Virginia's sixty-fifth birthday, her sister Winnie made her cupcakes and brought them to where she was last seen. Winnie told Virginia that they had not forgotten her. She told Virginia that they never would.

Lana Derrick's aunt Sally Gibson still searches, too. Each year when the snow melts, she finds herself scanning roadsides looking for her niece. And Marge still hears her daughter calling out to her when she's at the mall or walking down the street, still catches glimpses of Lana from the corner of her eye. She waits for a daughter she knows will never come home.

Mary Beaubien thinks every day of her sister as she raises her children and grandchildren, who Delphine never got the chance to know. In the nearly thirty years since Delphine disappeared, not a day has gone by when Mary did not wish she had more time with her little sister.

Audrey and Aielah were in a car accident when Aielah was little. They hit black ice and spun into a ditch. Aielah struck her head on the dashboard and was momentarily unconscious. Audrey thought her youngest child was dead. When Aielah came to, she said to her mom, "Look, I think there's an angel up there." Audrey looked up to the clouds her daughter pointed to; she saw it, too.

Afterward, Aielah brought it up sometimes, asking her big brother if she would ever have angel wings. They watched the movie *Ghost*, in which a murdered man returns as a spirit to exact revenge for his death and protect his love. That's what Tim would do. "If I ever get murdered, I will stick around and make it right," he told Aielah. She said, "I don't want to be a ghost, I want to be an angel." He told her she already was. "I don't have wings so no, I'm not," she replied. "Well, you just have to grow them," he said.

Darrell remembers seeing his family together—Aielah, Audrey and nephews who have since died. He hopes they are together now. "I believe everything is done for a reason on this earth to us. I don't know. It's hard to say because we're not God. We're just people. We just live the lives that we're given, that's all.

"She was brave, she was so brave. She was full of life. I miss that. I really miss that."

Ray Michalko passed away in 2017. He is sorely missed by families who describe him as a beacon of hope in a difficult time. "He keeps me grounded, I don't know where I would be without him," said Claudia Williams not long before his death. "He gives me hope." He was, said Gladys Radek, the only person she trusted with information. He did so much for so many along the Highway of Tears, and he is remembered with love and gratitude.

Girls and women continue to go missing along the Highway of Tears. In 2017, Frances Brown vanished while picking mushrooms north of Smithers. The next year, eighteen-year-old Jessica Patrick went missing from Smithers and was found dead not far from town. Shortly afterward, Cindy Martin disappeared from Hazelton. Indigenous women and girls continue to go missing and be murdered across Canada, too. Yet, as a May 2019 APTN story notes, there is still no database to track cases, and numbers have not been updated since the RCMP's 2015 report.

In March 2018, the national inquiry asked the federal government for an additional two years and $50 million on top of its existing $53.8 million budget to complete its work. The government denied the request, granting instead a six-month extension. In response, Chief Commissioner Marion Buller accused the government of putting politics "ahead of the safety of our women and girls."

Gladys moved home to Terrace in 2017 to be closer to her family. She worked as a support person for families throughout the national inquiry, as well as an adviser to the commission. The walk in 2017 was to be her last, but when the inquiry released its final report in June of 2019, she crossed the country once again to be there. This time, she drove.

The final report, called *Reclaiming Power and Place*, concluded that the violence against Indigenous women, girls and 2SLGBTQQIA people in Canada is a genocide. Colonial violence, racism, sexism, homophobia and transphobia, it noted, has "become embedded in everyday life," in interpersonal relationships, institutions and the laws and structure of society. "The result has been that many Indigenous people have grown up normalized to violence, while Canadian society shows an appalling apathy to addressing the issue.

The National Inquiry into Missing and Murdered Indigenous
Women and Girls finds that this amounts to genocide."

The commission issued 231 "Calls for Justice," which demanded
a sweeping range of measures. Among them are that Canada develop
a national action plan to address violence against Indigenous
women, girls and 2SLGBTQQIA people; that it implement and
comply with international human rights laws and treaties
designed to protect them and create a national police task force to
review and re-investigate cases. It called for changes to the justice, health and education systems, as well as to police departments, media and industry. And it challenged all Canadians to
act by denouncing violence against Indigenous people, learning
about and celebrating Indigenous history and culture, listening
to the stories shared by the families of missing and murdered
women and girls and recognizing the burden they carry, being
an ally to Indigenous communities and holding government
accountable to act. Commissioner Michèle Audette walked part
of the Highway of Tears with families on the way to the hearings
in Smithers in 2017. Shortly before the release of the final report,
I asked her what message she most wanted to convey to Canadians.
She said some might find the commission's evidence and conclusions difficult. "Some of us will feel guilty," she said. "[But] let's
acknowledge, let's recognize, that the past, yes, we cannot change
the past. But let's not deny that this happened. Let's not deny.

"Let's change."

When the report was released, Brenda Wilson spoke on CBC
Radio, pointing out how little had changed since the 2006 symposium meant to stop the deaths on the Highway of Tears. "How
many times are we going to have to do this over and over before
there is an action plan?" she asked. Days later, on a Saturday afternoon in June of 2019, Matilda Wilson stood beside the highway. It
was the twenty-fifth time she had done so since her daughter was
found murdered a few hundred metres away. It was the twenty-fifth

time she had addressed a group of supporters with tears in her eyes and resolve in her voice. Trucks roared by on the highway and wind rustled in the aspens overhead.

Ramona's dream was to be a psychologist. Someone, or several people, took that from her. But no one could take her power to help others, to be a force for good in this world. She has been here all these years: in the courage in her mother's eyes, the strength in her sister's voice, in all the work they've done. "She never died for nothing," her uncle Frank Sampson said several years before. "She's still with us and she's helping to make this world a safer place for our children. We just gotta keep on trying. We can't give up."

Kristal Grenkie, Ramona's best friend from high school, sees the difference Ramona has made. And she thinks that Ramona would have sacrificed herself if it meant change would happen, justice would be served, other lives saved. Ramona would have given her life to stop the killing.

The question that remains is whether she has.

The answer lies with all of us.

ACKNOWLEDGEMENTS

THIS BOOK IS THE RESULT of many people who generously and courageously shared their stories. Many also kindly reviewed sections of the book to ensure its accuracy.

I am deeply grateful to the families and friends of those taken, including: Brenda and Matilda Wilson; Kristal Grenkie; Mary Beaubien; Claudia and Francis Williams; Ida, Peter, Crystal and Vivian Basil; Marge and Darvin Haugan; Sally Gibson; Wanda Good; Michelle, Jack and Barb Hoar and Dave Gowans; Gladys and Stephanie Radek; Mary Teegee; Tim, Kyla, Sarah and Darrell Auger; Angeline Chalifoux; Sharon, Vanessa and Dean Joseph; Vicki Hill and Zoey Hill-Harris; Winnie, Rodney and Violet Sampare; Lucy Smith; Willie, Herbert and Norman Williams; Florence Naziel; and Val Bolton.

I am also indebted to many investigators, from the RCMP and other organizations: Wayne Clary, Garry Kerr, Rick Ross, Steve Pranzl, Dave Aitken, Rhonda Morgan, Ray Michalko and Scott Whyte.

Staff members at museums and libraries along the Highway of Tears were accommodating and helpful in their support of research for this book. A special thanks to Kira Westby, curator of the Bulkley Valley Museum, along with its staff and volunteers.

I am thankful to the faculty and students at the University of Kings College for their wisdom and support as the idea for this book was germinating. A special thanks to Stephen Kimber, Harry Thurston, Tim Falconer and David Swick.

I am forever grateful to my editors at Doubleday Canada, Martha Kanya-Forstner and Ward Hawkes, who understood this project from the start and whose commitment to the families and the story was unwavering as they deftly took a rough manuscript and shaped it into a book. I could imagine no better people to work with and much of what this has become is due to their efforts. And I am thankful to my agent, Chris Bucci, who embraced this project and supported it wholeheartedly throughout.

I am deeply grateful to Ophelia John for reading various versions of this book and offering insightful, incisive feedback. The support, belief and kindness of many friends saw me through this project. A huge thank you to Kim and Raven Besharah, Chantal Goguen, Rebecca Bulmer, Alanhea Vogt, Robbie Lowry, Jamie Munson, Kym Gouchie, Francesca Albright, Jane Lloyd-Smith and Mark Perry. And especially to Graham Blake, who has served as a cheerleader, editor, sounding board and so much more. Lastly, I thank my family, whose support and belief throughout my life makes everything possible, most especially my mom and dad.

THIS BOOK IS A work of non-fiction. All names, places and events are real; no aliases were used.

In putting together this book, I relied heavily on the recollections of many people who generously and bravely shared their time and stories. Where possible, I sought to confirm accounts through a variety of sources, including others who were present, newspaper articles, official reports and authorities. Memories are tricky things, particularly when it comes to traumatic events; where conflicting accounts existed that I could not confirm, for the most part, I excluded the information. In some instances, I opted to go with what seemed most plausible. Any errors are my own.

I also benefited tremendously from the work of many journalists before me, as well as the libraries and museums along the Highway of Tears that have stored decades worth of old newspapers that are otherwise largely unavailable to the public. Those articles, and the willingness of library and museum staff to dig them out, were invaluable in piecing together what happened long ago.

Quotations used are directly what was said in interviews or when I was present at events; drawn from newspaper articles or other written sources, referenced in the end notes; or derived from what people involved in the conversations recounted to me. In those instances, where possible, I confirmed the dialogue with the others who were part of the conversations.

INTRODUCTION: THE HIGHWAY OF TEARS

4 **NWAC research into 582 cases** Native Women's Association of Canada, "Fact Sheet: Missing and Murdered Aboriginal Women and Girls," 2015; based on data collected up to March 31, 2010.

5 **As one long-time activist put it** Bernie Williams, comments at Kasiks Wilderness Resort, September 18, 2017.

A BRIGHT LIGHT

8 **Ramona Lisa Wilson was born** The story of Ramona's birth and childhood was told during interviews with Matilda Wilson in Smithers, B.C., on February 17, 2016, and December 2, 2016, with further detail derived from interviews with Brenda Wilson in Prince George, B.C., on July 23, 2015, and November 16, 2018.

11 **Arthur Sampson, Matilda's father** The story of Arthur and Mary Sampson and their children was shared by Matilda Wilson in interviews in Smithers, B.C., on February 17, 2016, and December 2, 2016.

14 **"Where's the longhouse at the end of Main Street?"** Jennifer McLarty, "Will the real alpine please stand up? Town grapples with its mandatory architectural theme," *Interior News*, June 26, 1995.

14 **said her best friend, Kristal Grenkie** Kristal Grenkie shared many memories and stories of Ramona, as well as her account of the weekend Ramona disappeared, during an interview in Prince George, B.C., on October 20, 2016, and interviews in Smithers, B.C., on November 12, 2016, January 24, 2018, and November 17, 2018.

17 **Ramona had spent Friday night** Rhonda Morgan contributed significantly to the timeline leading up to Ramona's disappearance during interviews in Calgary, Alberta, on January 9 and 10, 2018. The majority of details about that weekend are from interviews with Matilda Wilson, Brenda Wilson and Kristal Grenkie.

22 **"We're not treating it as foul play"** Phillipa Beck, "Smithers girl, 16, goes missing," *Interior News*, June 22, 1994.

22   **"we don't know where she is"** "RCMP continue search for girl," *Interior News*,
     June 29, 1994.

A BRICK WALL

25   **It was the day after the second anniversary of her daughter's disappearance**
     Rhonda Morgan provided a timeline of Delphine's disappearance and the
     Missing Children Society of Canada's investigations during interviews in
     Calgary, Alberta, on January 9 and 10, 2018, along with subsequent phone con-
     versations and emails.

26   **"I wish we had a longer time with her"** Information about Delphine's child-
     hood, family background and disappearance was provided by her sister Mary
     Beaubien in an interview in Smithers, B.C., on April 28, 2017, as well as her
     aunt, Teresa Nikal, in an interview in Smithers, B.C., on September 2, 2016.

27   **Kristal Grenkie was about twelve when she met Delphine** Kristal Grenkie
     shared memories of Delphine and her disappearance during interviews in Prince
     George, B.C., on October 20 and November 12, 2016, and in Smithers, B.C., on
     January 24 and November 17, 2018.

31   **"Pushed from their lands"** Tyler McCreary, *Shared Histories: Witsuwit'en-Settler
     Relationships in Smithers, British Columbia, 1913–1973* (Smithers, B.C.: Creekstone
     Press, 2018), 36.

31   **In the 1920s, a public petition called for a ban** McCreary, *Shared Histories*, 53.

31   **The hospital was segregated** McCreary, *Shared Histories*, 10.

32   **"Railways, roads, farms, fences, and sawmills interfered"** McCreary, *Shared
     Histories*, 71.

32   **"With decreased demand for Witsuwit'en workers"** McCreary, *Shared Histories*, 131.

32   **"settler authorities continued to blame Indigenous families"** McCreary,
     Shared Histories, 176–77.

32   **Some of its residents moved into Smithers** McCreary, *Shared Histories*, 177.

33   **The treaty process amplified racism in Smithers "big time"** Interview with
     Bill Goodacre in Smithers, B.C., on December 8, 2016.

34   **Another recounted how a group of Kitwanga "locals"** "Tensions rise over
     roadblocks," *Interior News*, August 22, 1990; "Violence erupts at Eagle," *Interior
     News*, February 12, 1992.

34   **"Some people won't even look us in the eyes"** "Anti-native feelings run high,"
     Interior News, October 12, 1994.

35   **"That's what I've been [dealing with] my whole life"** Interview with Brenda
     Wilson, November 16, 2018.

35   **"There was not a lot of integration"** Interview with Kristal Grenkie, November 17,
     2018.

35   **"A lot of the violence here stems from racism"** "Racism in Smithers a hot topic
     with teens," *Interior News*, June 8, 1994.

36   **"We have no indication of foul play"** "Search expands for missing Telkwa girl,"
     Interior News, October 10, 1990.

36 **Nationally, more than 90 per cent of kids are found within a week** National Centre for Missing Persons and Unidentified Remains, "2018 Fast Fact Sheet," http://www.canadasmissing.ca/pubs/2018/index-eng.htm.

36 **Judy had searched in Granisle and as far away as Quesnel** "Search expands for missing Telkwa girl," *Interior News.*

36 **"So far, attempts to raise money or get help have proved unsuccessful"** "No clues turned up in missing teen case," *Interior News*, April 10, 1991.

37 **"When distraught parents initially complained"** Ian Mulgrew, "Clifford Olson—Canada's national monster—dead at 71," *Vancouver Sun*, October 3, 2011.

37 **Fred arrived in Smithers** Rhonda Morgan described Fred Maile's activities, referencing his reports, during interviews on January 9 and 10, 2018.

39 **"One cannot help but feel that someone must have witnessed her"** "Long wait: Four years and still no word about missing Telkwa teen," *Interior News*, June 22, 1994.

40 **"I can't say yes or no because I don't know"** "U.S. psychic joins search for two missing local girls," *Interior News*, July 13, 1994.

40 **"they might have found her"** "Long wait," *Interior News.*

41 **"All I can say is why me?"** "Life in limbo—coping after a daughter disappears," *Interior News*, August 3, 1994.

41 **"My name is Judy Nikal"** Judy Magee, letter to the editor, *Interior News*, July 5, 1995.

PART OF YOU IS MISSING

42 **a Missing Children Society of Canada team** Rhonda Morgan described search efforts for Ramona during interviews in Calgary, Alberta, on January 9 and 10, 2018, as well as in subsequent phone conversations and emails.

44 **"It's important for the integrity of witnesses"** Phone interview with Wayne Clary, November 2, 2018.

44 **"The RCMP cannot get the media thing right"** Phone interview with Garry Kerr, October 2, 2018.

45 **"They're not the CIA"** Phone interview with Michael Arntfield, November 22, 2018.

45 **"There's a bit of a lack of respect, honestly, for the families"** Phone interview with Lorimer Shenher, November 1, 2018.

47 **"It just all fell apart"** Interview with Brenda Wilson, November 16, 2018.

47 **"The best thing these people can do to get that 'part of you' back"** Brenda Wilson, "A part of you is missing," *Interior News*, January 18, 1995.

48 **"It prepares the groundwork for demagogues"** Pete McMartin, "Carpenter case: 'Unsavory' media show?" *Vancouver Sun*, February 3, 1995.

49 **But investigators needed more information** "Mother sends out plea for help: Anonymous tipster sought in Ramona Wilson case," *Interior News*, March 29, 1995.

50   **"I know it's hard to know or witness something you didn't want to be involved in"** "Loving mother misses daughter," *Interior News*, March 29, 1995.

52   **"Nobody gets away with murder"** John Young, "Murder probe launched after body found," *Interior News*, April 19, 1995.

FALLING THROUGH THE CRACKS

54   **Kristal was terrified as the police berated her** Kristal Grenkie shared her recollections of the police interrogation during interviews in Prince George, B.C., on October 20, 2016, and in Smithers, B.C., on November 17, 2018.

55   **Roxanne bounced back and forth between her mother's home and her foster home** Information about Roxanne's life is derived from newspaper articles, which are noted, along with a phone interview with Rene Beirness on October 11, 2018.

55   **"She was quite a good kid"** Paul Strickland, "Life on the street cut short: Dead teenager wanted to kick drug habit," *Prince George Citizen*, August 27, 1994.

56   **Mildred said she was "always our family"** Strickland, "Life on the street cut short."

56   **"A very nice person"** Lori Culbert and Neal Hall, "These are the stories of the victims," *Vancouver Sun*, December 12, 2009.

56   **"That's when she started turning"** Neil Horner, "Roxanne Thiara: Is there a killer lurking on Highway of Tears?" *Quesnel Cariboo Observer*, June 5, 2002.

56   **Things became a "constant battle" with her** Strickland, "Life on the street cut short."

56   **"I stepped on a lot of toes"** Horner, "Roxanne Thiara."

56   **After her release, she "went wild"** Interview with Rene Beirness.

57   **"This is such a fail"** Kristal Grenkie shared her recollections of Roxanne during interviews in Prince George, B.C., on October 20, 2016, and in Smithers, B.C., on November 12, 2016.

58   **"They are generally members of families"** Representative for Children and Youth, *Too Many Victims: Sexualized Violence in the Lives of Children and Youth in Care* (Victoria, B.C.: 2016), 8.

58   **The true total, the report noted** Representative for Children and Youth, *Too Many Victims*, 1.

59   **"Indigenous scholars have described the intense psychological distress"** Cedar Project Partnership et al., "The Cedar Project: Negative health outcomes associated with involvement in the child welfare system among young Indigenous people who use injection and non-injection drugs in two Canadian cities," *Canadian Journal of Public Health* 106, no. 5 (July/August 2015): 268.

59   **"Perpetrators of this violence may also believe"** Representative for Children and Youth, *Too Many Victims*, 8.

61   **the early 1900s in Prince George were a chaotic time** CBC News, "Moonshine, pulp mills and Communists: The history of Prince George's bad reputation,"

updated January 7, 2018, https://www.cbc.ca/news/canada/british-columbia /prince-george-crime-history-1.4475535.

61 **Ray Michalko recalled the city being known as** Interview with Ray Michalko in Surrey, B.C., on April 13, 2016.

61 **"If you had had a hundred bucks in your pocket in the back alley"** Interview with Rick Ross in Chilliwack, B.C., on December 8, 2017.

61 **One police officer estimated the number of users in the city** Marilyn Storie, "Use of heroin soars in city," *Prince George Citizen*, December 14, 1994.

62 **"Many young people leave home to escape abuse"** McCreary Centre Society, *Against the odds: A profile of marginalized and street-involved youth in B.C.* (Vancouver, B.C.: 2007), 39.

62 **Children as young as nine were out there** Arn Keeling, "A look at life on the streets," *Prince George Citizen*, June 13, 1995.

62 **"You have to be numb"** Keeling, "A look at life on the streets."

63 **Another spoke of dozens of people descending on someone** Paul Strickland, "Rally explores violence here," *Prince George Citizen*, December 19, 1994.

63 **"I hoped to the very end she was going to change"** Strickland, "Life on the street cut short."

63 **"She had dreams"** Horner, "Roxanne Thiara."

64 **"That was the last time we seen her"** Strickland, "Life on the street cut short."

64 **"When she did want to change, she wasn't given the chance"** Strickland, "Life on the street cut short."

64 **Examples of over-policing abound** See, for example: Canadian Press, "Groups alleging racial profiling demand probe into Vancouver street checks," June 14, 2018; Andrea Huncar, "Indigenous women nearly 10 times more likely to be street checked by Edmonton police, new data shows," CBC News, June 27, 2017; Bryan Labby, "Lethbridge police accused of 'racist' carding practices," CBC News, June 20, 2017.

64 **The same report, gleaned from a series of workshops** David Eby, *Small Town Justice: A Report on the RCMP in Northern and Rural British Columbia* (Vancouver, B.C.: British Columbia Civil Liberties Association, 2011), 95–96.

65 **Fourteen per cent had been assaulted by the police** McCreary Centre Society, *Against the Odds*, 40.

65 **In Prince George, 4 per cent of youths reported non-consensual sex** Stephen W. Pan et al., "The Cedar Project: Impacts of policing among young Aboriginal people who use injection and non-injection drugs in British Columbia, Canada," abstract, *International Journal of Drug Policy* 24, no. 5 (September 2013), https://www .ijdp.org/article/S0955-3959(13)00053-4/fulltext.

65 **"the courts tend to respond to Indigenous girls as though"** Justice for Girls and Justice for Girls International, *Submission to UN Committee on the Elimination of All Forms of Discrimination Against Women at its 7th Periodic Review of Canada* (October 2008), 9.

65 **"The terms of probation are often so unrealistic"** Native Women's Association of Canada and Justice for Girls, *Gender Matters: Building Strength in Reconciliation* (Ottawa: 2012), 25.

66   **"Aboriginal ancestry remained independently associated with incarceration"**
      Brittany Barker et al., "Aboriginal street-involved youth experience elevated risk
      of incarceration," unedited manuscript, December 1, 2016, 5, https://www.ncbi
      .nlm.nih.gov/pmc/articles/PMC4688204/pdf/nihms715971.pdf.

66   **"Today, Canadian police officers are accorded substantial discretionary
      power"** Barker et al., "Aboriginal street-involved youth," 6.

67   **He paid for sex numerous times over several years** The description of David
      Ramsay's crimes against these girls, his background and the reasons for judg-
      ment are derived from R. v. Ramsay, 2004 BCSC 756, https://www.courts.gov
      .bc.ca/jdb-txt/sc/04/07/2004BCSC0756err1.htm.

68   **A girl on the street in Prince George told a reporter** Canadian Press, "Teen
      hookers say they know to keep quiet," June 3, 2004.

68   **The worker said she had seen the judge with a girl in his car** Jane Armstrong,
      "Rumours swirled about jailed judge," *Globe and Mail*, June 3, 2004.

68   **"We didn't have any substance"** Armstrong, "Rumours swirled about jailed
      judge."

69   **"We weren't going to rush to judgment"** Jane Armstrong, "RCMP seek to
      reinstate case against constable," *Globe and Mail*, December 13, 2006.

69   **"I don't think his capacity to abuse those young women was sustained by him
      alone"** Gerry Bellett, "Prince George probe sought: Sex abuse scandal case raises
      questions with advocacy group," *Vancouver Sun*, May 21, 2005.

69   **Years later, "reports continue to circulate in Prince George"** Human Rights
      Watch, *Those Who Take Us Away: Abusive Policing and Failures in Protection of
      Indigenous Women and Girls in Northern British Columbia, Canada* (Toronto:
      2013), 33.

70   **"At times the physical abuse was accompanied by verbal, racist or sexist
      abuse"** Human Rights Watch, *Those Who Take Us Away*, 8.

70   **The researchers heard allegations of rape or sexual assault by police officers**
      Human Rights Watch, *Those Who Take Us Away*, 34.

70   **"I just kept thinking, 'But this is Canada'"** Phone interview with Meghan
      Rhoad, June 30, 2015.

70   **"We're hopeful someone saw her"** "Death treated as homicide," *Prince George
      Citizen*, August 24, 1994.

70   **"It's a good possibility the person knew the area very well"** Lindsay Kines,
      "Highway 16 road of death for Indian teenagers: A serial killer is considered a
      possibility in three slayings and two disappearances," *Vancouver Sun*, December 5,
      1995.

71   **"We're still having a hard time coming to terms"** Strickland, "Life on the street
      cut short."

71   **fled a "tumultuous home life" at twelve** "Police seek tips in killing of teen,"
      Prince George Citizen, December 12, 1994.

71   **"She was really very sensitive"** David Heyman, "Trying to go straight," *Prince
      George Free Press*, December 22, 1994.

73   **"She had potential"** Culbert and Hall, "These are the stories of the victims."

73   a resident wrote that she didn't "give a damn if the coverage of the murder
      puts us in a bad light" "Readers' views on plight of street kids," *Prince George
      Citizen*, December 16, 1994.

74   "We're concerned that the victims are being vilified" Paul Strickland, "Recent
      murders spark concern: Violence topic at coffeehouse," *Prince George Citizen*,
      December 15, 1994.

74   "There hasn't been anything about Roxanne in the press for a while" "Poster
      campaign started for murdered girl," *Quesnel Cariboo Observer*, March 29, 1995.

75   "Obviously, we're concerned that there is [a serial killer]" Kines, "Highway 16
      road of death for Indian teenagers."

THE NOT KNOWING

77   In the days Marge was growing up Marge Haugan described her history, along
      with Lana's, during an interview in Terrace, B.C., on December 7, 2016, in which
      Darvin Haugan also participated, adding his memories of Lana's teen years
      and disappearance.

78   Wanda Good, her older cousin, remembered the toddler Wanda Good shared
      memories of Lana as well as her insight on systemic issues surrounding missing
      and murdered Indigenous women and girls, policing and community response
      in an interview in Kitwanga, B.C., on September 1, 2016.

79   "You have to leave here if you want to work" Sally Gibson shared her memories
      of Lana's life and disappearance during an interview in Gitanyow, B.C., on
      August 21, 2015.

80   It was a rainy evening in late October when they pulled into the driveway
      Darvin Haugan shared the story of Lana arriving in Haugeyville as he spoke at
      a memorial vigil for her in Terrace, B.C., on October 17, 2015.

81   Clarice and Lana spent many weekends when Lana was visiting running
      around Clarice Dessert recalled her youth with Lana, the last night she saw her
      and its impact during a phone interview on November 26, 2015.

85   "We feel that's where she was heading" "Volunteers seek clues to Lana," *Terrace
      Standard*, November 8, 1995.

86   "There's a lot of ground to cover" "Lana Derrick search set for an expansion,"
      Terrace Standard, November 22, 1995.

86   "We said we would go until the snow fell" "Lana Derrick search set for an
      expansion."

87   Police brought in a hypnotist "Hypnotist unlocks clue to Lana," *Terrace
      Standard*, December 6, 1995.

87   police later said neither man was relevant to the case "Lana vigil planned,"
      Terrace Standard, October 2, 1996.

90   Families told reporter Lindsay Kines Lindsay Kines, "Highway 16 road of death
      for Indian teenagers: A serial killer is considered a possibility in three slayings
      and two disappearances," *Vancouver Sun*, December 5, 1995.

91 In Terrace, Sgt. Randy Beck called it "an awful leap" "Serial killer report called 'irresponsible,'" *Terrace Standard*, December 6, 1995.

AN INCH SHY OF A MILE

92 **Garry Kerr was a relatively new detective** Garry Kerr shared his background and the course and results of his investigation into the murder of Alberta Williams, as well as reviews of other cases, during an interview in Duncan, B.C., on August 27, 2017, and subsequent phone interviews on September 13, 2017, and October 2 and 20, 2018, along with various email communications. All comments and information attributed to him are derived from these conversations unless otherwise noted.

95 **The Department of Fisheries and Oceans would notify the local RCMP detachment** Garry Kerr provided his memories of what Prince Rupert was like during the late 1980s, as did RCMP member Rick Ross during an interview in Chilliwack, B.C., on December 8, 2017, and Francis Williams during an interview in Kitwanga, B.C., on October 31, 2016.

97 **For sisters Claudia and Alberta Williams** Claudia Williams shared the story of Alberta's life, disappearance and death during an interview in Vancouver, B.C., on April 14, 2016, as well as in subsequent phone conversations and email exchanges. She also spoke publicly about Alberta during a session of the National Inquiry into Missing and Murdered Indigenous Women and Girls in Smithers, B.C., on September 28, 2017.

100 **Francis Williams was already in bed when his phone rang** Francis Williams shared his memories during an interview in Kitwanga, B.C., on October 31, 2016, and in subsequent phone conversations and email exchanges.

103 **Rick started looking for her, too** Rick Ross spoke about the investigation into Alberta's disappearance and murder, including reading passages from his notes, during an interview in Chilliwack, B.C., on December 8, 2017.

107 **Fellow fishermen noticed a cloud that seemed to move with him** Interview with Murray Smith in Prince Rupert, B.C., on June 2, 2016.

108 **Scott Whyte, who served twenty-three years in the RCMP** Scott Whyte shared his recollections during an interview in Ladysmith, B.C., on January 7, 2019.

108 **Michael Arntfield, a criminologist and former police officer** All comments attributed to Michael Arntfield are from a phone interview on November 22, 2018.

BLATANT FAILURES

112 **"If an answer does exist to Lana's 1995 disappearance"** Jason Proctor, "The shadow of death: One grieving mother says the only thing that keeps her going is knowing that one day God will judge her daughter's killer," *The Province* (Vancouver), February 6, 2000.

113 **"What are we doing about it now?"** Proctor, "The shadow of death."

113 **"It's frustrating"** Proctor, "The shadow of death."

113 **"We always like to think we are close to solving it"** "Murder case proves frustrating for RCMP," *Interior News*, May 8, 1996.

113 **"He can't follow up everything on his own"** "Families wait for new leads in old cases," *Terrace Standard*, December 2, 1998.

113 **"in many cases, we just don't have the manpower or the money"** Proctor, "The shadow of death."

113 **"It's a big chunk of cake to bite off"** Comments attributed to Scott Whyte are taken from an interview in Ladysmith, B.C., on January 7, 2019.

115 **"To settle the west meant dispossessing the aboriginal people"** Peter Maurice German, "Federal-provincial contracting for Royal Canadian Mounted Police services: A survey utilizing the interplay model of public policy analysis" (MA thesis, Simon Fraser University, 1990), 126.

115 **Macdonald "sought the amalgam of an army and a police presence"** German, "Federal-provincial contracting for Royal Canadian Mounted Police services," 127.

115 **As its website notes, "Our mandate is multi-faceted"** RCMP, "Programs and services," http://www.rcmp-grc.gc.ca/en/nu/programs-and-services.

116 **"The key problem—one that has bled into the RCMP's culture"** Ken Hansen, "The problem at the root of the RCMP's dysfunctional culture," *Maclean's*, January 19, 2018.

117 **Garry worked in the North District Major Crime Unit** Garry Kerr shared memories of the structural changes within the RCMP and the file review undertaken during an interview in Duncan, B.C., on August 27, 2017, and subsequent phone interviews on September 13, 2017, and October 2 and 20, 2018.

117 **she had no information about a potential task force in the '90s** Email communication with Janelle Shoihet, December 3, 2018.

118 **"The real annoying thing is, they should have thrown these resources at this case"** Comments in this chapter attributed to Kim Rossmo are taken from a phone interview on November 8, 2018.

118 **there were "enough similarities at that time"** Bernice Trick, "Serial killer stalked Highway 16, two former RCMP officers say," *Prince George Citizen*, February 18, 2006.

119 **An investigation review released in 1996** Justice Archie Campbell, *Bernardo Investigation Review: Summary Report* (Toronto: Solicitor General, 1996), https://www.attorneygeneral.jus.gov.on.ca/inquiries/cornwall/en/hearings/exhibits/Wendy_Leaver/pdf/10_Campbell_Summary.pdf.

120 **"There is a good chance a serial killer is at work"** Stevie Cameron, *On the Farm: Robert William Pickton and the Tragic Story of Vancouver's Missing Women* (Toronto: Vintage Canada, 2010), 211.

120 **"without bodies—the physical evidence—there were no cases"** Cameron, *On the Farm*, 212.

121 **"If they had followed [Rossmo's] analysis"** Cameron, *On the Farm*, 213.

122 **said officers harboured stereotypes** Comments attributed to Lorimer Shenher come from a phone interview on November 1, 2018.

123 **certain factors seem to influence how cases are prioritized** Email from Steve Pranzl, January 15, 2019.

124 **Staff Sgt. Zalys made the following observation** Brian Hutchinson, "Police foresaw Pickton inquiry, noted bungled investigation, almost two years before serial killer's arrest," *National Post*, January 20, 2012.

125 **"Funding isn't an issue at all"** "Families wait for new leads in old cases," *Terrace Standard*, December 2, 1998.

126 **Oppal made an important point in his final report** Wally Oppal, *Forsaken: The Report of the Missing Women Commission of Inquiry: Executive Summary* (Victoria, B.C.: 2012), 95–96, http://www.missingwomeninquiry.ca/obtain-report/.

IT DEPENDS WHO'S BLEEDING

127 **Nicole Hoar's creations are full of whimsy** Michelle Hoar and Dave Gowans shared their memories of Nicole during an interview in Vancouver, B.C., on March 8, 2018.

131 **"All she kept talking about was how excited she was to see her sister"** Deborah Tetley, "'All we do all day, every night, is think of Nicole': Camp not same without missing tree planter," *Calgary Herald*, July 23, 2002.

132 **"We need our daughter home, we need to have her back"** Canadian Press, "Missing woman's parents plead for help: Tree-planter, 25, last seen two weeks ago," July 6, 2002.

132 **the heavy coverage "sparked a tremendous amount of recollection"** Canadian Press, "Search for woman missing in B.C. winds down," July 7, 2002.

132 **Police said they would shift their focus toward the "investigative aspect"** Mark Hume, "Search widens for missing B.C. student: 300 volunteers involved, police downplay link with six others who disappeared," *National Post*, July 8, 2002.

132 **RCMP investigators had traversed Highway 16 "talking to anyone who had a view of the highway"** Hume, "Search widens for missing B.C. student."

133 **"They are covering every metre of every forestry road"** Hume, "Search widens for missing B.C. student."

133 **"I'm doing this to get as much publicity and get people talking about her"** Daryl Slade, "Olympic skater laces up to find friend: Missing woman Steven Elm's prom date," *Calgary Herald*, July 9, 2002.

134 **"What you did for the search was admirable"** "Treeplanters show heart in search for colleague," *Prince George Citizen*, July 11, 2002.

134 **Nicole did not fit the same profile** Hume, "Search widens for missing B.C. student."

135 **"The more media attention on a case, the more pressure is going to be on police"** Phone interview with Kim Rossmo, November 8, 2018.

136 **"A lot of these things [task forces] are brought on by thorough reporting"** Phone interview with Dave Aitken, November 9, 2018.

136 **"Police bureaucrats are fundamentally concerned about their own well-being and advancement"** Phone interview with Michael Arntfield, November 22, 2018.

136 **In a 2010 paper titled "'Newsworthy' Victims?"** Kristen Gilchrist, "'Newsworthy' victims?: Exploring differences in Canadian local press coverage of missing/murdered Aboriginal and White women," *Feminist Media Studies* 10, no. 4 (December 2010): 376.

137 **three white women accounted for 187 stories, versus 53 stories about the Indigenous women** Gilchrist, "'Newsworthy' victims?," 379.

137 **Indigenous women were usually described "impersonally and rarely by name"** Gilchrist, "'Newsworthy' victims?," 382.

137 **"Beyond superficial details, readers did not get the same sense of who the Aboriginal women were"** Gilchrist, "'Newsworthy' victims?," 383.

138 **"The lack of coverage to missing/murdered Aboriginal women appears to suggest"** Gilchrist, "'Newsworthy' victims?," 384.

138 **"That was the big talk, about Nicole and how she went missing"** Interview with Kyla Auger at Alexis First Nation, Alberta, on April 10, 2017.

138 **"When our families first went to police reporting our girls missing"** Peter Smith, "Vanished: Somewhere along the Highway of Tears Nicole Hoar simply disappeared," *Calgary Sun*, July 14, 2002.

139 **"I don't want to say that now this girl is missing maybe they will do more"** Patti Edgar, "Hunt for missing woman rekindles old fears in B.C.: Relatives of missing, murdered women still look for answers," *Ottawa Citizen*, July 18, 2002.

139 **"One of the main reasons is lifestyle differences"** John Bermingham, "Could a serial killer be roaming Highway 16? Family calls for task force after 6 young females vanish along the route in 12 years," *The Province* (Vancouver), July 22, 2002.

140 **"It would be very, very easy, given the history of the other cases"** Deborah Tetley, "Hard journey down Highway of Tears: Missing woman's brother searches frantically, but fears what he may find," *Calgary Herald*, July 28, 2002.

141 **"Our unit got gutted and sent to the pig farm"** Canadian Press, "Pig farm pulls officers away from other murder cases," July 9, 2002.

141 **"Every time we dig a hole and plant a tree, she's in our thoughts"** Tetley, "'All we do all day, every night, is think of Nicole.'"

141 **"We have to ease our way back into our real world"** Patti Edgar and Mark Hume, "A sixth family feels the pain: Not 'a single thread of evidence,' police say," *National Post*, July 19, 2002.

RISING TIDES

144 **"despite the fact that First Nations people did not knowingly enter into any such arrangement"** Lynda Gray, *First Nations 101* (Vancouver, B.C.: Adaawx Publishing, 2011), 30.

145 **"conceived and implemented in part as an overt attack"** Amnesty International, *Stolen Sisters: A Human Rights Response to Discrimination and Violence against Indigenous Women in Canada* (2004), 8.

146 **the Indian Act was "a piece of colonial legislation"** Truth and Reconciliation Commission of Canada, *Honouring the Truth, Reconciling for the Future: Summary of the Final Report of the Truth and Reconciliation Commission of Canada* (Toronto: James Lorimer and Company, 2015), 55.

146 **"It was absolutely part of a larger project to assimilate and eliminate"** Interview with Dawn Lavell-Harvard in Ottawa, Ontario, on January 29, 2016.

147 **"acculturated into believing they had to think like white men"** Beverley Jacobs quoted in Jessica Riel-Johns, "Understanding Violence Against Indigenous Women and Girls in Canada," in *Forever Loved: Exposing the Hidden Crisis of Missing and Murdered Indigenous Women and Girls in Canada*, eds. D. Memee Lavell-Harvard and Jennifer Brant (Bradford, Ont.: Demeter Press, 2016), 38.

147 **"The resulting vulnerability of Indigenous women"** Amnesty International, *Stolen Sisters*, 2.

148 **Tamara was born in Prince Rupert** Gladys Radek told Tamara's story during an interview on Georgina Island, Ontario, on January 25, 2016.

150 **"She was just going through a really hard time at that point"** Lori Culbert and Neal Hall, "These are the stories of the victims," *Vancouver Sun*, December 12, 2009.

152 **noted her "colourful wigs or short-cropped hair, tall stature and fiery personality"** Stuart Hunter, "'She's been gone too long': Family refuses to give up hope as Tamara Chipman is the latest young woman to vanish on a northern highway," *The Province* (Vancouver), November 24, 2005.

152 **many dropped their work when the call came across the radio** Several fishermen recounted their memories of the search at a feast for walkers at Kitsumkalum Hall in Terrace, B.C., on September 23, 2017.

153 **"We were forced to stop searching only because the weather"** Tom Chipman testified before the National Inquiry on Missing and Murdered Indigenous Women and Girls in Smithers, B.C., on September 26, 2017.

153 **he heard the tip that Tamara was in Vancouver** Gladys recounted the time Tom and Christine spent with her in Vancouver searching, as did Tom, in a 2006 article by Maurice Bridge and Darah Hansen, "'Highway of Tears' claims 14-year-old: Women have vanished and been killed along stretch of No. 16 route near Prince George," Canwest News Service, February 16, 2006.

BREAKING A SPIRIT

156 **The hill was one of Tim Auger's favourite places** Tim Auger described his sister, their childhood and her disappearance and murder during interviews in Edmonton, Alberta, on February 28, 2017, and January 7, 2018.

156 **"She wouldn't suspect the worst of anyone"** Kyla Auger shared her memories of her sister during an interview at Alexis First Nation in Alberta on April 10, 2017.

158 **"She'd go through these points where she was strong"** Sarah Auger shared her memories of her mother, sister and growing up during an interview in Edmonton, Alberta, on February 27, 2017.

158 **Darrell Auger, Audrey's older brother, has a memory** Darrell Auger described the family's background and shared memories of his sister and of Aielah during interviews in Edmonton, Alberta, on February 28, 2017, and January 7, 2018.

164 **"things would be at ease for my daughter"** Angeline Chalifoux shared copies of letters Audrey wrote when she was seeking funding for her memorial walks.

166 **"Tragedy once again hit my family hard"** From Audrey's fundraising letters.

168 **"She was last seen getting into a black van"** Frank Peebles, "Missing teen sought," *Prince George Citizen*, February 7, 2006.

169 **"I remember one incident"** Bernice Trick, "High school mourns murdered classmate," *Prince George Citizen*, February 16, 2006.

169 **"I understand they're all individual investigations"** Susan Lazaruk, "Cops launch murder probe: Body of school girl found near Highway of Tears," *The Province* (Vancouver), February 17, 2006.

170 **"We are counting on PG residents"** Gail Marong, "Show grieving family you care," letter to the editor, *Prince George Free Press*, February 22, 2006.

THIS WE HAVE TO LIVE WITH EVERY DAY

172 **Aielah's death hit home for Rena in a major way** CBC Radio, *The Current*, Prince George, B.C., October 17, 2016.

173 **find a way "to put an end to these horrific murders"** Mark Hume, "Task force to probe Highway 16 deaths: RCMP investigation will focus on killings, disappearances of nine young women," *Globe and Mail*, March 1, 2006.

173 **"There are nine women listed as victims of the Highway of Tears"** Frank Peebles, "Carrier Sekani kick in $10,000 for Highway of Tears forum," *Prince George Citizen*, March 3, 2006.

173 **"This has been a long time coming"** Hume, "Task force to probe Highway 16 deaths."

173 **"I hope the government and all its agencies will seriously participate"** Peebles, "Carrier Sekani kick in $10,000 for Highway of Tears forum."

174 **Florence Naziel also felt she had to do something** Florence Naziel described the 2006 Highway of Tears walk and symposium during interviews in Witset, B.C., on November 3 and 24, 2016.

175 **Betty Joseph, Florence's sister, responded decisively** Betty Joseph described how she joined Florence on the 2006 walk during an interview in Terrace, B.C., on September 22, 2017.

176 **Matilda Wilson was considering a 370-kilometre walk** Matilda Wilson described the walk and symposium during interviews in Smithers, B.C., on February 17, 2016, and December 2, 2016.

176 **"It brings back how much it hurts"** Frank Peebles, "Pain and sorrow on the Highway of Tears," *Prince George Citizen*, April 1, 2006.

176 **Gladys Radek, Tamara's aunt, got a message on Facebook from Florence**
     Gladys Radek shared her memories of the walk during an interview at Georgina
     Island, Ontario, on January 25, 2016.

176 **"an issue that has been haunting not only communities along the highway"**
     James Vassallo, "Highway 16 walkers hope to find answers," *Prince Rupert Daily
     News,* March 13, 2006.

180 **Jean Virginia Sampare had been headed toward that road when she dis-
     appeared** Virginia's family—Roddy, Violet and Winnie Sampare—told her
     story to the National Inquiry into Missing and Murdered Indigenous Women
     and Girls in Smithers, B.C., on September 28, 2017.

182 **"I feel overwhelmed by the whole thing"** Frank Peebles, "Marchers arrive to
     open forum," *Prince George Citizen,* March 30, 2006.

185 **"First, you have to make people believe your child is lost"** Peebles, "Pain and
     sorrow on the Highway of Tears."

185 **Communities, she stressed, had to stop blaming victims** Peebles, "Pain and
     sorrow on the Highway of Tears."

185 **"Justice is what I want"** Dirk Meissner, "Hear our cries, victims' families say:
     'Justice is what I want,' mother tells symposium," Canadian Press, April 1,
     2006.

185 **"She is not just a name on a list of missing people"** Peebles, "Pain and sorrow
     on the Highway of Tears."

186 **"I know that one of the biggest memories"** Michelle Hoar, "Support meant
     a great deal," letter to the editor, *Prince George Free Press,* April 5, 2006, http://
     www.pgfreepress.com/support-meant-a-great-deal/.

186 **"I never thought I'd be standing up here"** Peebles, "Pain and sorrow on the
     Highway of Tears."

186 **The *Prince George Citizen* summarized the first day** Peebles, "Pain and sorrow
     on the Highway of Tears."

187 **"This is a daily issue"** Peebles, "Pain and sorrow on the Highway of Tears."

187 **The front page of the *Prince George Citizen*** Bernice Trick, "Organizer thrilled
     with Highway of Tears symposium," *Prince George Citizen,* April 1, 2006.

187 **"without question the most powerful gathering"** Dirk Meissner, "A collective
     cry to stop the killings: Police, politicians and aboriginals gather to share con-
     cerns about 'highway of tears,'" Canadian Press, April 1, 2006.

187 **"people feel a sense of abandonment"** Peebles, "Pain and sorrow on the
     Highway of Tears."

187 **he would take "the messages from this conference to Ottawa"** "Highway of
     Tears symposium ends with promises," *Prince Rupert Daily News,* April 3, 2006.

187 **"We hear you," he told the symposium** Frank Peebles, "Police examine murder
     suspects," *Prince George Citizen,* April 4, 2006.

188 **"It is the sincere wish of the First Nation and non-First Nation communities"**
     Highway of Tears Symposium Recommendations Report, June 16, 2006, https://www
     .highwayoftears.org/uploads/Highway%20of%20Tears%20Symposium%20
     Recommendations%20Report%20-%20January%202013.pdf.

189 **"There's a lot communities can do"** Leanne Ritchie, "Action urged along
     'Highway of Tears,'" *Prince Rupert Daily News,* June 22, 2006.

191 **"cost is secondary when it comes to nine lives"** Frank Peebles, "Report calls for efforts to prevent more victims," *Prince George Citizen*, June 22, 2006.

192 **"bite-sized and in some cases . . . doable"** Frank Peebles, "Police endorse Highway of Tears report," *Prince George Citizen*, June 23, 2006.

192 **"None of these recommendations come across as being problematic"** Peebles, "Police endorse Highway of Tears report."

192 **"God knows we need to do something"** Neal Hall, "Call for RCMP action on highway of tears: Report urges wider murder investigation, more free public transit," *Vancouver Sun*, June 22, 2006.

192 **"I can tell you it will be given heavy consideration"** Frank Peebles, "Report's recommendations praised," *Prince George Citizen*, June 22, 2006.

192 **An editorial in the *Prince George Citizen* stressed the importance** Dave Paulson, "Making report into reality," *Prince George Citizen*, June 23, 2006.

193 **"the workload coming out of the recommendations . . . is quite a massive amount"** James Vassallo, "'Highway of Tears' plan taking shape," *Prince Rupert Daily News*, July 21, 2006.

193 **"I am really happy"** Frank Peebles, "Highway of Tears position filled," *Prince George Citizen*, October 19, 2006.

WHERE WERE YOU TWENTY YEARS AGO?

195 **Steve Pranzl joined the Vancouver Police Department in 1976** Steve Pranzl shared his recollection of E-Pana's formation and work during interviews in Langley, B.C., on January 8, 2019, and over the phone on February 1, 2019.

196 **according to an RCMP report** Royal Canadian Mounted Police, *Working Together to End Violence Against Indigenous Women and Girls: National Scan of RCMP Initiatives* (May 2017), 12.

197 **"We started doing the review"** Lori Culbert and Neal Hall, "Highway of Tears case began with three teens," *Vancouver Sun*, March 6, 2014.

197 **David Dennis, then the vice president of the United Native Nations, called it** Suzanne Fournier, "Aboriginal leaders demand Highway of Tears task force," *The Province* (Vancouver), October 27, 2007.

197 **"There's absolutely no reason in the world to connect [cases from the early 1970s]"** Phone interview with Kim Rossmo, November 8, 2018.

199 **Dave Aitken sat down for a beer with Steve** Dave Aitken spoke of his experience with the E-Pana project in a phone interview on November 9, 2018.

199 **"They're the tough ones"** Wayne Clary described the challenges the cases presented investigators, along with the formation and work of E-Pana, during interviews in Surrey, B.C., on October 13, 2015, and by phone on November 2, 2018, and March 21, 2019.

200 **"In a homicide investigation, there is normally a logical, chronological progression"** Don Adam, "Top Robert Pickton cop breaks his silence: The former head of the missing women task force speaks out exclusively to The Vancouver Sun, defending his team in response to this summer's scathing review of the Robert 'Willie' Pickton case," *Vancouver Sun*, November 26, 2010.

200   **Michael Arntfield called it "an uphill battle"** Phone interview with Michael
      Arntfield, November 22, 2018.

202   **"There's more information in those notebooks"** Garry Kerr discussed RCMP
      practices during an interview in Duncan, B.C., on August 27, 2017.

206   **"It was good because we got to see other people, other families"** Interview with
      Sally Gibson in Gitanyow, B.C., on August 21, 2015.

207   **"It was very hard, difficult, to grasp everything"** Interview with Matilda Wilson
      in Smithers, B.C., on February 17, 2016.

207   **private investigator Ray Michalko was watching the news** Interview with Ray
      Michalko in Surrey, B.C., on April 13, 2016.

208   **He told the *Calgary Herald*, "I've been watching this over time"** Deborah Tetley,
      "Private investigator starts search into fate of missing women in B.C.," *Calgary
      Herald*, March 13, 2006.

208   **Ray accused the police of failing to follow up on tips** Ethan Baron, "Cops
      not probing Tears tips, PI says: Private detective began looking into murder/
      disappearance cases during March," *The Province* (Vancouver), June 2, 2006.

208   **"We're taking this very seriously"** Deborah Tetley, "Tips not followed up, PI
      alleges: RCMP say they're doing all they can," *Calgary Herald*, June 14, 2006.

208   **By the fall, Ray said he'd identified five persons of interest** Dirk Meissner,
      "Highway of Tears private eye probing 9 cases has serious tips on 1 death,"
      Canadian Press, September 10, 2006.

208   **"If you were one of the people that was present during this horrific crime"**
      Ethan Baron, "Highway of Tears private eye announces break in case," *The
      Province* (Vancouver), October 25, 2006.

208   **He was, he said, trying to "rattle some people up"** Baron, "Highway of Tears
      private eye announces break in case."

209   **"The RCMP are not convinced that Michalko's tips are bona fide clues"**
      Deborah Tetley, "New search for missing woman: Tips spur private eye to launch
      volunteer effort," *Calgary Herald*, May 1, 2007.

209   **"We hoped that we would come across something"** Deborah Tetley, "Mother's
      hopes dashed by failed search for daughter: Hunt in B.C. for fresh clues comes
      up empty," *Calgary Herald*, May 13, 2007.

209   **Ray said he was "disgusted and embarrassed"** Suzanne Fournier, "Aboriginal
      leaders demand Highway of Tears task force," *The Province* (Vancouver), October
      27, 2007.

209   **"That is the kind of information that should only come from the official
      investigators"** Frank Peebles, "RCMP deny break in Highway 16 cases," *Prince
      George Citizen*, March 13, 2008.

210   **The man took Ray "to the alleged crime scene"** Ray Michalko, *Obstruction of
      Justice: The Search for Truth on Canada's Highway of Tears* (Markham, Ont.: Red
      Deer Press, 2016), 179.

210   **"no one else, including E-PANA investigators, had spoken to or re-interviewed
      him"** Michalko, *Obstruction of Justice*, 184.

210   **"Your reluctance to comply with my request"** Michalko, *Obstruction of Justice*,
      186.

211 **families sent a letter to media outlets praising Ray's work** Frank Peebles, "Highway of Tears victim families defend sleuth's efforts," *Prince George Citizen*, June 9, 2008.

211 **"The truth is that I applaud Mr. Michalko's commitment and resolve"** Frank Peebles, "RCMP praises private investigator," *Prince George Citizen*, June 23, 2008.

211 **"It is the break investigators, family members and the public have been waiting for"** "Isle Pierre search may bring closure in Nicole Hoar case," *Prince George Citizen*, August 29, 2009.

212 **"investigators excavated dozens of sites in densely wooded sections"** Justine Hunter, "Police mum about probe into missing hitchhiker," *Globe and Mail*, August 31, 2009.

212 **"Your violence has included other family members, neighbours and dogs"** Parole Board of Canada decision, December 6, 2016.

212 **he "terrorized and threatened everyone in Isle Pierre"** Sam Cooper, "Police search dry well as B.C. missing women's case expands," Canwest News Service, August 29, 2009.

212 **The *Prince George Citizen* described Switzer** Frank Peebles, "'A little bit haywire': People who knew Leland Switzer paint disturbing picture of an unpredictable man," *Prince George Citizen*, September 1, 2009.

213 **"Switzer told police about this"** Neal Hall, "Possible Highway of Tears suspects haunt detectives: There has never been an arrest in this mystery," *Vancouver Sun*, December 13, 2009.

213 **In between two old grave markers, Vicki was searching for another one** Author met with Vicki Hill in Prince Rupert, B.C., on May 3 and 4, 2017.

215 **"I've been trying to find out myself"** James Vassallo, "Daughter of Highway of Tears' first victim wants answers: Woman still pursuing case 29 years after her mother's murder on a famed B.C. stretch," *Prince Rupert Daily News*, September 16, 2006.

216 **foul play had to be confirmed** Lori Culbert, "Siblings hope to put missing sister to rest one day: Virginia Sampare vanished without a trace in 1971, but doesn't meet the criteria to be added to Highway of Tears caseload," *Vancouver Sun*, December 12, 2009.

216 **Pauline Morris was fourteen years old in 1978** Laura and Ted Morris shared Pauline's story during a community hearing of the National Inquiry into Missing and Murdered Indigenous Women and Girls in Smithers, B.C., on September 27, 2017.

CANADA'S DIRTIEST SECRET

218 **Gladys Radek returned to Vancouver after the 2006 symposium** Gladys Radek described the advocacy work she continued to do after the 2006 symposium during an interview on Georgina Island, Ontario, on January 25, 2016.

220 **"Their cause is our cause"** Kerry Benjoe, "Walkers seek to stop violence," *Regina Leader-Post*, July 23, 2008.

220 **According to a** *Globe and Mail* **analysis** Matthew McClearn and Jeremy Agius, "Probing the mystery of Edmonton's killing fields"; Matthew McClearn, "The monsters in their midst," *Globe and Mail*, August 5, 2016.

220 **"Since I started organizing this in January"** Frank Peebles, "Justice walk headed for Ottawa," *Prince George Citizen*, June 4, 2008.

220 **"I kind of knew how big Canada was"** "B.C. residents bring unsolved-murder campaign to Ottawa," CBC News, September 15, 2008.

221 **Gladys vowed that "one way or the other"** Kris Schumacher, "Long march for justice nears end: Women confident they have raised profile of missing and murdered," *Prince Rupert Daily News*, September 9, 2008.

221 **"This is Canada's shame"** Chris Lackner, "Missing aboriginal women a 'human rights tragedy': Sisters in Spirit calls for gov't probe," *Edmonton Journal*, March 23, 2004.

221 **"We were starting to get a lot of international attention"** Interview with Dawn Lavell-Harvard in Ottawa, Ontario, on January 29, 2016.

222 **The government claimed the initiative had achieved its aims** Jorge Barrera, "Need for 'action' behind funding cut to Sisters in Spirit: Cabinet ministers' letter," APTN News, December 1, 2010.

222 **"the ability of NWAC to continue to use the Sisters in Spirit name"** Barrera, "Need for 'action' behind funding cut to Sisters in Spirit."

223 **Audrey Auger also began to walk** Details of Audrey's walk are gleaned from interviews with Kyla Auger at Alexis First Nation, Alberta, on April 10, 2017; Darrell Auger in Edmonton, Alberta, on February 28, 2017, and January 7, 2018; and a letter to the editor by Audrey Auger titled "Support for our walk welcome," *Prince Rupert Daily News*, July 4, 2007.

224 **"And we will keep walking"** Robert Matas, "Activists call for inquiry into the Highway of Tears," *Globe and Mail*, June 23, 2009.

224 **"It just seems like we complain"** Interview with Sally Gibson in Gitanyow, B.C., on August 21, 2015.

225 **"Throughout each and every journey we gained momentum"** Gladys Radek and Bernie Williams "Walk4Justice Summary: 2010," https://www.unbc .ca/sites/default/files/assets/northern_fire/email_attachments/walk4justice _summary2010.pdf.

226 **"It's going to be up to the people"** Beth Hong, "Missing Women Commissioner Oppal survives uncomfortable pre-hearing," *Vancouver Observer*, January 21, 2011.

227 **"She was always a stay-at-home mother, she was always happy"** Indyeyah Tylee shared her memories of Bonnie Joseph and Mackie Basil during an interview in Tachie on June 16, 2017.

227 **A diary kept by Bonnie and her husband** Bonnie's sister, Sharon Joseph, and cousin Vanessa Joseph spoke about Bonnie during interviews in Tachie, B.C., on May 6 and June 16, 2017. Sharon also shared Bonnie's diary.

228 **"Children from low income families"** Aboriginal Children in Care Working Group, *Aboriginal Children in Care: Report to Canada's Premiers* (Ottawa: Council of the Federation Secretariat, 2015), 11.

228 **then federal minister of Indigenous services Jane Philpott described the country's child welfare system** "We must disrupt the foster care system and remove perverse incentives, says Minister Jane Philpott," *The Current*, CBC Radio, updated January 26, 2018, http://www.cbc.ca/radio/thecurrent/a-special -edition-of-the-current-for-january-25-2018-1.4503172/we-must-disrupt-the -foster-care-system-and-remove-perverse-incentives-says-minister-jane -philpott-1.4503253.

229 **the system has been called "a second generation of residential schools"** Arlen Dumas, grand chief of the Assembly of Manitoba Chiefs, quoted in Kyle Edwards, "How First Nations are fighting back against the foster care system," *Maclean's*, January 9, 2018.

229 **A study published in the** *Canadian Journal of Psychiatry* Elizabeth Wall-Wieler et al., "Suicide attempts and completions among mothers whose children were taken into care by child protection services: A cohort study using linkable administrative data," *Canadian Journal of Psychiatry* 63, no. 3 (2018).

229 **Another study found these mothers were** Elizabeth Wall-Wieler, "Losing children to foster care endangers mothers' lives," *The Conversation*, March 29, 2018.

230 **"She's been fighting for her kids since day one"** Frank Peebles, "Disappearance worries family," *Prince George Citizen*, December 19, 2008.

231 **"They wouldn't say why they wanted to know"** Mark Hume, "'A terrible wait' along B.C.'s Highway of Tears: Father's worst fears confirmed day after body found," *Globe and Mail*, December 13, 2010.

232 **Cynthia's family released a public letter** Ian Austin and Sam Cooper, "Prince George man charged in deaths of three more women," *The Province* (Vancouver), October 17, 2011.

232 **Police ruled out his involvement** Ken MacQueen, "The country boy at the heart of four murder investigations," *Maclean's*, October 24, 2011.

232 **When it comes to Bonnie's disappearance** Email from Cpl. Madonna Saunderson, RCMP North District Media Relations, April 29, 2019.

233 **a crowd began to gather on the morning of June 13** Information in this chapter derives from the June 13, 2017, vigil in memory of Immaculate Basil with members of her family, as well as interviews with Ida, Crystal, Peter and Vivian Basil in Tachie, B.C., on May 6 and June 16, 2017.

235 **"She really loved her boy"** Rita Pierre shared her memories of Mackie during an interview in Tachie, B.C., on June 16, 2017.

235 **"She was a good person"** Maureen Felix shared her memories of Mackie in Tachie, B.C., during an interview on June 16, 2017.

235 **William and Elsie had enjoyed getting to know her** William and Elsie Pierre shared their memories of Mackie during an interview in Tachie, B.C., on June 16, 2017.

237 **In a media release asking for public assistance** "It's been three years—please help us locate Mackie," Fort St. James RCMP media release, June 13, 2016, http://nationtalk.ca/story/its-been-three-years-please-help-us-locate-mackie.

239 **The RCMP said it has conducted "a large investigation"** Email from Cpl. Madonna Saunderson, RCMP North District Media Relations, April 29, 2019.

WINDING DOWN

240 **"I had to lose my sister to be who I am today"** Brenda commented on her role during her remarks at a forum in Prince Rupert, B.C., on June 1, 2016, and at the start of the walk on June 2, 2016.

241 **when Brenda sat down with Angeline Chalifoux** Angeline Chalifoux described her involvement in the walks and advocating for Aielah during remarks in Prince Rupert, B.C., on June 1 and 2, 2016, and in interviews in Burns Lake, B.C., on June 14 and 15, 2016.

245 **The changes came the year after a Human Rights Watch report** See Human Rights Watch, *Those Who Take Us Away: Abusive Policing and Failures in Protection of Indigenous Women and Girls in Northern British Columbia, Canada* (Toronto: 2013).

245 **"the overall approach to missing person investigations"** "Missing Persons," B.C. Government, https://www2.gov.bc.ca/gov/content/safety/public-safety /missing-persons.

246 **"North District supervisors failed to comply with the policy requirements"** Civilian Review and Complaints Commission for the RCMP, *Chairperson-Initiated Complaint and Public Interest Investigation Regarding Policing in Northern British Columbia: Chairperson's Final Report After Commissioner's Response* (Ottawa: 2017), 12.

246 **"This response," noted the CRCC** Civilian Review and Complaints Commission for the RCMP, *Chairperson-Initiated Complaint and Public Interest Investigation*, 4.

246 **The 2014 "operational overview" reported** Although the 2014 National Operational Overview did not explicitly state the timeframe for which it included missing cases, the 2015 update clarified that it "included data about reported missing Aboriginal women cases dating back to 1951, and reported homicides of Aboriginal women over a 33 year period, (1980-2012)." Royal Canadian Mounted Police, *Missing and Murdered Aboriginal Women: 2015 Update to the National Operational Overview*, http://www.rcmp-grc.gc.ca/en/missing-and-murdered -aboriginal-women-2015-update-national-operational-overview.

246 **missing women and girls from along the Highway of Tears during that time period would account for** Author's calculations, counting seven missing cases (Virginia Sampare, Cecilia Nikal, Delphine Nikal, Lana Derrick, Tamara Chipman, Bonnie Joseph and Mackie Basil) and five murders (Aielah Saric-Auger, Roxanne Thiara, Alishia Germaine, Ramona Wilson and Alberta Williams).

247 **Indigenous women were significantly less likely to be killed by a spouse or former partner** Royal Canadian Mounted Police, *Missing and Murdered Aboriginal Women: A National Operational Overview* (2014), http://www.rcmp -grc.gc.ca/en/missing-and-murdered-aboriginal-women-national-operational -overview.

247 **Investigators had submitted exhibits from the scene** With the exception of several details provided by Steve Pranzl in an interview in Langley, B.C., on January 8, 2019, the description of how the RCMP connected Bobby Jack Fowler to the E-Pana cases was derived from interviews with Wayne Clary in Surrey, B.C., on October 13, 2015, and by phone on March 21, 2019.

248 **"This is a moment I've waited for for thirty-nine years"** "Senior charged in cold case murders of two young B.C. girls," CTV News, December 1, 2014, https://bc.ctvnews.ca/senior-charged-in-cold-case-murders-of-two-young-b-c -girls-1.2127782.

249 **notes the ruling that allowed the confession in the Jack case** R. v. Handlen, 2018 BCSC 1330, https://www.courts.gov.bc.ca/jdb-txt/sc/18/13/2018BCSC 1330cor1.htm.

249 **"The termination of funding for project E-PANA would impair"** James Keller, "RCMP warned budget cuts would hamper Highway of Tears probe," Canadian Press, February 4, 2015.

250 **The project's expenditures from 2015 onward** RCMP Access to Information and Privacy Branch, file A-2018-09574, February 15, 2019.

250 **Steve Pranzl, who spent twelve years on the task force, takes a different tack** Steve Pranzl described the work of E-Pana in an interview in Langley, B.C., on January 8, 2019, and in a phone interview on February 1, 2019.

251 **Wayne confirmed that investigators looked closely at her friends and associates** Phone interview with Wayne Clary on March 21, 2019.

256 **the issue of missing and murdered Indigenous women "isn't really high on our radar, to be honest."** "Full text of Peter Mansbridge's interview with Stephen Harper," CBC News, December 17, 2014, https://www.cbc.ca/news /politics/full-text-of-peer-mansbridge-s-interview-with-stephen-harper-1 .2876934.

257 **Although a follow-up study three years later showed little improvement** Journalists for Human Rights, *Buried Voices: Changing Tones: An Examination of Media Coverage of Indigenous Issues in Ontario* (Toronto: 2016), 2, 3.

257 **"Not because the issue itself was new"** Journalists for Human Rights, *Buried Voices: Changing Tones*, 15.

258 **released a report on missing and murdered Indigenous women in British Columbia** Inter-American Commission on Human Rights, *Missing and Murdered Indigenous Women in British Columbia, Canada* (2014), https://www.oas .org/en/iachr/reports/pdfs/indigenous-women-bc-canada-en.pdf.

258 **"Canada has committed a 'grave violation' of the rights of Aboriginal women"** United Nations, Office of the High Commissioner for Human Rights, "Canada's failure to effectively address murder and disappearance of Aboriginal women 'grave rights violation'—UN experts," March 6, 2015, http://www.ohchr.org /EN/NewsEvents/Pages/DisplayNews.aspx?NewsID=15656.

THE LAST WALK

261 **"The fact that so many Indigenous women and girls have been lost"** "Speaking notes for the Honourable Patty Hajdu, Minister of Status of Women, on the launch of the Inquiry into Missing and Murdered Indigenous Women and Girls," August 3, 2016, https://www.canada.ca/en/status-women/news/2016/08 /speaking-notes-for-the-honourable-patty-hajdu-minister-of-status-of-women

-on-the-launch-of-inquiry-into-missing-and-murdered-indigenous-women
-and-girls.html.

262 **"Since the failure of the police and the justice system"** Feminist Alliance for
International Action and Native Women's Association of Canada, "Reply to
Issue 17: Implementation of CEDAW Recommendations from Article 8 Inquiry
on Missing and Murdered Indigenous Women and Girls" (2016), 10, http://
tbinternet.ohchr.org/Treaties/CEDAW/Shared%20Documents/CAN/INT
_CEDAW_NGO_CAN_25418_E.pdf.

263 **"the Commission was gifted with the opportunity to find a new path"**
"Statement from Marilyn Poitras," July 11, 2017, https://www.documentcloud
.org/documents/3892277-Poitras-Words-of-Resignation-FINAL.html.

263 **One former staff member contended** Jorge Barrera, "MMIWG inquiry lacked
family aftercare plan, HR staff, says fired health manager," CBC News, November
18, 2017, http://www.cbc.ca/news/indigenous/mmiwg-millward-hr-1.4408690.

263 **It was an easy job, "a social," he called it** Garry Kerr described how the CBC
podcast came to be, along with his reconnection to the Williams family, in interviews in Duncan, B.C., on August 27, 2017, and over the phone on October 2, 2018.

265 **"It can jeopardize an ongoing investigation"** Interview with Rick Ross in
Chilliwack, B.C., on December 8, 2017.

265 **Wayne Clary told CBC the investigation was "very active"** Marnie Luke, "CBC
podcast uncovers new information in unsolved murder of Alberta Williams,"
CBC News, December 19, 2016.

265 **"It was great to connect with Garry"** Email from Claudia Williams, March 4,
2019.

265 **Vicki Hill, Mary Jane's daughter, was smiling, standing at the rest area** Unless
otherwise noted, details about and comments from the September 2017 walk
were gathered by the author.

269 **This happens whenever the coroner** "Death Investigations and Panels,"
BC Coroners Service, https://www2.gov.bc.ca/gov/content/life-events/death
/coroners-service/death-investigations-panels.

270 **a man named Peter Hunt went for a drive** Details about the discovery of Mary
Jane Hill and subsequent investigation are gleaned from the transcript of the
inquest on the body of Mary Jane Hill held before Coroner Darryl L. Stephens,
Prince Rupert, June 7–19, 1978.

271 **"She'd be in a drunken state and be beat up"** Inquest transcript, 14–15.

271 **"It could be that the body had been dragged or moved"** Inquest transcript, 25.

279 **Although they were on the same flight from Vancouver** Details and comments
as Claudia and Garry met in the Smithers airport were observed by the author
on September 26, 2017.

280 **"None of those details were given to us"** Beverly Williams's family testified
before the National Inquiry into Missing and Murdered Indigenous Women and
Girls in Smithers, B.C., on September 28, 2017.

282 **Beverly Williams was born on May 6, 1953** Details about Beverly's life and
death are derived from an interview with Lucy Smith, Herbert Williams, Norman
Williams and Willie Williams in Burns Lake, B.C., on September 2, 2016, as well

as the family's meeting with RCMP investigators in Burns Lake, B.C., on September 25, 2017, and the Williams' testimony before the National Inquiry.

284 **suggested at parole hearings that it was someone else** Parole Board of Canada, decisions from numerous dates.

EPILOGUE: A SAFER PLACE

291 **putting politics "ahead of the safety of our women and girls"** Alex Ballingall, "MMIWG inquiry gets six-month deadline extension to finish its work," *Toronto Star*, June 5, 2018.

292 **"this amounts to genocide"** National Inquiry into Missing and Murdered Indigenous Women and Girls, "Executive Summary" in *Reclaiming Power and Place* (2019), 4.

292 **I asked her what message she most wanted to convey to Canadians** Phone interview with Michèle Audette on May 10, 2019.

281 **RCMP Staff Sgt. Wayne Clary and Brenda and Matilda Wilson** Jessica
     McDiarmid, 2017
285 **Cross erected on the side of Highway 16 where Aielah Saric-Auger was found
     in 2016; the grave of Ramona Wilson; Wanda Good at a memorial cross
     placed for Alberta Williams in 2017; Tamara Chipman's family marching
     into Terrace in 2017** Jessica McDiarmid
287 **Brenda Wilson and Gladys Radek** Jessica McDiarmid, 2017

INDEX